God and Caesar at the Rio Grande

The U.S.–Mexico border region. Drawn by Linda Marston. Reprinted from Oscar Martínez, *Troublesome Border* (Tucson: University of Arizona Press, 1988), with permission of University of Arizona Press.

R

God and Caesar at the Rio Grande

Sanctuary and the Politics of Religion

Hilary Cunningham

 University of Minnesota Press
Minneapolis
London

An earlier version of chapter 1 was published in *ARC: The Journal of the Faculty of Religious Studies* (McGill University) 21 (1993). Reprinted with permission.

Published by the University of Minnesota Press
111 Third Avenue South, Minneapolis, MN 55401-2520
Printed in the United States of America on acid-free paper

Library of Congress Cataloging-in-Publication Data

Cunningham, Hilary.
    God and Caesar at the Rio Grande : sanctuary and the politics
of religion / Hilary Cunningham.
        p.   cm.
    Includes bibliographical references and index.
    ISBN 0-8166-2456-9 (alk. paper)
    ISBN 0-8166-2457-7 (pbk. : alk. paper)
    1. Sanctuary movement—Arizona—Tucson.   2. Church and state—
Arizona—Tucson.   3. Religion and sociology—Arizona—Tucson.
4. Urban anthropology—Arizona—Tucson.   I. Title.
BV4466.C86   1995
261.8'32—dc20   94-31786

The University of Minnesota is an
equal-opportunity educator and employer.

And they sent to him some of the Pharisees and Herodians, to entrap him in his talk. And they came to him and said to him, "Teacher, we know that you are true, and care for no man; for you do not regard the position of men, but truly teach the way of God. It is lawful to pay taxes to Caesar, or not? Should we pay them, or should we not?" But knowing their hypocrisy, he said to them, "Why put me to the test? Bring me a coin and let me look at it." So they brought one. And he said to them, "Whose likeness and inscription is this?" They said to him, "Caesar's." Jesus said to them, "Render to Caesar the things that are Caesar's, and to God the things that are God's."   —Mark 12:13–17*

When Caesar, having exacted what is Caesar's, demands still more insistently that we render unto him what is God's—that is a sacrifice we dare not make.
                                                                —Alexander Solzhenitsyn

Contents

Acknowledgments

This manuscript is the product of eight years of study and research, and I am particularly grateful to John Szwed, Marc Edelman, and especially Helen Siu of Yale University for their encouragement and insightful advice. I would also like to thank Micaela di Leonardo for suggesting this manuscript to the University of Minnesota Press, and Owen Lynch of New York University for his helpful comments and guidance as I began my study of Sanctuary. I also thankfully acknowledge the patience and skill of Janaki Bakhle and Robert Mosimann of the University of Minnesota Press, as well as the financial support provided by Yale University, the Institute for Intercultural Studies, the Social Sciences and Humanities Research Council of Canada, and the Leylan Dissertation Fellowship.

I am especially grateful to my husband, Stephen B. Scharper, for joining me in my fieldwork, for his insightful contributions in the writing of this manuscript, and for his deep and steady accompaniment. We both would like to acknowledge and thank the Sanctuary community in Tucson—especially Gary MacEoin, Mary and Darrel Wilson for "getting us started," Amy Shubitz and Marianna Neil for "keeping us informed," and Ricardo Elford for "keeping us going." I am grateful to Jim Corbett and John Fife for generously sharing their time and insights with us. I also thank all the Sanctuary workers, North American and Central American, who graciously extended their friendship and trust to us. Over the course of our fieldwork, Stephen and I discovered many wonderful and wise people, whose commitment to ending injustice was both inspiring and challenging. This entire manuscript has been possible because of their kindness in welcoming us, as "strangers," into Sanctuary.

Introduction

On the Steps of Sanctuary: Religion and Politics in the United States

All at once he [Quasimodo] was seen to reappear at one extremity of the gallery of the kings of France. He ran along it like a madman, holding his conquest aloft, and shouting: "Sanctuary!" Fresh plaudits burst from the multitude. Having traversed the gallery, he plunged again into the interior of the church. A moment later he reappeared upon the upper platform, with the gypsy still in his arms, still running wildly along, still shouting "Sanctuary!" and the throng applauded. Finally he made a third appearance on the top of the tower of the great bell: from thence he seemed to show exultingly to the whole city her whom he had saved; and his thundering voice, that voice so rarely heard by any one, and never by himself, thrice repeated with frenzy that pierced the very clouds: "Sanctuary! Sanctuary! Sanctuary!"
—Victor Hugo, *The Hunchback of Notre-Dame* (1831)

We are writing to inform you that Southside United Presbyterian Church will publicly violate the Immigration and Nationality Act, Section 274 (A). . . . We take this action because we believe that the current policy and practice of the United States Government with regard to Central American refugees is illegal and immoral. . . . We beg of you, in the name of God, to do justice and love mercy in the administration of your office. We ask that "extended voluntary departure" be granted to refugees from Central America and that current deportation proceedings against these victims be stopped.

Until such time, we will not cease to extend the sanctuary of the church to undocumented people from Central America. Obedience to God requires this of all of us.
—Rev. John Fife, pastor of Southside United Presbyterian Church (letter to Attorney General William French Smith, March 23, 1982)

If you stand on the steps of Notre-Dame Cathedral in Paris, it is not so difficult to imagine it as a sanctuary. The lofty spires, the towering stone walls, the solemn stares of the sculptured saints—all these seem to command respect and reverence. The edifice speaks of a powerful and wrathful God—one that a state might violate only with trepidation.

If you stand on the steps of Southside Presbyterian Church in Tucson, Arizona, the impression is quite different. You have to strain your imaginative powers to think of *it* as a sanctuary. There is nothing remotely "grand" about the church building. Its walls are thin and cracked. The interior is plain: there are no saints and no gilded altar. A flimsy wire fence surrounds the church property and in one corner a dusty, hand-painted sign proclaims, "Este es el santuario para los oprimidos de Centro América" (This is a sanctuary for the oppressed of Central America). You have the feeling that the whole scene—the church, its frayed doors, the rusty fence—could be blown away during the "monsoons" that annually sweep through the dust and dilapidation of the Sonoran Desert. The poverty and decrepitude of the building suggest a church that is insignificant, weak . . . hardly worthy of notice.

But it is indeed "noticed." If you linger in Southside's doorway for a while, you might see the pale green of a U.S. Border Patrol car edge its way along the street in front of the church. The dark-haired strangers speaking Spanish or an indigenous language near you fall silent as they watch its progress. Their talk resumes only as the taillights of the "state" disappear from view of the "church."

Notre-Dame's spires probably did much to legitimate its status as a sanctuary, and Southside's wire fence did little to buttress its, but what makes both these churches sanctuaries extends far beyond statuary and impressive architecture. Although a sanctuary is a physical place—a sacred site—it is also a cultural practice, one that is embedded, as the presence of the Border Patrol car attests, in a "conversation" about power.

In many ways, this conversation about power remains at the heart of the U.S. Sanctuary movement. Originating in Arizona, California, and Texas, the movement drew church and state into a bitter and often confrontational dialogue not only about how religion and politics are interrelated in American society, but also about which institutions can define the parameters of their relationship. Yet the discourse about power that one witnesses in Sanctuary—and indeed from Southside's very steps—is part of a much broader polemic between church and state in the United States, one that extends to the very beginnings of American statehood and to the constitutional debates over the proper place of religion in a democratic society. Unlike many modern nation-states in Europe, the United States did not entirely shed its religious carapace; it chose instead to enshrine a separation of church and state in its constitution, but at the same time retained a rhetorical fusion of religion and politics in its political culture. The historical result of this simultaneous church-state separation and fusion has been a confusing, often contradictory, interplay between religious and political domains.

The Context for U.S. Sanctuary

The research for this ethnography began on the cracked and weather-beaten steps of Southside Presbyterian Church in Tucson, Arizona, the birthplace of the U.S. Sanctuary movement. Broadly speaking, this movement can be defined as a religiopolitical coalition that began as a network of churches and synagogues that decided to offer "safe haven" or "sanctuary" to Central American fugitives denied political asylum by the U.S. Immigration and Naturalization Service (INS). The movement was officially inaugurated during the March 1982 public declaration of Sanctuary by Southside Presbyterian Church, and at its height in 1986-87 it spanned Mexico, the United States, and Canada, included more than four hundred religious congregations, and claimed between sixty and seventy thousand participants.[1]

A group of twenty-six Salvadorans, abandoned by a professional smuggler in Arizona's punishing Sonoran Desert, sparked the U.S. movement in July 1980. Half of the group succumbed to the desert's blistering heat before being found by the U.S. Border Patrol. The thirteen survivors were arrested, and, being "undocumented," were immediately processed for deportation. The incident received a great deal of public attention and several churches in Tucson and Phoenix became involved in assisting the fugitives. For many, their first encounter with the Central Americans became exposure not only to the INS's treatment of undocumented aliens along the U.S.-Mexico border but also to the violent political culture of Central America and the U.S. government's support of repressive regimes in Guatemala and El Salvador.

Between March 1981 and May 1986, what began as a collection of mostly church people deciding, for humanitarian reasons, to help the wave of Central Americans migrating to Tucson was transformed into a highly volatile church-state confrontation. In response to what they perceived as the immoral deportation of Central American political refugees, and in defiance of the INS, this group of church people developed an underground network that transported and crossed Central Americans into the United States. When the INS learned of these activities, it infiltrated the movement through undercover agents in order to stop what it claimed was an alien-smuggling ring. In September 1985, the government put eleven Sanctuary workers on trial; nine months later eight of them were convicted. In an ironic twist, the trial served to publicize the movement as well as the political turmoil engulfing Central America and, as religious groups in the United States rallied around Sanctuary, the movement blossomed.

Religion and Politics in the 1980s

Sanctuary emerged at a moment of both religious revival within and deep division between conservative and progressive churches in the United States. Underlying the ideological differences polarizing these factions were broad concerns regarding religion's proper relationship to politics and questions about how churches should function in relation to government. The presidency of Ronald Reagan during this period profoundly shaped the ways in which these issues were addressed by the churches; under his leadership, religion and politics adopted dramatically new contours.

Reagan's powerful link to conservative churches, for example, established an unprecedented alliance between right-wing religious groups and presidential politics in the postwar period. Although this alliance favored conservative Christians, it also restructured the American religiopolitical world in a broader sense. Reagan's manipulation of religion for political ends created an important ideological niche for Christian churches in a general way, and gave Christianity a singular relevance for, and power in, U.S. society during the 1980s.[2] This religiopolitical niche was not merely or solely an ideological space, however, but entailed new economic roles for the churches. Conservative churches, for example, promoted their ideological platforms (while securing their ties to the executive branch) through well-financed lobbies and substantial campaign contributions. Many progressive churches, on the other hand, assumed new economic responsibilities owing to the effects of Reagan's social policies—namely, the privatization of social services. As Reagan's reforms stimulated drastic cuts in social programs (such as food stamps, low-income housing, and school lunch subsidies), various church organizations found themselves bearing the brunt of funding and managing social programs that hitherto had been federal jurisdictions. Consequently, many churches—whose involvement in these programs had greatly expanded—became the principal advocates of those most affected by the cutbacks: the dispossessed and marginalized.

In this sense, Reaganism's new niche for religion restructured both the ideological and the material nature of church involvement in national politics. Although the "right" and "left" churches occupied this niche in different ways and with different agendas and financial resources, both—taking advantage of Reagan's paradigm for a fusion of faith and politics—appropriated "religion" as a resource to critique existing government policies and to promulgate new ones.

Sanctuary appeared at a time when Nonviolent Direct Action (NVDA) movements in the United States were undergoing a revivification, particularly among religious communities.[3] Tracing their origins back to post-war peace, civil rights, and antiwar groups, NVDA movements formulated a strong anti-nuclear-weapons platform in the late 1970s, but by the 1980s had spread into the ecology, feminist, gay and lesbian rights, and peace movements. Reaganism powerfully influenced the organization and political programs of many of these communities through its aggressive foreign policy in Central America. Largely in response to Reagan's interventionist agenda (and specifically in reaction to the invasion of Grenada in 1983), several NVDA movements (most of them Christian in orientation) articulated an anti-interventionist platform that attacked U.S. imperialism in the Third World, especially Central America. Sanctuary developed during a period when Christian groups began to mobilize first around stopping U.S. military aid to the Salvadoran and Guatemalan governments and the contras, and second, preventing a U.S. invasion of Nicaragua. Sanctuary, along with groups such as Witness for Peace and Pledge of Resistance, became part of the NVDA network, which included faith-based groups that rejected U.S. foreign policy in Central America.

Refugee Reforms

The U.S. Sanctuary movement also developed at a time when refugee determination in the United States was undergoing significant changes. In many respects, Sanctuary represents a concatenation of conflicting interpretations about Central American refugees in the United States. U.S. refugee laws did not formally emerge until after World War II when the United States, principally for humanitarian reasons, began to admit thousands of displaced Europeans. From the 1950s to the 1970s, however, asylum practices tended to favor individuals fleeing from communist or Middle Eastern countries. It was not until 1980 that the United States adopted a comprehensive and permanent position on refugee determination—one that brought the U.S. definition of a refugee more into line with the United Nations 1967 Protocol Relating to the Status of Refugees and that (indirectly) addressed the political biases inherent in U.S. asylum policy. The new laws, titled the Refugee Act of 1980, adopted the United Nations definition of a refugee and made it illegal for the U.S. government to return a refugee applicant to a country where the applicant's life or freedom might be threatened on account of race, religion, nationality, membership in a social group, or political opinion. This last reform, in particular, was intended to address the foreign-policy considerations that often undergirded decisions to admit or reject asylum applicants.

The connections that Sanctuary participants began to develop between asylum and Central American fugitives entailed not only an appreciation of these reforms, but also an awareness of the religious and political issues that lie at the heart of U.S. refugees laws. These issues are pregnant within U.S. refugee policy largely because the practice of asylum itself is grounded in Judeo-Christian traditions of compassion for the destitute and dispossessed; consequently, church groups perceive their refugee work as a *moral* responsibility. Refugee policy, therefore, is an arena in which religious and political concerns have often mixed, and, not surprisingly, in the post-World War II period, church and state frequently have worked together to address refugees issues. As historian Bruce Nichols notes, however, the postwar connection between church and state over refugees—originally conceived of as a "zone of cooperation" between government and private religious groups—has increasingly become an "uneasy alliance." Nichols observes that "the humanitarian cooperation [between church and state] in the postwar world . . . worked as long as no one directly questioned the exercise of international U.S. power" but that when "the legitimacy and humanity of that power fell under suspicion . . . the consensus between Church and State fell apart" (1988: 101). By 1980, just as Sanctuary was emerging, many of the religious-based refugee agencies had established greater independence from government programs, and several groups were questioning the continued political (i.e., anticommunist) orientation of U.S. refugee policy.

The persistent anticommunist direction of U.S. asylum practices—despite laws designed to eliminate it—was particularly salient in the government's treatment of Central American refugees in the 1980s. These refugees were especially "problematic" for the Reagan-Bush administrations, both of which had adopted foreign-policy programs that sought to protect U.S. national-security interests in Central America by supporting the region's military dictatorships and turning a blind eye to human rights violations. Admitting that the thousands of Central Americans seeking safe haven in the United States were legitimate refugees ran counter to the political and economic support the government espoused for regimes that were brutally oppressing their own populations. Predictably, the Reagan-Bush response to Central American fugitives was to deny that they were refugees fleeing violence in their homelands. Instead, they were deemed "economic" rather than "political" fugitives.

The fugitive Salvadorans and Guatemalans who became the first asylees in the U.S. Sanctuary movement raised both moral and political issues for a society already deeply embedded in contradiction. The United States had signed the 1967 UN protocol and had legislated domestic laws ostensibly insulating refugee determination from foreign-policy considerations. But the United States was also supporting, funding, and arming the brutal regimes that were propelling people northward. These contradictory realities produced opposing interpretations about the presence of Central Americans in the United States, and engendered conflicting visions of American society, U.S. national security interests, and the relationship of one's faith to one's political views. Sanctuary therefore encompassed not only acts of compassion toward Central American refugees but also a much deeper questioning of the relation of faith to nationalism, Christianity to Americanism, and individual conscience to the law.

Researching Sanctuary

Epistemological Issues

When I began to study the U.S. Sanctuary movement—first as graduate student at New York University and then at Yale University—I realized that it represented a research area largely ignored by social scientists. The reasons for this are too complex for me to draw any definitive conclusions, but I suspect that this lacuna in academic literature is linked to more general biases among social scientists—which tend to perceive religion largely as a conservative social force.

I am, of course, also implicated in my own conjectures about the social sciences. Like many of my North American colleagues, I had been raised by parents who had become disillusioned with institutional religion and had grown up in a fairly areligious climate. I had also been exposed to, and "turned off" by, the family values rhetoric of the Christian right— and found much in the speeches of fundamentalist preachers to support the definition of religion as conservative ideological manipulation. Yet at the same time, as an anthropology student, I kept bumping into dedicated Christians at rallies protesting U.S. imperialism in the Third World, nuclear proliferation, and other issues that had become staples of a "leftist" diet. How, I wondered, could such different groups with such different agendas be part of the same religion?

As my path continued to cross those of "leftist Christians," I began to read social-scientific literature on conservative Christian groups but found virtually nothing on progressive churches. This picture of religion and American political culture was decidedly skewed. Consequently, I recognized the need to document some of the activities of this "other" church, if only to balance the historical record. As my project matured, I also realized that Sanctuary raised important epistemological questions about the way anthropologists and other social scientists have studied religious phenomena. Here was a project that challenged not only the predisposition to view religion solely as a conservative social force and/or as a tool of powerful elites, but also more deeply held assumptions within anthropology about the place and importance of religion, as a medium of experience and change, in the contemporary world.

A second influence shaping this research stems directly from my experience as a graduate student in Yale's department of anthropology. At the time that I began to formulate a research strategy for Sanctuary, I became involved in a series of seminars conducted by a group of anthropologists and political scientists. These scholars took as their starting point an epistemological disjuncture between *agency* and *structure*—which, they argued, characterized much of social-scientific research—and endeavored to formulate new approaches through a culture and political-economy paradigm. Attempting to link macro- and microprocesses through concrete ethnographic studies, these scholars were particularly interested in the state and encouraged projects that centered on how different social groups participate in "discourses" over state power. Although many of these scholars shared an interest in peasant societies, much of their research resonated with my own interest in complex societies, and specifically in the role of religion in shaping U.S. political culture. As a result of these seminars, I developed a much broader framework for exploring the U.S. Sanctuary movement, and located my own study in a wider examination of power structures, cultures of resistance, and the complex forces at work in the creation of state hegemony.

Choosing a Research Site

Because the U.S. Sanctuary movement extended to almost every major geographical region (with the exception of the South), I had the choice of studying the movement in several locations. I chose Tucson, Arizona, as a primary base for two main reasons: (1) because of its historical importance as the first Sanctuary community, and (2) because the underground was still active there and gave me the opportunity to focus on dramatic church-state interactions. Originally, I had planned to conduct fieldwork in Tucson and Chicago, two centers of Sanctuary activity, but altered my plans after discovering that by 1990 the Chicago-based movement had greatly diversified its activities and was no longer focusing solely on Sanctuary. (I also changed my research agenda as I realized that my financial resources were not going to accommodate my original, overly ambitious, travel plans.) Consequently, and because of my increasing fascination with the underground, I ended up conducting fieldwork for ten months in

Tucson (1990-91), and then spent three more months in southern Mexico and Guatemala, where I met with Sanctuary contacts.

The choice of Tucson as a field site ended up being "politically" problematic for a variety of reasons—some of which did not become apparent to me until after I was deep into the research and the writing of this ethnography. Because of severe ideological splits within the movement—splits that have isolated Tucson from other centers of Sanctuary activity—my association with Tucson has strong political implications for certain Sanctuary participants. For some critics of Tucson's style of Sanctuary, research on this wing of the movement—particularly research that is not explicitly engaged in Sanctuary polemics—is decidedly biased; some Sanctuary participants view Tucson-based research as mere political propaganda for one wing of the movement. Part of this critique emerges from a resentment that journalists and religious leaders have shown considerable interest in Tucson's Sanctuary to the neglect of other Sanctuary centers; some feel that even doing research on the Tucson sector simply perpetuates a "media fiction" and serves only to "silence" the other voices of Sanctuary.

I am in general agreement that a comprehensive study of Sanctuary—one that entails the perspectives and experiences of a broad variety of groups across the country—would be of great benefit, but I am not so sure that the ideological differences that pervade Sanctuary narratives can be avoided. The "telling" of Sanctuary is unavoidably "contested terrain," and it is therefore important for me to clarify my own agenda in this ethnography.

It is my feeling that the Tucson experience represents not only a fruitful ethnographic topic for the study of U.S. religiopolitical culture, but also an important lens onto the Sanctuary movement itself. This narrative is not *the story* of the U.S. Sanctuary movement; it is not my intention to totalize the Tucson experience and present it as an expression of Sanctuary as a whole. The Tucson experience is *one* Sanctuary practice within a larger, diverse, and multivoiced movement; as such, it represents a particular "take" on Sanctuary from a particular location in the Sanctuary network. Admittedly, then, this research is "biased," but—in terms of my own objectives—only in the sense that I treat Tucson as *both* a specific narrative and a phenomenon that can yield broader insights into religion and politics in the United States.

A second problematic that emerged in developing a Tucson-based narrative is related to the issue of *voice*. Although the standard issues of authorial authority haunt this text (as they do all narratives), there are other issues of voice that are distinctive to Sanctuary politics. Most of these are related to the *kinds* of voices reproduced in Sanctuary narratives, and focus on the problem of *privileged* voices within the movement. I have, for example, included in this narrative historical quotes and my own interview material from John Fife and Jim Corbett—two "founders" of Sanctuary—because both have played a central role in shaping Tucson's Sanctuary culture. For many Sanctuary participants, however, especially those who critique the Tucson model, Fife and Corbett are "disenfranchising" voices—voices that dominate Sanctuary discourse and are linked to issues of male hegemony within the movement. This is a particularly sensitive problematic for me because I do not share the ideological position that Fife and Corbett are *simply* manifestations of male dominance in the Sanctuary movement; nor am I unappreciative of the culture of male power that contributed to their prominence. Fife and Corbett are both important historical figures in Sanctuary and products of specific sexual politics. Their position as leaders of the movement is the result of a complex interplay of circumstance, personality, and political economy. For the most part, however, I have made a conscious decision in this ethnography not to analyze Sanctuary from the perspective of prominent individuals but to explore the movement through the experiences of everyday participants—the North Americans and Central Americans with whom I associated on a daily basis.

Study Design

The study design I eventually adopted for fieldwork on Tucson's Sanctuary movement followed a "social network" paradigm. This decision was framed, to a large extent, by the nature of the Sanctuary movement in Tucson itself. Sanctuary is not a "community" or "neighborhood" phenomenon (thereby precluding neighborhood and community models of research), but rather a network of people whose lives intersect around specific events and activities. Consequently, I endeavored to involve myself in the world of Sanctuary by developing ties with individuals active in four interlocking networks—three of which were connected to Catholic, Presbyterian, and Quaker Sanctuary churches, and one to the underground.

My fieldwork began by attending (and tape-recording) three religious services each weekend, showing up for demonstrations at the local congressman's office, and attending a weekly prayer vigil protesting U.S. aid to Central America. After my third week in Tucson, I began to participate in Bible study and prayer groups, did refugee-related volunteer work, attended refugee court hearings, and participated in social events such as birthday parties, dinners, trips to Mexico, and gatherings at bars. I was also permitted to attend the weekly meetings of the underground and eventually participated in "border activities." Throughout these events, I conducted informal interviews and conversations with Sanctuary participants; as people became accustomed to my presence, I was able to take notes (and in some cases tape-record) during these discussions.

In Tucson, I circulated within a community of 168 people and developed intimate ties with a core group of 53 individuals. Within this core group, I conducted 67 taped interviews,[4] most of which revolved around life history, religious background and upbringing, and discussions of involvement in Sanctuary. The majority of my "informants" were married women between the ages of 50 and 75, or single men and women between the ages of 22 and 29. Only a handful of people in my sample had financially dependent (i.e., young) children, and roughly one-third were retired. With the exception of three persons, all of those in my core group were practicing Christians, but they reflected diverse religious backgrounds—ranging from hard-core evangelical to mainline liberal. The political backgrounds of my informants were also quite diverse: many claimed that they had always espoused "radical" political views, whereas others (sometimes sheepishly) acknowledged that they had voted for Ronald Reagan in 1980 and expressed conservative attitudes on capital punishment, abortion, and homosexuality. All, however, were committed to helping Central American fugitives in their midst, and many were risking imprisonment and fines by doing Sanctuary work.

With the exception of two months, I conducted all my fieldwork with my husband, Stephen Scharper, who, in addition to being an invaluable coworker and companion, ended up having a critical influence on my work. Several Sanctuary participants were initially reserved, somewhat suspicious of me as an anthropologist, and frequently reluctant to speak with someone intent on "recording" their words. As a result, developing trust was of the utmost importance. (The memory of government infiltration was, for many, still strong.) As it turned out, my husband's "personal credentials"—being the son of a prominent Catholic publisher who had introduced liberation theology to North American and European audiences—were extremely helpful in overcoming this reserve among Sanctuary workers. One prominent Sanctuary worker, for example, took us under his wing upon learning of Stephen's connection with Orbis Books and liberation theology, and consequently exposed us to many important Sanctuary personalities and activities.[5] My husband's "family ties" and his willingness to let me "piggyback" on his religious background, were thus critical in the process of my becoming involved in the Sanctuary network.

A central theme repeatedly underscored in this ethnography is that the U.S. Sanctuary movement represents a strand in a larger cultural process—one that is embedded in a "discourse" about U.S. church-state relations and the "articulating presence" of religion and faith in American society. Consequently, this study's conceptual issues involve questions about how a particular group of people used religious beliefs and practices to interpret and respond to state authority, and how, in doing so, they reconstituted their cultural world—from their place in the family and church to their identity within the nation and global community. Such a project has theoretical, historical, and ethnographic dimensions; each of these aspects of Sanctuary is discussed in this book.[6]

Chapter 1 focuses on some of the epistemological and theoretical issues that the U.S. Sanctuary movement raises for the study of "religious" phenomena. By way of a brief historical review, I analyze some salient anthropological conceptions of religion and explore how these have changed in the past fifteen years. I argue that Sanctuary raises important social-scientific questions about the relationship of religion to power and social change, and give some examples of works that have parted from traditional, static paradigms in order to underscore religion both as a dynamic social force and as a powerful medium of experience.

Chapters 2 and 3 are a historical account of the Sanctuary movement (focusing on Tucson's place within it) between 1980 and 1991. These chapters familiarize the reader with the main actors and events surrounding the movement, as well as with the culture of church-state conflict framing the declaration of Sanctuary, the creation of an underground railroad, and the government's indictment of eleven Sanctuary workers.

Chapters 4 and 5 focus on two questions: (1) How did the participants in the U.S. Sanctuary movement challenge state hegemony regarding undocumented Central Americans? and (2) How did they attempt to reconfigure U.S. church-state culture? Echoing some of the theoretical themes developed earlier, I analyze Sanctuary as a historical "process" and illustrate how participants in the contemporary movement reached deep into the wells of history to revive, retrieve, and ultimately rehistoricize a tradition that had existed in Judeo-Christian culture for centuries. I discuss the different church-state cultures underlying ancient Hebrew, medieval Christian, and U.S. sanctuary practices, and look at how each culture uniquely shaped the nature of the sanctuary "space" at different times in history. I trace how "liminality" and the "sanctity" of place, person, and community—as core cultural features of sanctuary—were manipulated in light of these different religiopolitical economies. These chapters examine the historical and cultural conditions underlying sanctuary traditions, and reveal sanctuary as an invented cultural practice, that is, an institution that changed as the religiopolitical culture in which it was embedded changed.

The remaining chapters take the reader into ethnographic terrain by returning to the sanctuary "spaces" of the contemporary movement. Chapter 6 focuses on Tucson's Sanctuary movement as a cultural phenomenon that articulated individuals into a novel social group, specifically by recasting the way in which they perceived and experienced themselves as a church. It explores the ideologies of social organization undergirding Tucson's Sanctuary community, patterns of participation in the movement, and Sanctuary theologies. Chapter 7 analyzes the unique experiences of Central Americans in Tucson Sanctuary and highlights how differences of language, class, culture, religion, and politics profoundly shaped the ways in which Sanctuary articulated Central Americans into the movement. Chapter 8 is an account of Tucson's underground and discusses how border work—the planning of runs (the transporting of undocumented Central Americans) and the evading of the Border Patrol—are expressions of both the broader Sanctuary church and a "faithful community."

Lastly, chapter 9 examines Sanctuary's relationship to, and impact on, the reconfiguration of U.S. church-state relations in the 1980s. In these pages, I discuss Sanctuary as the formulation not simply of "protest" but as "church"—that is, as a type of Christianity that fostered a new understanding of the church's relation to the state, as well as the role of Christianity in the global order.

Chapter 1

Sanctuary and Theoretical Frameworks: Anthropology, Religion, and Power

The evolutionary future of religion is extinction. Belief in supernatural beings and in supernatural forces that affect nature without obeying nature's laws will erode and become only an interesting historical memory. To be sure, this event is not likely to occur in the next generation; the process will very likely take several hundred years, and there will always remain individuals or even occasional small cult groups who respond to hallucination, trance, and obsession with a supernaturalist interpretation. But as a cultural trait, belief in supernatural power is doomed to die out, all over the world, as a result of the increasing adequacy and diffusion of scientific knowledge . . . the process is inevitable.

—Anthony Wallace (1966: 264-65)

By all the normal indicators of religious commitment—the strength of religious institutions, practices, and belief—the United States has resisted the pressures toward secularity. Institutionally, churches are probably the most vital voluntary organizations in a country that puts a premium on "joining up." A 1980 tabulation by the National Council of Churches listed approximately 340,000 churches in the United States with a total membership of 135 million. . . . the 135 million church members amount to somewhere between 60 and 75 percent of all Americans old enough to join.

—Kenneth Wald (1987: 51)

For those who followed American social and political developments in the 1980s, religion does not appear to be anywhere near "extinction" in the United States, and as a "cultural trait" seems to be surviving with vigor. This state of affairs runs counter to predictions made by social scientists during the 1950s and 1960s, when it was still fashionable for Western social scientists to aver that religion would disappear as "modernization" and its twin "secularization" steadily advanced. According to this line of thinking, countries like the United States would witness a decline in religiosity, and Third World governments, imitating their First World exemplars, would "increasingly utilize secular as opposed to religious symbolism to legitimate and consolidate their rule" (Sahliyeh 1990: 4). Social theorists confidently maintained that "nationalism, rather than

1

religion," would "provide citizens with a locus for their political allegiance and identification" (ibid.).

Yet in the gaze of what is perhaps a more humble social science—informed by two decades of intense worldwide religiopolitical activity—the secularization thesis has receded, giving way to a new set of questions about the role of religion in the contemporary world. The rise of liberation theology in Latin America; the role of the Catholic bishops in overthrowing the Marcos regime in the Philippines; church involvement in the apartheid struggle in South Africa; the Islamic revolution in Iran; the Catholic church's support of Solidarity in Poland; the emergence of militant religious nationalism among the Shia in Lebanon and the Sikhs in India; and the tragic conflict between Bosnia's Muslims and Christians—all of these suggest that religion continues, secularization theories notwithstanding, to be a powerful medium through which peoples of *both* the First and the Third Worlds experience social change.

In light of these events and queries, social scientists have—after "decades of neglect"—renewed their interest in religion and social movements (Guth et al. 1988: 357). Among the many phenomena to stimulate social-scientific interest was the emergence of grass-roots, politically oriented Christian groups in the United States during the 1970s and 1980s, which caught many social scientists off guard because of America's presumed status as a paragon of secular modernity. The groups that have received the most attention are the fundamentalist and charismatic Christian coalitions (e.g., the American Coalition for Traditional Values, the Moral Majority, and the National Conservative Action Committee), referred to collectively as the New Christian Right (NCR). These coalitions not only played a significant role in the election of Ronald Reagan, but also obtained a powerful influence in American political culture. According to some scholars, the fundamentalist surge of the past two decades represents a "renewal of religious commitment in American life comparable in scale and intensity to the 'Great Awakenings' of the eighteenth and nineteenth centuries" (Wald 1990: 51).

Alongside of the NCR's rise has been the emergence of another, less-noted religious movement, one that is also Christian-based and oriented toward national politics. The groups in this tradition (e.g., Clergy and Laity Concerned, the National Council of Churches, Pax Christi [U.S.A.], Sanctuary, the Sojourners Community), are located on the "left" of the American political spectrum and were engaged in organizing, demonstrating, and committing civil disobedience against the Reagan-Bush administrations. While the NCR groups sought political reform on abortion, school prayer, gay rights, "deviant" sexuality, pornography, and recreational drugs, the religious groups of the "left" confronted the government on such issues as foreign policy, nuclear weapons, apartheid, homelessness, economic policies, and Central American refugees. All of these churches, from both the "right" and the "left," have promulgated novel ideologies of religion and politics in American society, and, despite diversity in their agendas, share a specific focus: *power*. In particular, they share a concern with the role of *state power* in shaping social behavior.

As groups engaged in critical debates about cultural authority, these movements also challenge social scientists to reconsider standard theories about religion and religious phenomena and to incorporate a careful consideration of power into their studies of religion. This chapter examines some of the epistemological assumptions undergirding anthropological studies of religious phenomena, particularly in light of how anthropologists have incorporated issues of power into their analyses of religion. It also explores paradigms about religion that directly confront problems of power, cultural authority, and social change.

Many features of anthropological theory have their immediate provenance in the Western Enlightenment and its complex legacy of modernism. The specters of the philosophes and other harbingers of a secular modernity linger as a backdrop to the current discussion, as does the notion that religion is primarily a feature of "primitive" and "peasant" cultures—the two traditional staples of anthropological inquiry. Although I acknowledge the length and depth of this intellectual history, I offer only a cursory overview of anthropological approaches to the study of religion. My focus here is more on the post-World War II period and, in particular, research conducted in the past two decades. It is only within the last fifteen years or so that anthropology has formulated radically revised approaches to religious phenomena—approaches that have had to come to grips not only with the persistence of religion in diverse "modern" contexts but also with the significant role religion continues to play in contemporary political processes.

Analytical Tools: Classical Approaches

Religions are basically concerned with problems of meaning and problems of power. Anthropologists have been recently much occupied with meaning problems—systems of thought and belief, classification of worldview, concepts of spirit and deity, image and apparition, cultic and symbolic communion. . . . But many issues in the power relations of religious affiliation are still not clear.
—Raymond Firth (1981: 583)

In anthropology it has been almost standard practice to treat religion and politics as the private preserves of separate sub-disciplines that almost invariably become mired in their own theoretical assumptions. Religion is approached largely from a symbolic or culturological point of view. It is conceptualized as a system of meaning (supported by symbols and rituals) concerning "ultimate goals." This approach does not leave much room for a systematic inquiry into the social conditions and forces that generate and change such systems of meaning.

—Mart Bax (1991: 8)

Traditional social-scientific understandings of "religion" (as belonging to the realm of "meaning") and "politics" (as belonging to the realm of "power") offer us models that are, to say the least, circumscribed in their usefulness. Most of these traditional perspectives do not recognize, or simply neglect, the importance of analyzing religion as a constitutive force in the creation and exercise of cultural power. Anthropologists have tended to treat religion not as a modern phenomenon but as a characteristic of "primitive" societies, as a *normative* condition for all preliterate peoples (Morris 1987: 1). As some anthropologists have noted, this association has often been marked by a condescending characterization of preliterate cultures. The nexus between religion and primitive culture suggests that, for anthropologists, religion has been part of a fascination for "other" cultures—a fascination that has depicted religion as "an affliction that *other* people have, a bizarre form of discourse for which . . . only bizarre explanations come to hand" (MacGaffey 1981: 230).

Along with its penchant to link religion with the primitive, social anthropology has tended to treat religion as a "static" concept in two fundamental respects. First, there has been a tendency to describe religion as an internal and psychic quality, as a way of thinking, or as a mode of rationality certain peoples use to explain the world around them. In this framework, religion is a largely abstract and metaphysical phenomenon (structuralist strains within anthropology, for example, ultimately depict religion as a system of "pure ideas"). Second, religion has often been depicted as a social force that functions in a uniform manner upon society. When anthropologists have studied the social effects of religion, for example, they have largely focused on religion as a uniformly *integrative* force or as a tool of dominant social groups (see Lincoln 1985a; Thompson 1986), and have neglected to study religion as source of social division or as a medium of protest.

Added to this litany of "faults" has been the theoretical inclination of anthropologists to separate religion and politics within their own studies. Although, as Raymond Firth notes, anthropologists have investigated both systems of meaning and systems of power, they have done so in a manner that, in many cases, merely preserves a distinction between religion and politics, thus promulgating the notion that religion and politics are disparate realms within the social fields they study. (Such a separation, of course, belies a Western, metaphysical distinction between the sacred and the profane.)

Although these static and ahistorical approaches form the theoretical heritage (or baggage) of anthropology, they are no longer popular or assumed in studies involving religion. Anthropological literature over the past ten to fifteen years shows a considerable shift from the synchronic and symbolic conception of religion to a more *ideological*, dynamic, vital, and socially transformative one—a perspective that discerns how religion is frequently caught up within processes of dramatic social change.

Although the "forces" behind this shift include myriad cultural and historical factors, the fact that they have emerged is partly the result of paradigmatic criticism within anthropology itself. The anthropological record holds a number of critical reflections on treatments of religion—many of which are not altogether "new" but which have found firmer footholds in the 1970s and 1980s. Evans-Pritchard, for example, has chastised anthropology for unquestioningly equating the study of religion with the study of human origins (1965: 4-5). Other critiques, such as those of Geertz (1964: 282) and Douglas (1966: 81), have focused more on how modernization theories have separated primitive from advanced societies, and associated religion only with the former. It is not my intention to reflect upon the entire history of this period, but it is significant to note that some of the most substantive reflections on religion emerged from the post-World War II years, when traditional zones of anthropological inquiry (namely, in Africa and Melanesia) were transformed—particularly as nascent nationalist movements erupted and the static "primitive" became the "colonized" subject actively seeking independence.

Religions of the Oppressed

Among the first studies to challenge static and ahistorical perceptions of religion were the cargo cult and millenarian ethnographies produced in the post-World War II period.[1] It is during this time that questions about the *manufacture* of meaning within different ideological communities became more prominent in anthropological treatments of religion.

For many anthropologists, however, often writing beneath the venerated mantel of Durkheimian functionalism, such issues were neither typical nor topical. The nexus between religion and the expression of social unrest, or even social change, was rarely explored by most anthropologists during the 1950s and 1960s, since religion was generally viewed as an integrating, rather than a divisive, social force.[2] Nevertheless, finding themselves in situations that contradicted dominant paradigms of religion, several anthropologists writing on cargo cults and millenarianism argued that the religious movements they were studying were liberation cults seeking to shed the carapace of colonialism. This perspective ultimately countered static, functionalist paradigms of religion and spawned a new interest in "acculturation" or the ways in which cultures change through contact (Lessa and Vogt 1979). Anthropologists also treated the subjects of these movements not as superstitious "primitives" but as people struggling for emancipation, that is, as individuals "affected by historical processes whereby they are altered and transformed" (Lanternari 1963). In this framework, religion adopted more overtly dynamic qualities that had to be analyzed in specific historical, cultural, and political contexts.

The emphasis in these studies on social unrest and change resonated with what became a broader epistemological movement within anthropology—a "processual" anthropology focusing on social change, which began to surface in the late 1950s as the hegemony of Durkheim's structural-functional paradigm waned. A central theme for some anthropologists wishing to break the harness of synchronic studies (e.g., Raymond Firth [1964], Victor Turner [1969], and Edmund Leach [1954]) was the generation and transformation of social forms, particularly in the areas of new nations, urban cultures, and what eventually became known as Third World development studies (Salzman 1988). The process or "movement" metaphor seemed to indicate to anthropologists that "just as we appreciate movement and the need for movement in ourselves, so we [must] appreciate it in those things we study" (Fernandez 1979: 38-39). This processual momentum eventually trickled into religious anthropology, where, in the hands of certain authors, it was linked to broader questions about political power. Middleton (1960), for example, along with others in the "action-oriented" branch of process studies, focused on how individuals use religion for political gain. Geertz (1964) tried to demonstrate how religious symbols can be vehicles for "revolutionary" action. Turner developed a "processual symbolics" in which he related the manipulation of religious symbols to struggles for power (1974). In a work that specifically explored religious change, Colson (1962) examined how shifting Tongan communities, ritually associated with land, generated political community through religious shrines.

As they coalesced into a cohesive area of research, post-World War II studies of cargo cults, millenarian movements, and the "syncretic" churches of Africa also challenged the structural-functional model of religion. Although the anthropologists involved did not uniformly or directly press for radical changes in the way religion was characterized in their discipline, their work, taken as a whole, shows a significant attempt to look at religion as a dynamic social process embedded in conflicts over power. In this way, these studies can be seen as part of the broader conceptual shift to "process" and "power" within anthropology during the aftermath of World War II.[3]

The data provided by postwar anthropological studies countered some of the traditional views of religion as static, integrative, or merely supportive of existing political structures. The challenge, however, met with only limited success. Lincoln notes that a series of meetings was held after 1956 around the publication of some provocative studies of these movements (Cohen 1957; Worsley 1968; Thrupp 1962), the most important being Eric Hobsbawm's influential *Primitive Rebels* (1959), in which he argued that even though religious groups might be "rebellious," they could not be truly "revolutionary." Hobsbawm's supporters, defending what had become a "classical Marxist" thesis, suggested that these religious-based uprisings were generally ineffective and that their religious elements (millenarianism, rituals, and symbols) led their members into "irrational modes of organization" and "rendered them incapable of success" (Lincoln 1985a: 5).

Kennelm Burridge has described how difficult it was to convince his contemporaries that religion was, in many instances, an important medium of social resistance, protest, and change:

> Millenarianisms were regarded as social "sicknesses,"
> "irregularities," or "madnesses," interesting perhaps, but not
> properly within the field of religion, which was thought of as the
> conservative and stabilizing element of society. . . . Religion was
> so embedded in the social consciousness as conservative that,
> despite experience, the idea of religion as revolution or of
> revolution as religion seemed totally perverse. (Burridge 1985:
> 220-21)

Unfortunately, the questions these studies raised about the relation of religious culture to systems of power went largely unexplored, eclipsed by the dominant paradigms of the 1960s and early 1970s: Lévi-Strauss's reified structuralism, as well as interpretive symbolics, discussed religion in largely phenomenological, apolitical, and ahistorical terms. These paradigms sidestepped questions that the cargo cult and revitalization literature had posed, in some cases only implicitly, about religion and the exercise of power.

A New Look at Religion and Social Change

If one looks at anthropological studies as a collected body of works, the 1980s show anthropological interpretations of religion and its relation to the practice of power changing. As we have seen, the reasons for this shift encompass historical and cultural factors, but one factor seems to be related to the significant political influence world religions have exerted in recent social and political events. The framework adopted here for studying the U.S. Sanctuary movement builds upon more recent anthropological approaches to religion, particularly those that argue that religion is not simply a static set of ideas that a group of people have about the world, but also a system of meaning unfolding in a history and a culture, in politics and economies. In these more recent approaches, religion is regarded as the effort of a group of people to interpret their experience and give it a coherent form through a set of specific beliefs and practices—which are themselves shaped by particular historical and cultural circumstances.[4]

The more recent anthropological research on religion has raised some significant theoretical issues about how systems of meaning (such as religious systems) are related to political economies, and about developing paradigms and methodologies that can address religion, social change, and power from both a political-economic and a phenomenological perspective.[5] Such an approach is essentially integrative and calls for a rapprochement between academic disciplines that have traditionally avoided one another owing to the dichotomy existing between "political-economic" and "symbolic" approaches to culture. In the former camp, scholars have tended to overemphasize how political and economic (and in some cases, ideational) conditions or structures shape human experience; in the latter, researchers have focused almost exclusively on the inner experiences, strategies, and actions of human agents as they mediate the world around them. Studies of religion have suffered acutely from this dichotomy. Often associated with the "symbolic" and the "cognitive," religious phenomena frequently have been divorced from their political-economic context.

During the late 1970s and the 1980s—thankfully, for analysts of religion—there was a movement toward breaking down the epistemological walls dividing human experience (or *agency*) and the social environment (or *structure*) (e.g., Giddens 1984; Abrams 1982; Bourdieu 1977; Sahlins 1981; Ortner 1989). According to some theories, those who focus primarily on culture as an *internal* phenomenon (something internalized and made meaningful by human actors) must examine how political, economic, and other *external* conditions "structure" the very generation of human meaning and experience. Consequently, those who focus more on how political and economic conditions shape the production of meaning systems must also explore how human beings creatively interpret their experiences in light of these limitations, and how they are able ultimately to transform the very structures engulfing them.

The paradigm—labeled by various authors "practice theory," "process theory," "structuring," and "structuration"—collapses the rigid conceptual disjuncture between human agent and social structure to suggest that both are organically and inextricably linked. Sherry Ortner has summarized this approach:

> Practice theory . . . is in itself a theory of translation between an objective world and a subjective one, between a world constituted by logics beyond actors' perceptions, and a world constituted by logics spun by thinking, acting agents. Practice theory always has two moments, one largely objectivist and one largely subjectivist. In the first, the world appears as system and structure, constituting actors, or confronting them, or both. . . . But in the second, the world appears as culture, as symbolic frames derived from actors' attempts to constitute the world in their own terms by investing it with order, meaning, and value. (1989: 18)

As a theoretical orientation, the practice paradigm has some important implications for the study of religion; I outline only two here. First, because this body of theory rejects any rigid conceptual posture that estranges human agency and social structure, traditional definitions of religion as a personal, internal, meaning-seeking activity or simply as a symbolic code functioning to keep society together ultimately have to be set aside. Instead, one must adopt an interpretation of religion that is essentially processual and contextual: people may construct meaning through a religious medium, but they do so within a world where economic, political, and symbolic forces are shaping the construction of their spirituality or religious sensibility. Religion, therefore, is neither an internal meaning-seeking event (a subjective moment) nor an external ideology simply shaping people's consciousness (an objective moment); it is both.

Second, practice theories fundamentally redefine traditional arguments that separate religious and political-economic discourses. Many of the practice-based studies of human society build on Weber's insight that ideological and political-economic systems are mutually constitutive. In the practice paradigm, religious systems, as particular kinds of "moral economies," are deeply tied to systems of production and distribution, and to the structures of power that pervade society. One can expect religion, then, to be very much at the heart of social discourse about power, politics, and economics. In the practice paradigm, religion is embedded within a field of social "discourses" whose interrelationships vary throughout history; which discourses religion is distinguished from, and which arenas of power it exerts an influence in, are an analytical problem for the social scientist. The result, from a practice perspective, is a sense of religion that spans and integrates three levels of analysis. Religion is (1) a *subjective* phenomenon—it is a hermeneutical medium through which creative human agents can interpret the world around them and their place within it; (2) a *social* phenomenon—it acts as a set of external, ideological, or social conditions that shape an individual's or group's subjective hermeneutics; and (3) a *dynamic* phenomenon—it is ultimately a cultural process that, although embedded in specific historical and social "moments," changes over time and can play a defining role in the direction of that change.

Some ethnographies have adopted issues of agency and structure, practice and process, moral and political economies in their treatments of religion. Pioneer works in this line of research are offered by Michael Taussig (1980) and June Nash (1979). Both works examine the impact of capitalism on South American laborers and attempt to combine political-economic and interpretive-symbolic approaches. Taussig and Nash illustrate how ideological systems (such as myth, ritual, religious beliefs) not only respond to, but also reformulate, macro political-economic processes, such as creation of a money economy and proletarian wage labor. More recently, Sherry Ortner, in her study of Buddhist monasteries among the Sherpa of Nepal, explicitly adopted a practice paradigm in order to illuminate religious phenomena (1989).[6] In each of these works, religious beliefs and practices are not divorced from their cultural context, and are treated neither as subjective, static, cultural characteristics nor as a uniformly functioning *external* social force. These studies, and their contemporary offshoots, indicate that religion is viewed as an indigenous system of meaning—as a dynamic "discourse"—embedded within particular economic, political, and historical circumstances, at whose core are creative human agents.

This ethnography of sanctuary utilizes a concept of "religion" that builds upon these more recent anthropological studies of religion and politics; it endeavors to convey a sense of religion as discourse and process, as a dialectic of agency and structure, as human experience *creatively contextualized* in a political economy, a culture, and a history. In this study of one Sanctuary community, I have appropriated a practice framework in order to analyze how a particular group of North Americans *interpreted*, *mediated*, and *changed* their historical, economic, political, and symbolic world, and how they attempted to re-create it by using their religious beliefs and values in a novel fashion. They began this process first by questioning, later by reconstituting, the relationship between faith and politics within U.S. culture. In the next chapter, we return to the steps of Sanctuary in order to explore the complex but undeniably dynamic contours of this religiopolitical phenomenon.

Chapter 2

Local History, Part 1:
Declaring Sanctuary for Central Americans
(July 1980 to December 1982)

The birthplace of the first declared sanctuary in the United States for Central Americans is the Sonoran Desert, a vast expanse of parched earth dotted with rugged mesquite bushes, sun-bleached rocks, and sundry species of cactus. The sanctuary's immediate home is the city of Tucson, located about sixty minutes north of the U.S.-Mexico border. Originally a Pima Indian village called Schookson (meaning "at the foot of the black mountain"), Tucson became a Spanish outpost in 1775 (Sonnichsen 1982: 7). It remained moderately populated for much of its history, but between 1950 and 1965, coinciding with the widespread introduction of air-conditioning and a "silver boom," the city's population grew 521 percent (from 45,454 to 236,877); today Tucson's population is around 670,000. Regarded as a "liberal university town," Tucson has never been dominated by a single industry or a political machine. Its population (which is 25 percent Hispanic) consists largely of professionals, university-related workers, small businesspeople, government officials (including a sizable number of INS and Border Patrol employees), and retirees—many of whom are military veterans from the nearby Davis-Monthan Air Force Base.[1] Politically, Tucson is quietly diverse: its left-wing constituency is characterized by a peculiar eclecticism, and its laid-back liberalism is often contrasted with the high-powered conservatism of its rival city to the north, Phoenix.

Visually, Tucson is a sprawling development of low-lying adobe buildings, trailer parks, shopping malls, and the ubiquitous Circle Ks—the local version of gas station minimarts. In the more affluent sections of town, the houses are surrounded by grass lawns and shady trees, or, if the owner has opted for a desert landscape, a yard of teddy-bear, prickly-pear, organ-pipe, and saguaro cacti. These last are the many-armed giants associated with the Southwest; their stately forms have been so decimated by rapacious development that it is now illegal to damage or remove a saguaro without permission from the city.

Although commercial developers have pockmarked much of Tucson with strip malls, parking lots, and condo developments, its natural beauty is still arresting. During the monsoon season, dramatic storms attack the city and the streets suddenly fill up with three or four feet of madly churning water. At dusk, the four mountain ranges that surround Tucson turn a deep purple, an unexpected breeze appears, and the entire sky, as far as one can see, lights up with a magnificent sunset. It is during these times of nature's sublime and wild moods—not during the scorching afternoons—that an outsider begins to understand the draw of the Sonoran Desert.

Yet many have come to Tucson for reasons other than its majestic scenery. Because of its proximity to the U.S.-Mexico border, wealthy Mexicans often visit Tucson's well-stocked shopping malls, and the city has seen its share of what locals commonly refer to as *mojados* or "wetbacks," undocumented Mexicans seeking work in Tucson's hotels, restaurants, ranches, and landscaping and construction businesses. Beginning in the 1980s, Tucson—along with Los Angeles and southern ports of entry in Texas—became a principal destination of many Central Americans headed for the United States. By 1990, the U.S. Border Patrol had arrested almost 1.5 million people trying to enter the country illegally—16,953 of whom were Salvadoran, 9,707 Guatemalan, and 1,092,258 Mexican (*Refugee Report*, December 21, 1990).[2] Thousands managed to evade the Border Patrol and make their way inland, while others became tragic statistics—the bloated and disfigured bodies of those who had succumbed to the Sonoran Desert while attempting to cross into the United States. The story of sanctuary begins with such a tragedy.

In the summer of 1980, a fugitive group of Salvadorans made their way into the United States via the Organ Pipe National Monument in Arizona. The reserve is a protected region where organ-pipe cacti (a plant related to the giant saguaros found throughout southwestern Arizona and northern Sonora, Mexico) grow. This region is one of the most dangerous habitats for human beings in the United States: daytime temperatures in July and August can reach well over 120 degrees Fahrenheit, and the desert vegetation offers little protection from the sun's deadly rays. Those familiar with the desert's dangers wear hats, long-sleeved shirts, and long pants, and carry plenty of water since dehydration can occur within half an hour.

The group of mainly middle-class, urban Salvadorans—students, housewives, factory workers, a bus driver, and a shoemaker—who entered the United States on July 3, 1980, were not aware of the Sonoran's perils. They had crossed into the United States via Sonoita, a Mexican village approximately 120 miles southeast of Yuma, Arizona, and were being guided by Salvadoran and two Mexican coyotes.[3] Following a trail that took them deep into the desert, and told by their guides that they would be walking only a short distance, the group had not brought along much water, nor had they taken any precautions to cover exposed skin. During their first day in the desert, one coyote disappeared along with two young men who were students at the University of San Salvador. A few hours later, claiming that he was going to get water, the second coyote also disappeared; he was accompanied by a Salvadoran woman called Berta. By late afternoon, none of the missing parties had returned and the Salvadorans (according to newspaper interviews) began to save and drink their urine, and, thinking it would relieve them, took off much of their clothing. By evening, one of the women in the party had died from heat exposure.

On the second day, the group realized that their guides were not going to return; it was decided that the men should go look for water. The Salvadoran coyote—who had made only one previous (and unsuccessful) trip up to the United States—remained with the women. As the afternoon wore on, two of the women died of heat exposure and dehydration. At roughly the same time, fewer than three miles away, the U.S. Border Patrol had begun a search for the survivors. They had picked up one coyote and two Salvadorans the preceding day, but all three had refused to tell the patrol that there were still people left out in the desert. Berta, the woman who had left with the second coyote, had also been caught and had told the Border Patrol about the others. She led them to an area she remembered passing, but once there changed her mind and refused to help the search party. That evening, the Border Patrol found the party of men who had left in search of water; only three were alive. The women who had stayed with the Salvadoran coyote were discovered the next morning around 10 A.M. Seven of the ten women were dead, as was the coyote, who, according to the survivors, had beaten several of the women to death before he collapsed. Three of the original twenty-six were never found; the thirteen survivors were arrested and taken to a jail in Tucson, where they awaited deportation hearings.[4]

Newspaper coverage of the horrific event sparked widespread interest in the fugitives—perhaps in part because these people were not destitute agricultural laborers but "well-dressed, obviously middle-class men and women travelling with Bibles, cold cream and toilet water" (Crittenden 1988: 3). The accounts of the survivors' ordeal, particularly the stories of the political violence in El Salvador, generated concern for the Central Americans among churches in the Tucson area.

The discovery of these Salvadorans in Arizona's blistering desert is one of those galvanizing events that profoundly alter people's lives. The desert tragedy brought together and focused many different individuals and streams of experience—Catholic, Presbyterian, Quaker, and Jewish. It is out of this context of intersecting events and experiences that the Sanctuary movement emerged.[5]

South Tucson and Southside Church: The Roots of Sanctuary Work

Many of Tucson's Hispanic and Native American poor are concentrated in South Tucson, a run-down but independent municipality of seven thousand wedged between a highway and the western perimeter of downtown Tucson. Located on the border of South Tucson's faded and scruffy corridors is Southside Presbyterian Church, its white adobe walls rising above ramshackle roofs, bent wire fences, and expanses of cracked, dried earth that serve as front yards. Southside has a history of involvement in "social justice" activities—ministries that focused on the Hispanic and Native American urban poor, and that, in the 1980s, dovetailed with Southside's response to Central American fugitives.

In the 1970s, a group of Chilean refugees was sponsored in Tucson, and several churches established a support network for them. These churches devised a system whereby a five-member team (a social worker, a lawyer, a doctor, a businessperson, and an interpreter) was assigned to each refugee or family to help them relocate in Tucson. Gary MacEoin, a writer and activist who lived in Tucson from 1974 to the mid-1980s, argues that this refugee-support system, originating with Chilean political refugees, became the infrastructure for the Sanctuary movement in one crucial respect: it brought together the Anglo and Latino constituencies in Tucson and developed a program of community concern and response. These became the principles of Sanctuary.[6]

The historical records on Sanctuary point to the presence of a few key individuals who assumed prominent roles in the creation of the movement. Given the gender structure of American Christian churches, it is not surprising that many of these individuals are male—priests, pastors, and elders who occupied positions of authority within their church communities. This aspect of Sanctuary diversified as the movement developed, and as other Sanctuary communities in the United States consciously opted for female-centered authority structures. (The Sanctuary coalition that developed in Chicago, for example, became a key critic of male-dominated Sanctuary, which, it argued, was exemplified by Tucson [see Lorentzn 1991].) In Tucson, however, public leadership in Sanctuary (particularly in relation to media coverage) remained predominantly male, while women tended to exert influence through more informal channels.

One of the churches that spearheaded the campaign to help the thirteen surviving Salvadorans was St. Mark's Presbyterian Church. Following the desert tragedy, and under the directorship of its pastor, David Sholin, the church raised two thousand dollars to bond out the Salvadorans while they awaited their deportation hearing. Sholin convinced the Tucson Ecumenical Council (TEC)—a coalition of sixty-five Catholic and Protestant churches—to form a special task force on Central America, the Tucson Ecumenical Council Task Force on Central America (TECTF) (see figure 2.1). The task force began to investigate U.S. refugee policy and educate its members about what was happening in Central America, particularly in terms of how churches should respond to the influx of Central Americans pouring into Tucson from the summer of 1980 on.[7]

One member of TECTF was a Redemptorist priest, Ricardo Elford, who had come to Tucson in 1967. Father Ricardo began to learn first-hand about Central American refugees in January 1981 when he helped to bail out a Salvadoran woman from the House of Samuel, one of many Christian groups that, on contract with the INS, housed undocumented aliens. As he became increasingly concerned about the violence in Central America, he organized a weekly, public demonstration alerting people to U.S. foreign policy in Central America (the first was held on February 19, 1981). The prayer service/demonstration, known as "the Vigil," consisted of a small group (usually twenty to forty people) who would stand during rush hour every Thursday with placards in front of Tucson's Federal Building, home of the offices of the local INS.[8] After roughly twenty minutes, those attending the Vigil gathered into a circle and read a prayer sheet consisting of biblical quotes, prayers, and newspaper selections on the violence in Central America. The entire demonstration, which concluded with announcements about upcoming political and religious events, usually lasted thirty to forty minutes. Although designed to draw public attention to happenings in Central America, it also became a center of prayer, reflection, and the sharing of information for a faith community that was coalescing around the issue of U.S. foreign policy in

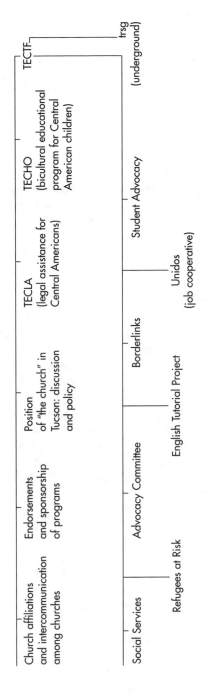

Figure 2.1. Structure of Tucson Ecumenical Council and subcommittees. All subcommittees under TEC have tax-exempt status through the parent organization. The underground (trsg [tucson refugee support group]), although affiliated with TEC, receives its funding separately through another Tucson-based, religious, and tax-exempt organization. *Source:* Tucson Ecumenical pamphlet, April 4, 1990.

Central America and the government's treatment of "alien" Central Americans.[9]

Rev. John Fife—another central figure in Sanctuary history—became an important figure in the evolution of the TEC task force. The forty-four-year-old pastor of Southside Presbyterian United Church had been trained at Pittsburgh Theological Seminary, had been involved in the civil rights and anti-Vietnam War movements, and had come to Tucson in December 1969. His new congregation, Southside Church, built in 1906 as a Presbyterian Indian Mission project, originally had been located in a shantytown called "Papagoville." When Fife arrived, the church consisted of a mixed fifty-six-member congregation consisting mainly of Pima, Tohono O'odham (Papago), and Mexican-Americans.[10] The Presbyterian Church U.S.A. had just decided to close the church down because it did not consider Southside a viable congregation, but Fife persuaded the parent body to keep it going.

In 1980, Fife, Father Ricardo, and other clergy in Tucson began to learn about social conditions in Central America through a "reporting network" consisting mostly of American priests and nuns stationed in Central America—a network of clergy that had become "in effect a private diplomatic corps" who sent back word to the churches in the United States that, "contrary to what American officials were saying, there was a bloodbath going on" (Crittenden 1988: 25). Tucson's churches were hearing similar reports from Manzo Area Council, a private social-service organization that mainly helped undocumented Mexican aliens with immigration problems. (Central Americans began showing up at Manzo in 1979.) The churches' connection with Manzo intensified through their work with refugees, and Manzo eventually joined with TEC to form the task force on Central America. (This alliance between church and legal agencies had a defining effect on the Sanctuary movement, particularly as the Tucson churches attempted to give Sanctuary a legal basis.)

The main objective of the TEC Task Force on Central America was to "harness and direct a response of faith at all levels" to the plight of Central Americans in the United States. This response eventually included "a formal proclamation of biblically based motivation; a weekly ecumenical prayer service outside the Federal Building that houses the INS offices . . . the support and expansion of community-based legal services to aid refugees and their rights . . . [and] the raising of three-quarters of a million dollars for bonds and legal expenses" (MacEoin 1985: 16). As TECTF expanded its base of operations and contacts, other communities became involved in its refugee advocacy work, first along the U.S.-Mexico border from Texas to California, and then north to Chicago, Seattle, New York, and Boston. For many of these mainly white, middle-class religious groups, "church" became a place where they obtained an education both about U.S. foreign policy in Central America and about the widening gap between governments and church groups over what was happening in Central America.

What *really* was happening in Central America? Not all of the thirteen dehydrated Salvadorans found in the Sonoran Desert were fugitives from political persecution (some were fleeing factory shutdowns, strikes, and bad economic conditions), but several bore ghastly stories of torture, rape, and murder. These accounts—what became standard testimonies of violence over the 1980s—helped stimulate concern among the churches for the safety of the Central Americans should they be deported back to El Salvador.[11] In order to understand fully the emergence of the U.S. Sanctuary movement, it is essential to examine the social, political, and economic wellsprings of the Central American exodus to the United States.

Central America and the "Feet People"

Although poverty alone did not produce massive migration from (and displacement in) Guatemala and El Salvador in the late 1970s, the economies of these nations—based on systems that favored less than 10 percent of their populations—profoundly undergirded the social and political conditions prompting the exodus. By the 1970s, the agro-export-oriented economies of the five Central American nations had diversified and industrialized compared to previous periods; yet this "modernization"—while it produced an increase in profits for the small number of entrepreneurial families, sectors of the middle class, and foreign interests—was accompanied by an expansion of the landless peasantry and a declining standard of living for the majority of the population. Between 1955 and 1975, for example, the average plot of land for a Guatemalan family decreased by one-half. A similar pattern held for Nicaragua, and in El Salvador the landless population grew from 11 to 40 percent between 1961 and 1975 (Berryman 1985: 16; see also Gorostiaga and Marchetti 1988).

In addition to the expansion of poverty, the mid-1970s saw growing activity and membership among the guerrilla groups of Guatemala and El Salvador. "Popular organizations"—groups such as FECCAS (the Christian Federation of Salvadoran Peasants in El Salvador) and CUC (Committee for Campesino Unity) in Guatemala—began to demonstrate against the economic, military, and political agendas of their governments.[12] Significantly, several popular organizations were linked with a rapidly changing Catholic church.

A Liberation Church

For most of its history in Central America, the Catholic church has been allied with traditional power structures, but in the 1960s a substantial theological shift occurred in the upper echelons of the church. Following Vatican II (1962-65)—the second modern meeting of the world's Roman Catholic bishops to discuss church doctrine and contemporary life—several indigenous Latin American clerics began to rethink traditional Catholic teachings and to formulate their own "contextual" theologies. At the same time, missioners and priests began to pour into Central America, bringing with them new paradigms regarding theology and ministry.[13] In 1968, the second meeting of the Latin America Episcopal Council (CELAM) was held in Medellín, Colombia. At this meeting, the Latin American bishops (who had had little input at Vatican II) not only began to explore the implications of what they termed "institutional violence" and a "preferential option for the poor," but also adopted a new "faith methodology" that reversed traditional Catholic patterns. Instead of beginning with doctrine and moving to its application, some bishops argued, faith must begin with reality itself, then move to reflection on reality, and finally to action. As it developed, this approach became a lay-intensive pastoral program, and its methodology (termed *concientización*) was practiced in small groups of fifteen to twenty families called *comunidades de base*, or basic Christian communities (BCCs). These groups usually began with a discussion of social problems, relating them to readings from the Bible, and then developed a plan of action to address them.

This pastoral methodology and the preferential option for the poor coalesced into a movement under the rubric "liberation theology"—a religious perspective premised on the notion that the poor should not be integrated into structures of oppression but become *autores de su propio destino*, subjects of their own destiny (Berryman 1984: 28). Advocates of liberation theology, some of whom incorporated a Marxist critique into their work, criticized the social, economic, and political structures oppressing the majority of Latin American peoples.[14] Focusing on "the non-subjects of history, those who have been denied any voice or identity in history by their fellow humans," they promulgated a "praxis of solidarity with those who suffer and . . . [work] for the transformation of human agency and social structure" (Chopp 1986: 3-4).[15]

Because liberation theology entailed a fundamental critique of existing power structures (including those of the Catholic church) and U.S. economic and political imperialism in the Third World, its appeal was hardly universal. Conservative members of the Catholic church, such as Belgian

Jesuit Roger Vekemans, denounced it; the Vatican Congregation for the Doctrine of the Faith twice "silenced" liberation theologian Leonardo Boff for twelve months; and the Reagan campaign's 1980 "New Inter-American Policy for the Eighties" (the "Santa Fe Document") singled out liberation theology as a force counterproductive to U.S. interests (Lernoux 1989: 90).[16] The Salvadoran and Guatemalan governments also felt threatened by liberation theology and, choosing to regard it as communist-inspired insurgency, began to target priests, nuns and church workers with campaigns of terror.

In the mid-1970s, as the popular organizations stridently began to voice discontent, the Guatemalan and Salvadoran security forces, along with the oligarchic groups they defended, unleashed a brutal "counterinsurgency" campaign designed to quell all opposition—a familiar approach to political opposition for the poorer classes of Guatemala and El Salvador.[17] The targets of these campaigns were most often peasants, students, leaders of cooperatives, labor leaders, human rights activists, priests, and lay catechists.[18] In El Salvador, for example, government repression was carried out by both the military and right-wing "death squads" linked to elite paramilitary organizations such as ORDEN (Democratic Nationalist Organization) and ANSESAL (National Security Organization). Around the same time, the Guatemalan army adopted a large-scale counterinsurgency program directed primarily at the Amerindian populations located in the El Quiché, Huehuetenango, El Petén, and other regions. By 1979, this form of governmental violence, which did not distinguish between civilians and combatants, was destroying entire villages and producing one hundred to two hundred deaths per month. In the wake of the violence, some two hundred thousand Guatemalans fled their country (Manz 1988: 7-14); thousands of others became "internally displaced."

The violence to which the civilian population was subjected during these counterinsurgency campaigns was horrific, systematic, and brutal. Individuals were often picked up by security forces, cruelly tortured, murdered, and then dumped on the roadside or in fields. Others were "disappeared"; still others were murdered in front of family and friends. In Guatemala and El Salvador, the civilian-directed campaign of violence adopted what one exiled missionary referred to as a sinister "hermeneutic of death":

People are not just killed by death squads . . . they are decapitated and their heads are placed on pikes and used to dot the landscape. Men are not just disemboweled by the Salvadoran Treasury Police; their severed genitalia are stuffed into their

mouths. Salvadoran women are not just raped by the National
Guard; their wombs are cut from their bodies and used to cover
their faces. It is not enough to kill children; they are dragged
over barbed wire until the flesh falls from their bones while
parents are forced to watch. . . . Their killing has sexual
overtones. Salvadorans are not shocked to learn that nuns are
raped by the National Guard, when teachers and health workers
are sexually molested by the Treasury Police or when peasants
are mutilated after they have been killed by the army. (Santiago
1990: 293)[19]

When international human rights organizations, such as Amnesty International and the Inter-Commission on Human Rights of the Organization of American States (OAS), condemned the state-sponsored carnage, the governments of Guatemala and El Salvador blamed "communists" and "guerrilla insurgents" for the violence.

Exodus

A major consequence of "counterinsurgency" was the death and displacement of thousands of Central Americans. Human rights groups have estimated that over the past two decades 80,000 to 100,000 Salvadorans and more than 200,000 Guatemalans have been killed in political violence in their countries, and even more have been uprooted. Currently, more than one million Central Americans are living in the United States, the majority of whom emigrated after 1979 (Hamilton and Pastor Jr. 1988: 6).

In 1981, just as the numbers of Central Americans entering the United States began to swell, Ronald Reagan took office. In the perception of the Reagan administration, Central America had become a seedbed of communist revolutionary movements—Nicaragua's Sandinistas had just ousted the U.S.-backed dictator, Anastasio Somoza, and the Salvadoran guerrilla coalition, the FMLN (Farabundo Martí Front for National Liberation) had boldly but unsuccessfully attempted to overthrow the government. U.S. State Department officials tended to attribute these actions to the influence of Soviet-Cuban communism, which they believed was threatening U.S. geopolitical hegemony in Mesoamerica and the Caribbean. Their response (after 1982) was to resume military support to the Guatemalan and Salvadoran governments and to pursue a policy of "low-intensity warfare" (LIW) against insurgent factions in these nations. The Reagan administration interpreted the tremendous influx of Salvadorans and Guatemalans as the flight of "feet people," that is, people primarily seeking greater economic opportunity in the "great North" (see Gomez 1984: 222-25).

Reaganite reasoning did not concur with the perspectives of many U.S. church groups, which were influenced by the stories of returning missioners who had served in El Salvador and Guatemala. These groups therefore adopted a new urgency in their critique of U.S. foreign policy in Central America: within the first five months of Reagan's first term, congressional letters were "running 600 to 1 against U.S. military aid to El Salvador" (Lernoux 1989: 89).[20]

The Development of a Sanctuary Underground

The Quaker Connection

In May 1981, as congressional letters opposed to U.S. military aid to El Salvador were piling up in the White House, a second defining moment for the Sanctuary movement occurred. On May 4, Jim Dudley, a Quaker, picked up a male hitchhiker in southern Arizona. Dudley did not know it, but the hitchhiker was a young Salvadoran who had just crossed into the United States via Nogales. As he drove the man toward Tucson, Dudley was pulled over at the Peck Canyon Road roadblock by the Border Patrol. The agents arrested the Salvadoran for EWI (entry without inspection) and nearly arrested Dudley. Perturbed by the experience, later that evening, Dudley told two Quaker friends living in Tucson, Jim and Pat Corbett, what had transpired.

A rancher, Jim Corbett had been forced into early retirement by a rare and crippling form of arthritis; he spoke Spanish fluently and knew the ins and outs of survival in the Sonoran Desert. He and his wife lived simply in a quiet, rather dusty corner of north-central Tucson. The Corbetts were disturbed by Dudley's story and, being somewhat informed about the violence in El Salvador, were concerned that the man might be a refugee. The next day, Jim Corbett decided to track the man down but had little luck with either the Border Patrol or the Immigration and Naturalization Service, which refused to give out information on detainees (Davidson 1988: 19). Corbett then contacted the Manzo Area Council, which directed him to Father Ricardo Elford. The priest, on his way out to help a group of Salvadorans arrested on the Papago Indian Reservation that morning, explained that he would need to find out the full name of the man and his location before the Border Patrol would allow Corbett to speak to him; Corbett could then present a G-28 form indicating that the Salvadoran had legal representation and entitling him to a deportation hearing.[21]

By a fortuitous coincidence, Corbett's name was the same as that of a previous mayor from Tucson, and in his second call to the Border Patrol he was mistaken for the politician. Consequently, he was given the Salvadoran's name ("Nelson") and his location in the Santa Cruz jail, on the edge of Nogales, Arizona, a border town that spreads over the international fence separating Mexico and the United States. Corbett drove to the jail only to discover that the man had been moved to El Centro, California, the main holding center for illegal aliens in the southwestern United States. At the Nogales jail, however, Corbett discovered several other Salvadorans being held for deportation in 20 by 20-foot cells crammed with thirty to forty men. He went to the Border Patrol office and requested G-28 forms, which he wished to file on behalf of Enrique Molina Parada and a second "Nelson," two Salvadoran detainees whom he had encountered in the jail. After finally receiving the forms, Corbett returned to the jail only to learn that the Border Patrol had removed both Salvadorans.

The Corbetts obtained a $4,500 lien on one of their trailers and, through the Manzo Area Council, bonded out four Salvadoran women and one baby. In one of a series of letters that Jim Corbett penned first to his fellow Quakers and then to a general audience, he intimated that helping Central Americans who were "illegally" crossing into the United States might lead to active resistance to the government.[22] Corbett's letter of May 12, 1981, reads in part:

Dear Friends,[23]
Imagine a moonless night and a group of about 15 fugitives who are groping their way through country that's terrifyingly alien to them. Two carry infants. Three are small children who clutch at their parents' hands and try not to cry.

The blinding stare of spotlights suddenly freezes them in place. An amplified voice blares orders. Uniformed men close in.

They will be sent back, maybe to be tortured or killed, at the very least to live under the daily threat of being assaulted or killed at the whim of any soldier. It needn't happen that way, though, if the people who live where they are captured would help them, but few of the local people seem to know it's happening. Maybe they don't want to know.

—Vichy France? It did happen there, as it has happened so many places before and since, but I'm writing to you because it's happening now, here in Arizona. . . .

What it all comes down to is that there's an immediate need for an enormous amount of bond money or collateral property for bonds, but there's also an urgent need to persuade the courts that they should follow the example of the San Francisco judge who is releasing Salvadoran refugees on their own recognizance. Because the alternative to meeting the bond requirement may be tantamount to a death sentence, refugee bonds have, in fact, degenerated into ransom . . . I'd like to hear from people who are willing to put up bonds and collateral or to help with associated expenses. . . .

Speaking only for myself, I can see that if Central American refugees' rights to political asylum are decisively rejected by the U.S. government or if the U.S. legal system insists on ransom that exceeds our ability to pay, active resistance will be the only alternative to abandoning the refugees to their fate. The creation of a network of actively concerned, mutually supportive people in the U.S. and Mexico may be the best preparation for an adequate response.

—A network? Quakers will know what I mean.

This letter is addressed primarily to Friends because their history presents them with special responsibilities. If the time does come when Quakers are once again being jailed in the U.S. for helping refugees, the implications will be clear to everyone. This is one reason the U.S. government is usually reluctant to jail Quakers for conscientious resistance and may sometimes even modify oppressive policies in order to avoid creating a confrontation, but to this special consideration entails an obligation not to abandon the victims of war and oppression, even when active resistance with all its risks becomes the only alternative to passive collaboration. (Corbett 1986: 1-3)

Just over a week after his encounter with the Border Patrol and the INS, Corbett began to envision a loose network of support and assistance for undocumented Central Americans—a network of "safe houses" reminiscent of the "underground railway" established by Quakers prior to the Civil War by which slaves escaped to "free" districts. As the Sanctuary movement matured, its participants frequently referred to this abolition underground, appropriating its language and imagery in an effort to give Sanctuary historical legitimacy. (INS rhetoric tried to counter this Civil War imagery by comparing the Sanctuary workers to slave traders who were importing "chattel" into the United States.)

Corbett's letter also conveyed what became a dominant motif in the movement: the comparison of Central American refugees to Jews fleeing persecution under the Nazis. This metaphor became a powerful symbol within the movement, reminding people that to "look the other way" as innocent men and women went to their deaths was to condone (and therefore participate in) their murder.

The "Mexican Connection"

In June 1981, Corbett was telephoned by a Salvadoran woman in Phoenix who said that a church person had told her that he might be able to help her. The woman explained that two of her family members, a brother and a cousin, were hiding in a house in Nogales, Sonora (Mexico). Could he do something for them? Corbett and two members of his goat-milking cooperative made the hour-and-fifteen-minute trip to Nogales, Mexico, where they found two Salvadorans hiding in a basement. Telling them to "sit tight," they wandered around Nogales and learned from the "locals" that people crossing into the United States from Mexico usually just crawled through one of the several holes in the international fence dividing the two countries. This, according to Corbett, seemed like the simple part of crossing the Salvadorans—the real difficulty would be trying to get them through the Border Patrol checks on the highway leading to Tucson. The next day, accompanied by Father Ricardo, Corbett looked for a rendezvous location on the American side of the fence and picked Sacred Heart Church, located up on a hill that was close to, and easily visible from, the border. In Sacred Heart Church, Corbett and Father Ricardo met a priest who was sympathetic to their agenda and referred them to a Mexican priest working in Nogales who was known to be helping Central Americans apprehended by the Mexican police. The priest, Ramón Dagoberto Quiñones, together with one of his parishioners, a widow named María del Socorro Pardo de Aguilar, eventually became the Mexican coordinators of the Sanctuary movement. (Their counterparts on the U.S. side of Nogales were Father Tony Clark, a priest at Sacred Heart Church, and Mary K. Espinosa, coordinator of the religious education program at the church.)

Father Quiñones and Doña María were members of Santuario de Guadalupe, a church that provided social services to the poor of Nogales, Mexico—a city swelling with people looking for jobs in the *maquiladoras*.[24] Paid around four dollars per day, Mexican workers and their families often had to live in cardboard shacks built upon the discarded skids from these assembly plants. Squatter communities dotted the garbage-strewn hillsides of Nogales, Sonora, and their inhabitants, bereft of running water and electricity, could look out across the border at the relative opulence of Nogales, Arizona, a stone's throw away. Quiñones's church, responding to the dire poverty of the town, had created a nursing home for homeless old people, and operated a free medical/dental clinic and a soup kitchen. One of the church's more recent ministries involved visiting the many Central Americans jailed in the Nogales penitentiary (Centro para Readaptación Social). According to Quiñones and Doña

María, the stories they heard from the Central Americans indicated that there was no way that a person could safely apply for political asylum at the border; many had approached U.S. Customs guards but had been promptly handed over to the Mexican immigration police, *la migra*, and then jailed for deportation. Quiñones, Doña María, and Corbett concluded that the only way for a Central American to apply for political asylum was within the United States. The trio therefore had few qualms about helping Central Americans cross into the United States, where, at least legally, they were entitled to apply for refugee status. Corbett eventually became part of the Mexican ministry and began to visit the jail in Nogales (dressed in clerical garb). As deportations of Central Americans became increasingly routine, Corbett clandestinely taught Salvadorans Mexican idioms and the street names of Nogales, Sonora, in case they were queried by the Border Patrol (Golden and McConnell 1986: 40); Doña María helped women change their hairstyles and clothing to look more Mexican (Crittenden 1988: 50-51). The main point behind this strategy was, in case of apprehension by the Border Patrol, to convince the officers that the Central Americans were Mexicans. If this worked, they would merely be sent back over the border (the usual procedure for dealing with illegal Mexicans) and could try to cross again at another time. If detained as Central Americans, they would in all likelihood be jailed and formally deported—which often amounted to being dumped by bus at a port of entry in Guatemala, where military personnel would systematically check and interview the passengers.

As Corbett perceived it, the real problem for Central Americans fleeing violence was that at the U.S. border the Mexican informal, church-based system of protection and transportation collapsed. What was required was a "border ministry"—a strategy of action that would safely move Central Americans into the United States where they could contact a lawyer and apply for asylum. In another open letter (July 6, 1981), Corbett detailed treatment of Central Americans by the INS and began to formulate a theology of an "underground" based on the notion of hospitality to strangers and incorporating elements of Latin American liberation theology, particularly the concept of *comunidades de base*. Corbett's letter also contained possibly the first reference in the movement's history to the concept of "sanctuary." In typical Quaker fashion, he treated Sanctuary not as a historical and legal institution but as a community activity (what he referred to as a church) whose members are gathered around a commitment to (or "solidarity" with) the dispossessed and the poor.

The first meeting of what became the Sanctuary underground was held in the fall of 1981 at the Santa Rosa mission church in Tucson's Yaqui Village (called Old Pascua).[25] The underground was named the tucson refugee support group (trsg)—all lowercase letters because the Quaker contingent did not believe in, nor wish to create, any kind of formal or official organization.[26]

Pursuing the "Legal Route"

So if you hear from the INS that what those churchpeople ought to do is try to work within the law first, we did it. And we did it with as much energy and imagination and creativity as we could.

—Rev. John Fife (quoted in "Conspiracy of Compassion,"
Sojourners [14], 1985: 16)

We began with an absolute belief in the system, a belief in the integrity of the system. . . . On that I'm very emphatic. And on my part I had no reason whatever to imagine that they [the INS] would descend to the tricks that they decided to.

—Gary MacEoin (interview, March 1991)

While Jim Corbett, Father Quiñones, and the members of the Quaker goat-milking cooperative were developing the infrastructure of a quiet underground railway, the TEC task force continued to pursue a legal and public way of aiding undocumented Central Americans. In June 1981, the TECTF group met to discuss a strategy for aiding Central Americans jailed by the INS and facing probable deportation. The group decided on a strategy of bailing out the Central Americans located in El Centro, California, but in a way that would attract as much media attention as possible. (This emphasis on media coverage and media-staged events became "a hallmark of Tucson's activist strategy" [Crittenden 1988: 43].) On July 10, 1981, after obtaining a court injunction that permitted them access to the Central Americans in El Centro, a group headed by Rev. Ken Kennon (pastor of Broadway Christian Church and the first chair of the TEC task force) traveled the five hours to the detention center. El Centro was built in 1973 to house a maximum of 250 inmates (usually undocumented Mexicans), but in 1981 when the TECTF group arrived, between three hundred and four hundred prisoners were being held there in very bad conditions (one example: inmates were locked outside in a corral during the day, often in 110 degree weather, with little access to shade). The inmates were also isolated from legal assistance (the nearest cities with legal aid for refugees were Los Angeles, San Diego, Phoenix, and Tucson—two, three, four, and five hours away, respectively, by car).

For two weeks, sixty rotating volunteers processed asylum forms and freed (on bail) ninety Central Americans.[27] For many, the process was a crash course in U.S. immigration and asylum law. This "education" produced the realization that the vast majority of Salvadorans (up to a thousand per month) were being routinely deported by the INS without ever having known that they could apply for political asylum (Golden and McConnell 1986: 41). Moreover, the number of Salvadorans who were granted political asylum was miniscule in proportion to the demand. It was becoming apparent to the task force that the legal route might be statistically doomed: bonding out the Central Americans "bought time" (approximately two years after all appeals had been exhausted) but by no means guaranteed political asylum (ibid.: 44).

An Expanding Network

As many of Tucson's churches and citizens began to organize resettlement programs for the bonded-out Central Americans, several California churches were working with the Central American refugees who had flooded into the Los Angeles area via Tijuana, Mexico—many of whom then moved northward into the San Francisco area. Tucson's contact with the Los Angeles and San Francisco network of lawyers and churches that were aiding refugees had already begun during the El Centro bailout. Significantly, one of the California contacts was a Lutheran pastor from the San Francisco Bay area, Gus Schultz, who had "pioneered sanctuary for conscientious objectors to the Vietnam War in Berkeley a decade earlier . . . [and who] was now talking to his weekly clergy reflection group about sanctuary for Central Americans" (MacEoin 1985: 19). In the fall of 1981, a group called the Sather Gate Churches—a coalition composed of the pastors of churches located near the University of California Berkeley campus—decided to form the East Bay Sanctuary Covenant. In October of that year, Lutheran Social Services distributed a letter detailing the idea of declaring Sanctuary for Central Americans fleeing violence in Guatemala and El Salvador. The letter was prompted by an incident in which an INS agent had chased a undocumented man into a church and arrested him there. The action provoked a public outcry, prompting the local INS director to respond with an administrative order to all agents: under no conditions were agents to pursue persons if they entered a church, hospital, or school (Crittenden 1988: 64). In November 1981, St. John's Presbyterian Church in Berkeley secretly began to shelter an undocumented Central American family (Bau 1985: 11-12).

Jim Corbett too was secretly harboring Central Americans on his property. The situation, however, was quickly getting out of hand: twenty-one Salvadorans were camping together in a little adobe house, with people sleeping in two tiny rooms and all sharing one modest, permanently dirty bathroom. Corbett asked John Fife if Southside Church could take in some of the refugees. Fife was sympathetic, but unable to make such a decision without consulting his congregation. He said that he would put it to the session of elders being held the following week. Corbett attended the session and made an eloquent appeal; Southside voted in favor of the proposal—two of only four abstentions were federal employees who felt that they could not support the resolution, but did not want to block it. The session, however, had reservations and queries both about how the INS would view their activities and whether helping the Central Americans constituted a violation of U.S. immigration laws.

After the vote, some of Corbett's Central Americans moved into Southside Church, and Fife became more actively involved in what the underground termed "evasion services." Fife and others in the movement assumed that what they were doing was illegal, but—following in the tradition of Martin Luther King Jr., Gandhi, and Dietrich Bonhoeffer—thought it was absolutely necessary to save lives. Although Fife did not publicize his work with the underground, he did announce to his congregation of 120 that the church was assisting Central Americans.

Declaring Sanctuary

Establishing a "Playground"

We decided to go public because we had all become aware that a full-scale holocaust was going on in Central America, and by keeping the operation clandestine we were doing exactly what the government wanted us to do—keeping it hidden, keeping the issue out of public view.
                    —Jim Corbett (quoted in Golden and McConnell 1986: 47)

The actual declaration of sanctuary in Tucson was profoundly shaped by the U.S. government's initial response to the church groups that were assisting undocumented Central Americans. Around Thanksgiving 1981, an INS attorney approached Margo Cowan of the Manzo Area Council while she was attending an asylum hearing at Tucson's Federal Building.[28] The lawyer told her that the INS knew "something" was going on with Corbett, Fife, and some Central Americans. The lawyer added that they had better stop what they were doing or the government would have to indict them. Shortly afterward, an "emergency meeting" was called for members of the TEC task force and those engaged in evasion services for the refugees.

The central problem for the group was the possibility of the government's immediately calling a grand-jury investigation that would grant immunity to those testifying before it. Since persons under immunity cannot refuse to testify on grounds of self-incrimination, TECTF members who did not cooperate could be jailed for contempt and end up behind bars before the turmoil in Central America even became a public issue (see Gillet 1984). Arguing that the churches would have to preempt the government's actions by making Central America a media issue, John Fife came up with the idea of declaring Southside Church a sanctuary for Central American refugees:[29]

> And so we sat around this very room [Fife's living room], about ten or twelve of us, saying what'll we do now? And at that point I opened my mouth and said maybe what we need to do is beat 'em [the government] to the punch. And take the initiative, and we'll go public. And then when we're indicted at least we'll have some interpretation. I think what I said was that they'll have to play in our playground. Maybe that's the best we can do out of it. Beat 'em to the punch. Sanctuary emerged out of this discussion. (John Fife, interview, June 1990)

Since many of those in the group had tried the "legal route" of assisting Central Americans and found it clearly unsatisfactory (not one of the fourteen hundred Central Americans bailed out of El Centro had received asylum [Golden and McConnell 1986: 14]), they supported the idea— with the exception of the Manzo Area Council lawyers.[30]

One of Fife's greatest fears was that the whole issue of undocumented Central Americans and the forces compelling them to leave their countries could be swept under the rug if the public were encouraged to see what they were doing simply as "breaking the law." As a result, he urged that Sanctuary become a media event, something that would garner regional, perhaps even national, attention and force the government to address their concerns. In an interview held just over ten years after this meeting, Fife conveyed the sense that there was no formal, premeditated envisioning of a "social movement" and that Sanctuary really was the product of INS pressure:

> We didn't think we were starting a movement—or anything! All I was trying to do was get the congregation through a process. I thought what we were doing was in isolation here in Tucson. And basically it was in self-defense. We didn't want to do it. It was all in response to Border Patrol and us scrambling to figure out what the heck to do now. That's not exactly sterling leadership! So there wasn't that much intentionality to it at all. We were just trying to keep our heads above water. And assumed that when we did the public announcement, we would be

indicted. The assumption was that they were just going to do it on our playground. We had no idea that it [Sanctuary] would go elsewhere. (John Fife, interview, June 1990)

Voting on Sanctuary

On the last Sunday in November 1981, John Fife announced to his congregation that, at their annual general meeting in January, he would be calling for a vote on whether or not to declare Southside a sanctuary. For the next two months, Southside buzzed with activity. The congregation held Bible study meetings and information sessions on U.S. immigration laws as part of an educational process so that by January the congregation would have a shared vocabulary for discussing the issue.

In January 1982, Southside held its general meeting—an occasion when the church usually approved an annual budget, elected its elders and deacons, and discussed projects for the coming year. At this meeting, however, the congregation faced a much more significant decision. After five hours of debate and prayer—in which many were extremely reluctant to condone the breaking of the law, and one man was completely opposed to the idea of Sanctuary—Fife called for a secret ballot in order to gain a sense of what direction the community was taking. The vote was seventy-nine in favor of Sanctuary with two against, and four abstentions (about 65 percent of the total congregation voted). It was decided that Southside would declare itself a sanctuary on March 24, 1982, the second anniversary of Archbishop Romero's assassination,[31] and that the declaration would be coordinated with as many other churches as possible that were willing to declare sanctuary at the same time. (The day after the vote, the member of the congregation so bitterly opposed to Sanctuary sent a letter to the FBI informing them of Southside's intentions.)

On March 23, 1982, Fife sent a letter to U.S. Attorney General William French Smith, U.S Attorney Melvin McDonald (Arizona), INS officer William Johnston, and Border Patrol director Leon Ring (Tucson sector). The letter informed the government of Southside's plans to declare sanctuary and called for change in U.S. immigration practices. The next day, as churches across the United States were honoring Archbishop Romero's memory with special events and services, Southside Church declared sanctuary. A six-foot table was set in front of Southside's front double doors, above which hung a four-foot cross. Two banners were placed on each side of the doorway: the one on the left (as you faced the church) stated, "La migra no profana el santuario" (Immigration, do not defile the sanctuary); the one on the right, "Este es el santuario de Dios para los oprimidos de Centro América" (This is God's sanctuary for the oppressed of Central America). Fife was seated in the middle of the table; to his right sat Alfredo (a Salvadoran man wearing a bandana over his nose and mouth) and Father Ricardo; to his left sat Gary MacEoin and Jim Corbett. Several others stood and sat behind the table, including the only woman present, Joanne Welter (president of TEC). At 10 A.M., in front of eight television cameras and forty newspaper reporters (including journalists from California and New York), Fife read the text of the letter he had sent to the U.S. Attorney General the day before.[32] He then welcomed and introduced Alfredo, a thirty-year-old Salvadoran who had worked for an agrarian reform program that had been crushed by the army. (Fife explained that Alfredo was wearing a bandana because he did not wish the Salvadoran military to discover his identity and take retaliation against his family back home. *Newsweek* [April 5, 1982] reported that Alfredo was "an underground tactician for the guerrillas in El Salvador.") Visibly nervous, Alfredo made a brief statement (in Spanish) about social conditions in El Salvador. (Jim Corbett, Gary MacEoin, Margo Cowan, and Father Ricardo Elford also made statements.)

While Southside Presbyterian declared sanctuary, a similar ceremony was conducted at the University Lutheran Chapel in Berkeley, California, where five churches publicly became sanctuaries.

That evening, Fife and several other clergymen, including one rabbi, led roughly 230 supporters on a march from downtown Tucson to Southside Church (about 1½ miles), where they celebrated an ecumenical service "in solidarity with Central American refugees." The INS undercover agent who attended wrote in a memo to his supervisors:

> Aside from old people, most of them looked like the anti-Vietnam war protestors of the early 70s. In other words, political misfits. . . . I attended the "service" to see what they were going to do. . . . The service appeared to be purely a political show with all the ministers, priests, etc. at the altar area. . . . Various times during the first part of the "service" while cameras were going good, the "Frito Bandito" [Alfredo] appeared in the front doorway. . . . I refer to an alleged El Salvadorian [sic] wearing a black mask, who has been used in various photos. . . . There was nothing really inflammatory or inciting said, it was rather bland. . . . It seems that this movement is more political than religious but that a ploy is going to be Border Patrol "baiting" by that group in order to demonstrate to the public that the U.S. government via it's [sic] jack-booted gestapo Border Patrol Agents think [sic] nothing of breaking down the doors of their churches to drag Jesus Christ out to be tortured and murdered.

I believe that all political implications should be considered before any further action is taken toward this group. (Thomas Martin, Tucson, March 24, 1982)

The government followed agent Martin's advice and pursued a quiet but vigilant "hands off" policy toward church sanctuary for Central Americans. While the state sat back to "watch," other churches joined the movement. Within a year of Southside's declaration, forty-five faith communities in the United States had declared themselves sanctuaries for Central Americans, and more than six hundred congregations and religious organizations were cosponsors of these sanctuaries (MacEoin 1985: 23). By December 1982, Tucson's underground extended south to Mexico City and was developing lines to Chicago, Los Angeles, San Francisco, Seattle, New York, and Boston. Along the Mexico-U.S. border at Nogales, Father Quiñones and Doña María were sheltering Central Americans (in private homes and the church) before they crossed into the United States, where they were picked up by Sanctuary workers and driven to Tucson. Within six months, volunteers had begun to arrive from the East and West Coasts, as well as the Midwest, in order to participate in Sanctuary work. Fife estimated that by year's end Southside Church alone had sheltered 1,600 Salvadorans (Bau 1985: 11)—roughly 0.3 percent of the INS estimate of 500,000 illegal aliens that crossed into the American Southwest from Mexico every year, and 0.5 percent of the 300,000 undocumented Salvadorans residing in the United States.

Chapter 3

Local History, Part 2: The U.S. Sanctuary Movement on Trial (January 1983 to July 1986)

In resurrecting the tradition of ecclesial asylum, Sanctuary church groups attempted to frame their activities as a church-state conflict. This framework gave the religious groups involved a powerful set of cultural resources with which to combat the threat of government prosecution. Through Sanctuary, offering food and shelter to Central Americans suddenly became a First Amendment issue (the right to practice religion free of government interference)—later it became a collective moral (church) critique of the government's actions. Because the issue of undocumented Central Americans was moved into a church—a cultural space and jurisdiction ostensibly protected from the arm of the state—Sanctuary severely limited the way in which the government could respond. Yet, precisely because the issue of Central American fugitives was framed as a church-state conflict, government representatives were able to formulate a counterframework—their own "playground," so to speak—for resolving the conflict. This framework underscored an equally powerful cultural tradition of separation between religion and politics, one that stressed strict adherence to the "laws of the land." The church-state dimensions of Sanctuary, then, were inherently ambiguous since they offered both government officials and Sanctuary participants a tradition with which to condemn the opponent. Consequently, the probable "winner" of this church-state conflict was difficult to predict.

State Responses to Sanctuary

If sanctuary is feeding and clothing persons in distress, then the INS does that. The

35

immigration service feeds more and clothes more Salvadorans than [does] anybody in the Sanctuary movement. If that is what sanctuary is, then I'm for it. I'd be a member. But if it is encouraging illegal immigration, or if it is helping the surreptitious entry of an alien, I'm not only against it, Congress is against it, and Congress is reflected in the statute. And if I catch a person doing this, then I'm going to prosecute them.

—INS official (interview, Tucson, September 1990)

Government surveillance of the Sanctuary movement began at the March 24 press conference on the sun-swept steps of Southside Presbyterian Church in 1982. The INS, which had no explicit policy regarding churches, decided to hold off from conducting a formal investigation—at least initially.

On December 12, 1982, the CBS television program "60 Minutes" aired a segment on Central American refugees that presented a rather sympathetic portrait of the Sanctuary movement. The government came off negatively; it appeared to be a callous institution that was persecuting women, children, and families who were fleeing terrible violence. (Then Assistant Secretary of State for Inter-American Affairs Elliot Abrams claimed on the program—after viewers had been exposed to the horrors of El Salvador—that Salvadorans fleeing to the United States had no well-founded fears of persecution and were entering the country primarily for economic reasons.) The program engendered a flurry of activity in the INS and letters to the western regional office of the INS requesting that an investigation into the Sanctuary movement be initiated.

The man assigned to lead the investigation was antismuggling agent James Rayburn, a forty-one-year-old veteran of the Border Patrol from Texas. Rayburn had served in the Vietnam War (where he had been captured by the Vietcong) and had a passionate hatred of communism (Crittenden 1988: 105-6). In January 1983, Rayburn contacted an INS intelligence agent, Dean M. Thatcher, about preparing a preliminary report on the movement. Thatcher's memorandum commented:

> The Sanctuary Movement does not appear to be a serious threat
> to enforcement efforts by the Service [INS] when viewed in its
> overall context. However, if the movement's growth is
> misinterpreted through lack of intelligence, the service image
> could be adversely affected. At this point, it appears that some
> churches are using the sanctuary concept to rally congregations,
> and create cohisiveness [sic] in Hispanic parishes. This type of
> movement is particularly attractive to pastors with a political
> bent that are seeking a cause. Those who are normally satisfied
> to vent their ill humors in the *Sojourners* [a progressive Christian

magazine] would consider refugee sanctuary as de rigor [*sic*]. Risks would be minimal, considering the reluctance of the state to incur the wrath of the church. Whatever liability that is incurred from Sanctuary can be written off by the relative merits of gaining martyrdom. (Thatcher, January 4, 1983, internal INS memorandum)

The memorandum conveyed the generally ambivalent sensibility of the INS and the Justice Department toward prosecuting Sanctuary. The government recognized the powerful cultural authority that churches possessed in the United States, and acknowledged the potentially explosive nature of becoming involved in a church-state conflict. Yet many government officials were offended (and irritated) by the ideological direction of the movement. Literature on Sanctuary produced by the Chicago sector of the movement—particularly with its liberation theology orientation and strong condemnation of U.S. foreign policy in Central America—was used by the government as evidence that Sanctuary was a "political" rather than a "religious" movement.

That same January, Rayburn began surveillance of the Sanctuary movement and hired four agents to conduct the undercover investigation: Salomón Graham (an undocumented Mexican who had been arrested for illegal entry and transporting aliens); Jesús Cruz, a Mexican-born permanent resident (also previously convicted for transporting illegal aliens); and two INS agents, John Nixon Jr. and Lee Morgan.

On July 12, 1983, "Frontline" aired a program on Central American refugees and the Sanctuary movement. Like the "60 Minutes" program, it was a powerful condemnation of the INS's treatment of Central Americans who were fleeing violence and was sympathetic to the work of Jim Corbett. Harold Ezell, INS director of the western region (the most prestigious of the INS's four regions), was infuriated by the program. In December, Ezell informed the Phoenix office of the INS that he wanted the Sanctuary investigation stepped up. The INS authorized an undercover operation (originally called the "Underground Railroad" but changed to "Operation Sojourner")[1] for a three-month period. The agents' mandate was limited; they could neither engage in illegal activities (though they were permitted to attend meetings with possible conspirators and transport aliens within the United States) nor participate in acts of violence or use unlawful investigative techniques to obtain information. The agents had to obtain authorization from the Justice Department for any clandestine collection of evidence. By March 1984, Rayburn decided that he "had no alternative" but to initiate an undercover investigation, and therefore requested authorization to secretly tape-record conversations between the agents and Sanctuary participants.[2] (Agent Jesús Cruz began taping conversations on April 22, 1984, although Rayburn did not receive official permission to do this until May 24.)

The agents infiltrated the Sanctuary movement at its three main points of "alien" activity: Nogales, Tucson, and Phoenix. The undercover agents became "volunteers" for the movement, and attended underground meetings and church services. They routinely taped private conversations in people's homes and in churches using concealed body bugs, and they transported Salvadorans and Guatemalans between Nogales, Tucson, and Phoenix. During these drives, the agents recorded conversations with Central Americans about why they were coming into the United States, how they had gotten there, and who had helped them. By the summer of 1984, many Sanctuary workers had become suspicious of these "volunteers," particularly Salomón Graham, John Nixon, and Morgan Lee. These individuals just did not seem to fit the profile of a Sanctuary participant. As Ann Crittenden noted, all three were in their late thirties or early forties, drove Trans Ams, were available twenty-four hours a day to do transporting, and seemed eager to take days off work to drive Central Americans to safe houses.[3] Many Sanctuary workers were willing to overlook their suspicions, however, because the men's availability was convenient; as one Sanctuary worker recounted, they could always be counted on to say yes to a job.

The involvement of undercover agents in the movement illustrates how the declaration of sanctuary forced the INS to define its status as a law-enforcement agency. The role it eventually adopted was based, perhaps predictably, on an adversarial model and, as a result, played into the church-state oppositional paradigm that the Sanctuary workers hoped to utilize. The tussle between the two camps became one of establishing—in the eyes of the "public" observing Sanctuary through media reports—which side represented legitimate authority.

Internal Divisions

The issues of communication, and control, and turf, and all those kinds of things have been with us since the very beginning. We were always fighting with one another, right from the beginning.

—Rev. Ken Kennon (October 1990)

As the movement spread, differences arose over the ideology of Sanctuary—its direction, goals, structure, and procedures. By September 1983, there were two main camps—"Chicago" and "Tucson." Although not the only divisions in the movement, these camps became paradigmatic labels referring to the main differences within the coalition.[4]

In July 1982, the Tucson Ecumenical Council task force approached the Chicago Religious Task Force on Central America (CRTF) about becoming a national coordinator for the Sanctuary movement—an organization that could act as a communications clearinghouse by publishing and distributing information about Sanctuary, develop a mailing list, and locate communities that would take a refugee into Sanctuary. The CRTF was a coalition of religious and social-action groups formed largely in response to the murder of four American churchwomen in El Salvador in 1980. Many of its thirteen steering committee members were ministers and Catholic missionaries (nuns and priests) who had served or traveled in Central America. Strongly influenced by Latin American liberation theology, CRTF had the primary objective of standing "with the cry of the dispossessed" and organizing the opposition of the U.S. religious sector to the government's financing of nominally civilian military regimes in Central America (see "Organization, Purpose, Faith Commitment and Composition of CRTF," *Basta!* January 1985: 6). The coalition hoped that by mobilizing public sentiment against the government, U.S. aid to El Salvador would cease (Golden and McConnell 1986: 51-52).[5] In 1982, CRTF convinced the Wellington Avenue United Church of Christ in Chicago to become a sanctuary for Central Americans. They contacted TEC and the underground, and told them that Chicago wanted a refugee to enter "public Sanctuary."

From the beginning of its involvement, the CRTF leadership envisioned Sanctuary as a "public event"—a set of activities that would draw the attention of the media and thereby alert the public to what was going on in Central America and propel them to action. Sanctuary, according to one of its steering committee members, "at its best has not been a place to hide in, but a platform to speak out from, as the poor of Central America bear witness to their reality. . . . Sanctuary is a place where refugees can speak the truth" (Golden and McConnell 1986: 2).[6] Once the CRTF became coordinator of Sanctuary's political advocacy campaign, it set up a network of Sanctuary churches, and distributed over thirty thousand copies of manuals and booklets instructing churches on how they could become involved in Sanctuary.[7] CRTF's "public Sanctuary" involved refugees who were processed through TEC, were interviewed by a CRTF representative in Phoenix, and, in some cases, were trained for public speaking about the social and political conditions in their countries. Sister Darlene Nicgorski, a Catholic nun who had lived in Guatemala, often conducted these interviews.

One of the main disagreements between the TEC and the CRTF was over civil disobedience. John Fife's March 23, 1982, letter to the INS indicated that the Sanctuary church was breaking the law—but, it suggested, so was the U.S. government. Who then, church or state, was violating the law? At first, the Tucson group assumed that it was following in the "civil disobedience" tradition of Henry David Thoreau and Martin Luther King Jr. After contact with secular legal groups, however, particularly the ACLU, members of Tucson's Sanctuary network began to explore the concept of "civil initiative." Civil initiative was rooted in the principles of the Nuremberg Trials, according to which citizens are legally obligated to disobey inhumane governments. Building on these principles, civil initiative argued that the Sanctuary workers were operating in accordance with international treaties that the United States had signed and was bound to uphold.[8] Since, on the basis of these treaties, the Central Americans had "rights" to be in the United States, Sanctuary workers were not breaking the law when they helped refugees enter the country and avoid INS interception. Rather, they were upholding laws that the U.S. government was violating; Sanctuary actions therefore constituted a "civil initiative."[9]

Some members of CRTF did not find civil initiative an appealing concept; they felt that it undercut the compelling political statement that only civil disobedience could make:

> Sanctuary by its very nature breaks the law and/or current
> implementation of law. All of us in the Sanctuary Movement
> have chosen to break the law, not as an end in itself, but to
> defend the powerless, the Central Americans in the U.S. and
> those still in their homelands. (*Basta!* Editor's note, January
> 1985: 21)

A second area of disagreement between the two camps emerged around the "kind" of refugees the Sanctuary network would assist. Factions within the larger coalition wanted to restrict the underground to those Central Americans fleeing right-wing violence and repression—it did not make sense to some to put refugees who were fleeing brutal violence in the same community of solidarity as their oppressors. (Theoretically, a fugitive could meet up with his or her torturer.) TECTF and trsg policy, however, did not wish to exclude *any* refugees from the Sanctuary network.[10]

Tensions over the political orientation of refugees spilled over into disagreement about the "religious" and "political" nature of the Sanctuary movement. In a letter to the TECTF (February 10, 1984), the CRTF steering committee articulated its understanding of the religious-political nature of the movement—one that not only underscored an explicit political orientation to Sanctuary but also echoed many of the statements made by Latin American liberation theologians about the church's need to address the *causes* and *structures* of oppression:

> Some call the sending of medicine to a war-torn country "humanitarian" but then label efforts to stop the flow of weapons that do the killing in the first place "political." . . . To separate the religious from the political in this fashion is to create a false dichotomy. . . . During the rise of the Third Reich, Dietrich Bonhoeffer said that the church must of course bind up the victims being crushed beneath the wheel, but there comes a time when the church must be the stick put in the spokes to stop the wheel from crushing the people. (quoted in Davidson 1988: 83)

Some Tucson members interpreted the CRTF statement as implying that their work along the border was merely "Band-Aid humanitarian" work. They regarded CRTF statements as a kind of "political harassment," a way of trying to impose a particular ideology by disparaging a certain "style" of Sanctuary. Members of the Chicago sector, in contrast, felt that Tucson refused to acknowledge the structural dimensions of Sanctuary work. On behalf of TECTF, Jim Corbett articulated a somewhat different concept of Sanctuary:

> [Tucson's] view contrasts fundamentally with the interpretation that would convert the growing network of Sanctuary congregations into a mass movement that is defined by its political objectives and distinguished by its religious identity. The Sanctuary covenant community that has formed in Tucson could never assimilate into such a movement because we provide Sanctuary for the persecuted regardless of the political origins of their persecution or of their usefulness in promoting preconceived objectives. We are convinced that whenever the covenant community's decision to stand with the oppressed is understood to mean it must place itself in a subordinate alignment with any creed, ideology, hierarchy, platform, armed force, or party, its prophetic role is betrayed and its reconciling role is abandoned. We disagree with any interpretation of Sanctuary that would shape it selectively into a factional instrument. (Corbett 1986: 112)

These conflicting interpretations of Sanctuary's theological and religiopolitical nature were linked to differences over the structural organization of the movement. In keeping both with a Quaker-influenced philosophy of a "church" (a community guided by the spiritual experiences of its members and resistant to any official doctrine or structure) and ideologies of nonviolent direct action (which favored fragmented organization), Jim Corbett and John Fife advocated a loosely linked, horizontal network of Sanctuary churches without one person or group directing the movement. The CRTF, frustrated by what it perceived to be a disorganized, and ultimately ineffectual, "just-let-the-movement-happen" model, called for a clarification of goals. While Tucson accused Chicago of trying to turn the movement into a hierarchical, bureaucratic "superstructure," Chicago chastised Tucson for ignoring the structural and political-economic causes that were producing the refugees and creating confusion by advocating organizational "anarchy."[11]

Differences between "Catholic" and "Quaker/congregationalist-Protestant" cultures may have played an important role in dividing the movement. Each group possessed a different set of cultural values about what a church movement was and how it should be organized. Dominated by Catholic clerics, nuns, and laypersons, the CRTF wanted a defined identity, a clear set of goals, and regulation of procedure. To a certain extent, the "structure of administration" and the "ideology of membership" it advocated resembled that of the Catholic church, itself a centralized institution directed by a steering committee. TECTF, strongly influenced by a group of unprogrammed Quakers and Presbyterians whose traditions rejected overarching creeds, doctrine, and hierarchical decision-making structures, pursued a vision of Sanctuary modeled on a congregational paradigm. In this model, the local community always acted on the basis of its own spiritual reflection and experience, independent of any central directorate.[12]

Relations between the two camps reached a low point in October 1984 when CRTF refused to release to Jim Corbett a mailing list of all the Sanctuary sites in the United States. Corbett wrote a letter back to the CRTF denouncing the formation of a directorate and acknowledging that the rift was becoming serious. Because CRTF animosity was directed principally at him, he indicated, he would no longer participate in a leadership role in the Sanctuary movement. A reconciliation was initiated by CRTF through a series of letters, telephone calls, and publication of Tucson opinions in its newsletter, but as of December 1984 the two streams continued to drift in different directions.

The Chicago Religious Task Force went on to form the National Sanctuary Alliance (NSA) and the National Sanctuary Communications Council (NSCC), which stayed linked to an independent fund-raising organization, the National Sanctuary Defense Fund (NSDF). Tucson's Sanctuary community generally maintained independence from the NSA, although dissenters within TECTF allied their activities with the Chicago-based wing. Hence, these ideological and structural differences were reproduced within Tucson's Sanctuary community.

Sanctuary Arrests and Indictments

In February 1984, Stacey Lynn Merkt along with a Catholic sister, Dianne Muhlenkamp, a *Dallas Times Herald* reporter, and three Salvadorans were stopped by the U.S. Border Patrol in Texas. Merkt, a Methodist in her mid-twenties, was a refugee worker for Casa Romero, a hospitality house for Central Americans (founded on December 2, 1981) run by the Roman Catholic diocese of Brownsville, Texas. Muhlenkamp pleaded guilty to a misdemeanor and was released on a year's probation, but Merkt was indicted and convicted in May 1984 on three federal felony counts: two of aiding and abetting the unlawful transportation of undocumented aliens and one of conspiracy to transport undocumented aliens. In June, Merkt was sentenced to a ninety-day suspended sentence and two years' probation, but a court of appeals for the fifth judicial circuit reversed and set aside the convictions.[13] Merkt was again arrested while transporting undocumented Salvadorans in December 1984. For her second arrest, she was convicted of one count of conspiracy and was sentenced to an eighteen-month prison term and three years' probation. She began serving her sentence on January 29, 1987 (after several appeals were rejected), at the Federal Correctional Institution in Fort Worth, Texas.[14] Stacey Lynn Merkt was the first person in the United States to be tried and imprisoned for her work with undocumented Central Americans (see Bosniak and Rasmussen 1984).

Merkt's arrest was a signal that the U.S. government was not going to take a passive stance toward Sanctuary. It was also seized upon and publicized by the churches as a case of Christian "martyrdom" in the face of an oppressive state—exactly what agent Dean M. Thatcher had predicted.

On March 7, 1984, approximately one month after Merkt's first arrest, the staff coordinator of TECTF, Phillip Willis-Conger, was stopped by the Border Patrol. Willis-Conger and another volunteer, Katherine Flaherty, had been in Nogales organizing a "crossing" of four Salvadorans. They were driving back to Tucson when they were pulled over and arrested. Willis-Conger's knapsack was confiscated and its contents were forwarded to James Rayburn in Phoenix.[15] The documents he had been carrying included the names and addresses of Sanctuary contacts along the U.S.-Mexico border, maps to safe houses, and a document by Jim Corbett titled "Some Proposals for Integrating Smuggling, Refuge, Relay, Sanctuary and Bailbond Networks." The five-page document included information on how the Sanctuary networks should be formed and coordinated, as well as on the four main refugee routes from Guatemala through Mexico and into the United States. Willis-Conger's indictment was dropped after a judge ruled that the Border Patrol had made an illegal stop and search, but his arrest sent warning tremors through Tucson that further indictments of Sanctuary workers might be imminent.

On January 14, 1985, the anticipated indictments came down: a grand jury in Phoenix returned a seventy-one-count indictment for sixteen people. Those indicted were Father Ramón Quiñones, María Socorro Aguilar, Sister Darlene Nicgorski, Sister Mary Waddell, Sister Ana Priester, Father Anthony Clark, Phillip Willis-Conger, Katherine Flaherty, Jim Corbett, Rev. John Fife, Mary Kay Espinosa, Peggy Hutchison, Wendy LeWin, Nena MacDonald, Bertha Martel-Benavidez, and Cecilia del Carmen Juárez deEmery. (The last two were Central Americans who had used agent Jesús Cruz to help them get family members into the United States via Nogales.)[16] At the same time, the INS rounded up and arrested several of the Central Americans whom the Sanctuary movement had helped cross into the United States, and who were among the 74 unindicted coconspirators (of whom 49 were Central Americans and 25 were U.S. citizens).[17] By the time of the trial, however, the counts had been reduced to 52 (later to 45 and then 30), and the indictments dropped to 11.

The charges against the Sanctuary workers involved five "substantive" offenses and two "shielding" offenses. The five substantive charges involved crossing illegal aliens (this included "masterminding an operation which aids an alien to walk across a border"); transporting illegal aliens; concealing, and harboring or shielding illegal aliens (three separate felonies). The derivative charges involved conspiracy, aiding, and abetting (Matas 1989: 67). Each charge involved a prison sentence and/or a fine (see tables 3.1 and 3.2).[18]

The spectrum of those indicted for Sanctuary work included both the leadership and the volunteer core of the movement. The prosecuting attorney and drafter of the indictments, Don Reno, wished to send a clear message of "deterrence" to those involved in the movement. Even the most peripheral Sanctuary activity (such as that of Nena MacDonald) would be treated by the government as a serious violation of immigration laws. The indictments were weighted toward those working in the Phoenix area so that the trial could be held there—a conservative and "law-and-order" city compared to Tucson.[19] (As it turned out, however, the judge allowed the trial to be held in Tucson.)

The indictments and the ensuing trial fostered the development of a local, church-based network of people who coalesced around the issue of

Table 3.1. Profiles of indicted Sanctuary workers at the time of the trial

Sanctuary worker	Age	Religious affiliation	Occupation	Location
Darlene Nicgorski	41	Catholic	Catholic sister	Phoenix, Ariz.
Wendy LeWin	26	—	Refugee volunteer worker	Phoenix, Ariz.
Katherine Flaherty	33	—	Refugee volunteer worker	Tucson, Ariz.
John Fife	45	Presbyterian	Pastor, Southside Presbyterian Church	Tucson, Ariz.
Jim Corbett	51	Quaker	Retired rancher	Tucson, Ariz.
Phillip Willis-Conger	27	Methodist	TECTF coordinator	Tucson, Ariz.
Peggy Hutchison	27	Methodist	Refugee ministry/ social work	Tucson, Ariz.
Anthony Clark	35	Catholic	Priest, Sacred Heart Church	Nogales, Ariz.
Mary Kay Espinosa	30	Catholic	Coordinator of religious education program, Sacred Heart Church	Nogales, Ariz.
Ramón Dagoberto Quiñones	50	Catholic	Priest, Santuario de Nuestra Señora Guadalupe	Nogales, Mex.
María del Socorro Pardo de Aguilar	59	Catholic	Volunteer, Santuario de Nuestra Señora Guadalupe	Nogales, Mex.
Nena MacDonald	38	Quaker	Volunteer refugee worker	Lubbock, Tex.

Sanctuary. True to the ideological orientation of the Tucson group, this network was not highly centralized and consisted of several simultaneously operating segments or teams that coordinated specific tasks. One participant described the expansion of Sanctuary from the summer of 1985 to the end of the trial:

> We went crazy! You had to do all your regular work, then you got added fifty jobs. Every single person who did anything—even if you were the person who brought paper here once a week—got handed ten other jobs that had to be done. You have to picture the normal work: refugees still came, runs still occurred. But media became absolutely crazy here because we had to open up a second Sanctuary office just for media.
>   You had to have every day lunches for the defendants, their

Table 3.2. Summary of counts for the indicted Sanctuary workers

Counts	Charges
1	Conspiracy. Five years' imprisonment and/or $10,000 fine.
2–4	Bringing an alien illegally into the United States. Five years' imprisonment and/or $2,000 fine.
5–15	Aiding and abetting in the commission of transporting an illegal alien. Five years' imprisonment and/or $2,000 fine.
16	Transporting an illegal alien. Five years' imprisonment and/or $2,000 fine.
17–21	Concealing, harboring, or shielding illegal aliens. Five years' imprisonment and/or $2,000 fine.
22–24	Encouraging or inducing or attempting to encourage the entry of an illegal alien. Five years' imprisonment and/or $2,000 fine.
25–30	Unlawful entry, eluding examination or inspection. Six months' imprisonment and/or $500 fine.

Counts as charged against defendants

Darlene Nicgorski	1–9–10–11–18–19
Wendy LeWin	1–16
John Fife	1–4–5–25
Jim Corbett	1
Phillip Willis-Conger	1–6–7–8–22–26–27
Peggy Hutchison	1–29
Anthony Clark	1–15–20
Mary Kay Espinosa	1–21–30
Ramón Dagoberto Quiñones	1–3–23–28
María del Socorro de Aguilar	1–2–12–13–14–24
Nena MacDonald	1

Note: Katherine Flaherty accepted a plea bargain from Prosecutor Don Reno two weeks before the trial. Charges were dropped against Sisters Priester and Waddell; the government claimed Sister Priester was too ill with Hodgkin's disease to stand trial and needed Sister Waddell to care for her. The two Salvadoran women pleaded guilty to reduced charges and were dropped from the case.

families, their attorneys, and the media. And that had to be served between noon and one, because you only had an hour's break in court. And then two times a week they had attorney-client meetings and you had to have dinner prepared for all these people.

Then you had to have all the people who were here for the trial housed someplace. And their families housed, and their relatives, and their sister's father . . . it was endless calling people and asking, "Do you have one more bed or couch?" And the transportation! You had to have them all in court in time. We had agreed that we wouldn't use taxis. So you had to make sure that everybody every day was picked up on time at whatever house they were sleeping at and make sure they had breakfast at the house. And for families who couldn't provide breakfast you had to pick them up, get them breakfast before they got to the courthouse.

Now you have to picture that every day you had to have people typing because as you got the news from the courtroom you had to have the daily decision typed on a computer and mailed out to the media service so that you could hand it to the media. And that was every day of the trial. It was usually two or three, four pages of condensed stuff. So every day you had to have a team there to do the mass mail. Friday you did a composite of five days of court on a computer and sent it to all the people who ever contributed, all the sanctuaries, the churches, whoever asked for info. So it got to be 4,000 by the end of the trial. But every Friday here was a mailing of 4,000 and you had to get it into the mail. You know what collating is like for 4,000 pieces! This was done all by volunteers.

And then you had to have all the refugees who were being subpoenaed brought in, and that was double work. Because you had to have somebody with them all the time. You have to have them sequestered someplace so that no one would find them. You had to feed them. You had to have babysitting. So we had a whole team for watching somebody else's kids. We had to worry about how to give a breather to the defendants. Like Nena with her two kids in Texas. A couple times we flew her home even though it cost a fortune. You were constantly trying to think of that. How to get Peggy and her husband-to-be some space away from reporters.

People wore many, many hats and it tested our caring for each other. We had a weekly service planned at the cathedral. Every Tuesday at eight o'clock was a different service that a different faith had prepared for the defendants, the attorneys, and their families. There were those kinds of weekly things that took so much time. When it was all over, it was almost like death. You had lost a part of you. You were relieved but you didn't know what to do. (Sanctuary worker)

These "activity teams" offered activists in Tucson numerous "points of entry" into the movement—with the exception of the underground segment, which "contracted" while other Sanctuary activities expanded:

In the underground railroad work there was this wave of paranoia after the indictments came out. I mean, it *really* went underground. You didn't know who was doing it. You didn't even know contacts who knew who was doing it. When I first got involved I didn't have the slightest idea who was working in the underground railroad and I didn't even know how to find out. And it was just hush-hush. And everybody was paranoid about their phones being tapped and so you didn't talk to anybody. I mean you didn't even mention that aspect of the work except in euphemisms. I mean it was wild. (Sanctuary worker)

The 1985-86 trial period was formative for the TECTF Sanctuary community in that the loosely linked segments of activity came to define the structural organization of Sanctuary in Tucson. The groups coordinated their work to some extent, but as one participant recalled, "It was easy to be off in a corner and not know what was going on in the other segments." This segmentation of activities, and indeed of information, later became a conscious political strategy of TECTF. The lack of centralization ensured that if one of the segments became jeopardized it would not mean the shutdown of the whole system, since each of the units was semiautonomous. Tucson activists argued that the dispersal of authority and knowledge in these segments effectively counteracted the government's strategy, which sought to diffuse the movement by removing key leaders. In a segmented model, there simply were too many "key leaders" who oftentimes did not know much about what was going on in the other centers of activity. Almost six years after the Sanctuary trial had ended, these semi-independent segments were still generally in place, and although not all were active, they continued to be points of potential mobilization for the Tucson religious community.

Media Coverage: Structuring Church-State Conflict

So where are the authorities?
                            —Beverly Medlyn, *Arizona Daily Star* (December 15, 1982)

Although the Sanctuary leadership intended to use the media as a way of arousing public support and pressuring the state to treat undocumented Central Americans fairly, the press ended up drawing government attention to Sanctuary in a way that many in the movement did not anticipate. Media coverage not only created a "cultural aura" for Sanctuary by establishing popular images of what the movement was, but also structured the emerging disagreement between the government and churches over the fate of undocumented Central Americans.

Pretrial print coverage of the Sanctuary movement in the mainstream press showed a pervasive fascination with the underground railroad.

Many early magazine articles on Sanctuary began by recounting the experience of accompanying a Sanctuary transporter on a "run."[20] The author "took" readers into the Sonoran Desert, sometimes into the heart of southern Mexico, and, with lavish description, tried to convey what it was like to be working for the underground. Many articles depicted the underground world as dangerous, wild, and full of intrigue and potential disasters:

> *Tapachula, Chiapas, Mexico*—Screaming jungle birds and bugs overpower the sputtering of the rickety motorboat snaking through the alleys of black water and choking mangrove trees. The unfolding trail resembles a scene from the movie "African Queen," when a boat is pulled through a torrid swamp by Humphrey Bogart's leech-covered body.
> "All the better," says Jim Corbett. He eyes the route ahead and nods approvingly. "No one will ever find this place." (Williamson 1984, August 26-30, *Sacramento Bee*)

Despite the movement's efforts to convince the press that what Sanctuary workers were doing was really legal, reporters—often referring to the antislavery Underground Railroad in the United States—continually placed emphasis on civil disobedience and breaking the law, which added to the romantic danger the media was weaving around the underground. The popular press also embellished its portrait of the underground with "outlaw" imagery. Sanctuary workers became a group of crafty outlaws who had been able, despite the openness of their actions, to outwit a plodding and clumsy law-enforcement agency:

> For nearly a year, they have publicly flouted the law without reprisal. Their contraband and their method of acquiring it have been publicized in the national media, where ringleaders detail their acts with impunity, almost daring officials to respond. (Medlyn 1982, December 25, *Arizona Daily Star*)

> The smuggling began when one refugee . . . asked Corbett for help in getting a relative who had made it as far as Nogales, Mexico, near the border. "We ended up in Nogales at 12 midnight on the slum side of the red-light district trying to find someone located in a basement." They finally found the person, hid him, and then, watching the patterns of the Border Patrol, sneaked him through a hole in a chain-link fence at 12:45 in the afternoon. "Most of the Border Patrol was at lunch," Corbett said. (Williamson 1984, August 26-30, *Sacramento Bee*)

> "They're really not very smart," she [the Sanctuary worker] says of the Border Patrol and INS.

"They're so predictable."

Like clockwork. Every day at two o'clock, the Border Patrol plane flies a sweep of the border between Nogales and Douglas. Every one of these days that Sanctuary workers happen to be bringing refugees across the line they simply check their watches, sit under preselected trees at the appointed hour and eat their lunch as they watch the plane fly by. (Smith 1986, February 26, *New Times*)

As the Sanctuary movement expanded into the interior of the United States, many journalists began to underscore the "everyday" quality of the movement in contrast to the outlaw imagery of border Sanctuary. In this coverage, Sanctuary was depicted as a "rapidly burgeoning" but mainly middle-class movement that was engulfing all kinds of people: Protestants, Catholics, Jews, Democrats and Republicans, lawyers, factory workers, and particularly "moms." This "everyday" imagery of the movement seemed to suggest that Sanctuary "could happen to anyone":

In Sunday silks and starched white shirts, the congregation of Central Presbyterian Church stands to sing Hymn 435—"In Christ There Is No East or West." Rich organ chords reverberate from the church's old stone walls. This is a scene of worship, but also one of deliberate law-breaking. . . .

The Massillon [Ohio] example is particularly striking. The manufacturing town of about 30,000 is part of a congressional district that hasn't sent a Democrat to the House of Representatives since 1948. Yet four churches in the district are harboring Salvadorans or Guatemalans. Central Presbyterian's middle-class congregation includes lawyers, retired military personnel and even a federal judge. (Brooks 1984, June 21, *Wall Street Journal*)

[Peter] and his wife, Nancy, had built a wonderful life together after years of hard work. They lived in a comfortable suburban house, close enough to catch the breeze off of Puget Sound. Their three children, nine-year-old Ryan, four-year-old Alex, and three-year-old Casey, were good boys who were growing up in a warm, loving and secure environment. Now, the threat of jail was very real. The Dormans, along with the rest of their congregation at Seattle's University Baptist Church, had joined the nationwide "Sanctuary" program, a network of churches set up to help illegal aliens who are escaping the repression of their native lands. (Pacheo 1984, December, *Ladies Home Journal*)

Journalists also turned the Sanctuary movement into a personality cult by focusing on Rev. John Fife and Jim Corbett as "founders" of the movement. This analysis ignored the complexity of Sanctuary's multiple origins and founders, and seemed to suggest that the charisma of these two men held the key to Sanctuary's emergence. Fife was usually depicted as the cowboy preacher, a smooth-talking, iconoclastic cleric (with a record of activism) who was practicing his own version of justice on the frontier:

> Reverend John Fife, extraordinarily long-legged, tips himself back in a chair, chain-smoking away the restlessness. With his neatly trimmed beard, cowboy boots, and irreverent, self-mocking sense of humor, he is not what you expect in a Presbyterian minister. He prefers calling himself a preacher. (Quammen 1984, August, *New Age Journal*)

> At forty-three, Fife is a tall, engaging man with an easy manner. For the past thirteen years, he has joined young couples in marriage, baptized their babies, and buried their loved ones. In his spare time, he kayaks and rafts the major rivers of the West. And his commitment to civil rights is strong.
> In the 1960s, Fife was arrested in Pittsburgh for trespassing while picketing in front of the suburban homes of slum landlords. He marched with blacks in Birmingham and Selma, Alabama. During the Vietnam War, he counseled draft resisters. And in 1981, he began sheltering illegal immigrants. (Bassett 1983, August 7, *Denver Post Magazine*)

Corbett (whom one journalist referred to as the "pimpernel of the desert") was associated more with the underground branch of the movement. He was portrayed in popular media as a mild-mannered, stoic, but tough Quaker who possessed an almost uncanny knowledge of the desert:

> [Jim Corbett] runs through the jungle like a deer, survives on one daily meal often consisting of tortillas and bananas—when he remembers to eat. Impervious to giant cockroaches, malaria-ridden mosquitoes, he prefers rooms that cost less than $3 a night when he travels on scout for the railroad. (Williamson 1984, August 26-30, *Sacramento Bee*)

> The gaunt-faced man followed the shimmering desert highway south to the Mexican border. His hands, painfully swollen by arthritis, rested lightly on the steering wheel of the ancient Chevy pickup, but no pain or weakness or uncertainty showed on his face. The fact that he was about to commit a federal crime troubled Jim Corbett not at all. (Witt 1982, August 9, *People Magazine*)

A philosophy graduate of Harvard, a retired rancher, and a
former goat-herder among the semi-nomadic tribes on the lower
Baja peninsula, the forty-nine-year-old Corbett had earned a
reputation as a new kind of outlaw in the American West. He
has been called a smuggler and a bandit, a forger and a master at
disguising refugees. (Bassett 1983, August 7, *Denver Post
Magazine*)

Despite the media cult forming around Fife and Corbett, one of the
most important functions of the press during this period was the exposure it gave the American public to the stories of Central Americans.
With almost predictable regularity, articles on Sanctuary included one or
two accounts from Central Americans about what had happened to them
in El Salvador or Guatemala. The accounts of torture, disappearances,
and exodus were common, everyday experiences for the Central Americans, but few in the United States were aware of how extensive and sys-
temic the violence was. These "testimonies," like the statements being
made by Central Americans in public Sanctuary, were most often a
straightforward listing of horrific events not usually accompanied by any
political analysis:

It was night and the family was sleeping. The commander of the
cadre ordered the father, mother and three children to lie down
on the floor. The commander accused them of aiding guerrillas
and asked, "Do you know why I'm going to kill you?"
The father answered, "Yes, yes, I know and I feel proud to die
for that." But the man's 17-year-old daughter began to cry and
roll on the floor pleading in the name of God for them to spare
her because she was young. The commander answered that the
family should have thought of that before. So they began to kill
them, little by little. First they took off their hands with
machetes. Then they took off their feet. Then their heads. Then
they cut them in half. (Miller 1982, December 12, *Minneapolis
Tribune*)

Several newspapers and journals, particularly after the indictments,
chose not to underscore the unique "people and culture" of Sanctuary
and focused instead on what they perceived to be a church-state conflict.
Many newspaper articles and television programs on Sanctuary accom-
plished this by using a contrapuntal format in which opposing positions
were systematically laid out as a conversation between Sanctuary workers and government officials. The question left to the reader was, "Who
is right, church or government?" This coverage of Sanctuary established
a structure of polar oppositions between Southside and the U.S.

government—church versus state, religion versus politics, conscience versus the law, humanitarian values versus national security/foreign policy, refugees versus economic migrants—that prepared the public for a dramatic confrontation, a "shoot-out," as it were, between church and state in the context of a courtroom trial.

These structural oppositions, especially as they pertained to a church-state conflict, were somewhat misleading. Many of those in the INS, the Border Patrol, and the Arizona attorney general's office were practicing Christians who publicly stated that it was a Christian's duty, first and foremost, to obey the law, and to keep religion and politics distinct. As it turned out, this structure of oppositions, publicized by the media, never really surfaced, because the presiding judge decided that Sanctuary was not going to be a church-state trial.

The Sanctuary Trial

Pretrial Motions: The Limiting of Evidence and Testimony

In bringing the Sanctuary workers to trial, the government established a "political space," a context that was conducive to establishing that Sanctuary had no legal basis and was therefore a simple case of "breaking the law." In a U.S. courtroom, the presiding judge has an extraordinary amount of power in shaping the kind of trial he or she is going to rule on. Perhaps the most significant element in this process is the judge's power to determine (1) what kinds of testimony and legal arguments are permissible during the trial and (2) what instructions are given to the jury so that it can determine a verdict. In both of these areas, the judge's rulings had a defining effect on the Sanctuary trial.

The judge for the Sanctuary trial (randomly selected by a clerk out of a pool of Phoenix judges) was Earl Hamblim Carroll, a registered Democrat appointed to the bench in 1980 by President Jimmy Carter. Carroll, whose background was in corporate not criminal law, had a reputation for being a staunch "no-nonsense" judge; his appointment to the case was received with apprehension by both the prosecution and the defense. Each of the defendants hired a separate lawyer so that during the trial there were eleven attorneys defending eleven defendants against one prosecutor, Donald Reno Jr.

Both the prosecution and the defense submitted preliminary motions regarding evidence and testimony to the court: the prosecution won its main points, while the defense failed to obtain almost all of what it requested.

Prosecutor Reno's strategy was to have Sanctuary tried as a simple, straightforward case of alien smuggling. Aware of the powerful cultural traditions and values underlying the concept of "asylum" and "freedom of religion," Reno did not wish to get involved in discussions of violence in Central America, the definition of a refugee, or religious convictions. As a result, he filed a motion *in limine* to preclude the introduction of defenses that claimed (1) that the aliens being assisted were legitimate refugees entitled to live in the United States; (2) that the defendants' actions were justified on the basis of religious belief; and (3) that the defendants' actions were justified on the basis of good motives and beliefs that would negate criminal intent.

Judge Carroll ruled in favor of Reno's motions and prohibited testimony and evidence that referred to (1) international law; (2) persecution and violence suffered by the aliens in their home countries; (3) comparative statistics pertaining to asylum policies for aliens from "either Communist-dominated countries and countries undergoing a Socialist or Communist revolution"; (4) comparative statistics regarding Central American aliens who have applied for or been granted asylum under the Refugee Act of 1980; and (5) religious convictions (Matas 1989: 69; Bau 1985: 85).[21]

These rulings virtually destroyed the defense's strategy of arguing for dismissal of charges on the basis of religious freedom and that the Central Americans assisted by Sanctuary workers were legitimate refugees legally entitled to political asylum. The prohibition of testimony and evidence of violence in Central America effectively canceled the second argument, and Carroll's ruling on international law and comparative statistics regarding Central American aliens meant that the defense could not develop an argument for "civil initiative" (i.e., that the government was violating international and domestic laws regarding refugee policy, in contrast to the Sanctuary workers, who were upholding these laws). This also meant that the defense could not demonstrate that the INS routinely violated U.S immigration laws through its systematic deportation of Central Americans, and thereby exonerate the defendants.

The defense moved to have the charges against the Sanctuary workers dropped on three grounds: first, that the prosecution was an unconstitutional infringement of the rights of the defendants to freedom of religion because Sanctuary work (the saving of lives) was a religious activity;[22] second, that the government's infiltration of the movement was "outrageous" and violated due process as well as the First Amendment right to free exercise of religion; and third, that the state was engaging in selective prosecution—why, for example, was it not prosecuting Arizona ranchers who were inducing undocumented aliens to enter the United States to work on their farms? (This reference to Arizona ranchers was based in a case—which the government had declined to prosecute—in which the Whitewing Ranch of southwestern Phoenix had allegedly sent company personnel into the Mexican border town of San Luis to recruit laborers and hire coyotes to lead them into the United States. A farmworkers' union had tried consistently to get the illegal traffic stopped, and had provided the government with a list of several witnesses to the illegal activities, but was told by the INS that the government could not prosecute without proof that the illegal workers had paid money to the U.S. company for their crossing.) The defense also brought up the fact that Salvadoran President José Napoleón Duarte's family was being moved into the United States with the help of high-ranking U.S. officials—why weren't they being prosecuted?[23] The selective-prosecution argument further sought dismissal on the grounds that the government was prosecuting Sanctuary workers because they were critical of its policies, that the Sanctuary trial was a case of political targeting, and that the state was trying to censor dissenting views.

Judge Carroll ruled against all of these defense motions, although he did admit that the government's undercover operation was "unacceptable" (though not outrageous). Investigator Rayburn was also forced to concede that the investigation had not been conducted properly, especially regarding the clandestine tapings that were done prior to official permission being given. Finally, Judge Carroll permitted defense on the grounds that the defendants did not have a specific intent to break the law because they might have believed, for example, that they could take the aliens to the INS at a "reasonable" later date (Crittenden 1988: 232).

Given these pretrial motions, an acquittal of the eleven Sanctuary workers seemed highly unlikely. The government had compiled a "statement of facts" for the period of March 26 to November 26, 1984, which, based on over one hundred hours of tapes, was a litany of felonies. Strikingly absent in the language of the government's account of the Sanctuary movement was any reference to the religious motivation of the Sanctuary participants and any potential information about the "aliens" that would indicate that they were "refugees." As the court date approached, it looked as though the prosecutor was going to run the trial as a simple alien-smuggling case. Limited in the kinds of evidence they could introduce, the defendants had no way of explaining their actions if asked questions such as "Did or did you not instruct illegal alien 'A' how to cross the border?" or "Did you or did you not conspire with others to avoid immigration interception when you drove illegal alien 'B' to Tucson?"

"America" on Trial: Establishing a Framework

The sense that "America" was also on trial was a theme that both prosecution and defense stressed throughout the Sanctuary trial, particularly in their press statements and during closing statements to the jury. As the lawyers framed it, two choices were proffered to the public: (1) "innocence" of the defendants, indicating that American citizens can practice their religious values freely without government interference (the corollary to this verdict was that the government was treating Central American fugitives unjustly and lying to the public about what was going on in Central America); and (2) "guilt" of the defendants, indicating that no person, religious or otherwise, was higher than the laws of the land (the corollary to this verdict was an affirmation of Congress, the U.S. Constitution, and the democratic system undergirding American society).

The Sanctuary trial quickly became a media event: ten radio stations (including Voice of America, National Public Radio, and Pacifica Network), fifteen television stations (including NBC, CBS, ABC, and ITV [Great Britain]), and thirty newspapers (including the *New York Times*, the *Miami Herald*, the *Washington Post*, the *Toronto Globe and Mail*, *Time*, and the *Nation*) had reporters covering the trial.

In his opening statement on November 15, prosecutor Don Reno presented the jury with an image of a tightly knit alien-smuggling operation. He divided the defendants into three groups: Corbett, Fife, Nicgorski, and Willis-Conger were placed in the first group as the "commanding officers" of the conspiracy; Hutchison, MacDonald, and LeWin, the second group, were the actual transporters and "smugglers"; and Clark, Espinosa, Quiñones, and Aguilar were referred to as the "Nogales connection." According to Reno, Rev. John Fife was the mastermind of the operation and his church was the headquarters of the criminal activities; and Phil Willis-Conger was the coordinator of the conspiracy—the man who assured the smooth running of the network; and Sister Nicgorski was the "travel agent," the person who organized the transportation of aliens and arranged places for them to stay. The second group, characterized as lackeys, did the pickups, driving, and delivery. Finally, Reno claimed that Quiñones, Aguilar, Clark, and Espinosa kept the conspiracy supplied with aliens by feeding them into the "pipeline."

In contrast to this portrait, the defense's opening statements—which were interrupted several times by Judge Carroll—focused on character profiles. Each of the defendants was depicted as a deeply charitable person with strong humanitarian motivations. Defense lawyer Ellen Yaroshefsky countered Reno's image of a smuggling ring by stating that "there is no . . . command structure here, there is but one leader here—

and that leader [God] is just beyond the reach of the immigration service" (quoted in Matas 1989: 72).

The prosecution endeavored to demonstrate a conspiracy by reference to overt criminal acts (eighty-four in all), and had to prove that the defendants actually had committed these acts. Prosecutor Reno had one hundred hours of tapes, but he was reluctant to use them since he anticipated a long, tedious battle with the defense lawyers over which words, lines, and paragraphs could and could not be submitted as evidence. Consequently, Reno decided not to submit the tapes as evidence, and planned instead to use the testimony of infiltrator Jesús Cruz to convict the defendants. A problem emerged, however, when the prosecution attempted to have the testimony of the Central Americans involved in the case represented solely through Cruz's reconstructions of his conversations with them. Judge Carroll ruled that the Central Americans involved in the case would have to testify in person, and, as a result, several Salvadorans and two Guatemalans testified before the court.

Reno began the government's case by calling Jesús Cruz to testify on November 21, 1985. As his testimony progressed, Cruz's performance became highly problematic for the prosecution: he frequently contradicted information he had given to the INS; his English was extremely poor and, because Judge Carroll ruled that conversations Cruz had heard in English had to be repeated to the court in English, much of his testimony was incoherent.[24] To make matters worse, the defense lawyers undermined Cruz's credibility as an agent of law enforcement by demonstrating that he had violated U.S. gun laws while working for the INS.[25] In cross-examination, the defense tried to depict Cruz as a "Judas figure" (the man who betrayed Christ to the Roman authorities by kissing him)—a person who had ingratiated himself to church people with gifts and lies, and then betrayed them to the government for money. To some extent, this strategy was successful; as it turned out, whenever the testimony of Cruz was the only incriminating evidence against a defendant, the jury dismissed those charges.

Supporting Testimonies

The Central Americans who testified in the case were not permitted to discuss political and economic conditions in their countries, nor personal histories of torture and political harassment, in the presence of the jury. Consequently, during their testimony the jury was frequently sent out of the room while the rest of the courtroom listened to prosecutors and defense lawyers wrangle with the judge over what testimony was admissible. Judge Carroll did allow some of the Central Americans to tell their whole stories, but not in front of the jury. Such was the case for a doctor named Francisco Nieto Nuñez, who, with his wife and three children, had fled political persecution in El Salvador. Nieto had been working with refugees in El Salvador when he and his wife were arrested by the national police, imprisoned, and tortured. His wife had eventually been released and reunited with the family, but police showed up at their home and abducted their infant. The baby, at the time less than a year old, had its head held underwater by the Salvadoran police in front of Nieto until he signed a statement confessing to being a subversive. After eighteen months in prison, at the intervention of the Red Cross, Nieto was released. He decided to flee the country with his family and went straight to the airport from the jail. The jury heard none of this, but was recalled to hear how the family had crossed into the United States and who had helped them to do it.[26]

Three North American coconspirators were also called to testify: George Lockwood, the 39-year-old minister at Peggy Hutchison and Phil Willis-Conger's church in Tucson; Kay Kelly, a 62-year-old deacon at Southside Church; and Mary Ann Lundy, 53, who was cochair of the Sanctuary committee at Riverside Church in New York City. All three refused to testify. They were held in contempt of court and placed under house arrest for the duration of the trial. As each of these coconspirators left the courtroom, the defendants, their lawyers, and their supporters stood up; Judge Carroll warned that he would hold them in contempt if such demonstrations continued.[27]

Throughout the interrogation of these witnesses, tensions intensified dramatically between the defense and the prosecution, and between the defense and Judge Carroll. Convinced that the court was biased, the defense team felt that it was being persecuted at every turn by a judge who favored the prosecution. One defense lawyer attempted to submit a tape recording comparing Carroll's admonishment of Reno to that of his chastisement of the defense. He pressed for dismissal on the grounds that the judge frequently scowled at the defense, thereby intimidating and prejudicing the jury. Taken as a whole, Judge Carroll's rulings clearly favored the prosecution. He frequently permitted Reno (who had his own interpreter for the Spanish testimony) to object to the court's official translations. In one instance, where a tape recording was introduced as evidence, Carroll ruled that what could have been either an "un-huh" (yes) or an "uh-uh" (no), was clearly an "un-huh," or yes. On the tape, a Salvadoran woman (Elba Teresa) was being asked by Jesús Cruz if Peggy Hutchison had brought her into the country. The defense lawyers claimed that "two felony counts and one misdemeanor hinged on admission of the sentences as evidence" (Crittenden 1988: 308).

The Verdicts: "Guilty of the Gospel"

The prosecution rested its case on March 7, 1986. In a move that amounted to a protest of the whole trial, the defense also rested—without calling any witnesses or permitting the defendants to testify. After a lengthy fight over instructions to the jury, and after closing statements by prosecution and defense, the twelve-member panel left the court to decide the verdicts on April 17, 1986. In its final statements to the jury, the defense team argued that the government had taken a simple case of people helping one another and turned it into a crime—the jury was deciding "for America" whether or not U.S. citizens would be able to pursue humanitarian and religious values without state interference. The prosecution called on the jury to "have the courage" to decide, as the framers of the Constitution would have wished them to, that there is "no higher law than that passed by Congress."

On May 1, 1986, the jury returned its verdicts. John Fife was convicted of conspiracy and two substantive counts; he faced a maximum of ten years in prison. Darlene Nicgorski, the hardest hit of the defendants, was convicted of conspiracy and four counts of harboring, which added up to a potential fifteen years in prison. Pardo de Aguilar was convicted of conspiracy and one charge of aiding the entry of an illegal alien. Hutchison was found guilty of conspiracy, as was Willis-Conger, who was also convicted of two acts of aiding and abetting entry and transportation of aliens. Father Quiñones was convicted of conspiracy and aiding entry, Father Clark of harboring, and Wendy LeWin of illegal transportation; all faced a maximum of five years in prison. Three defendants—Jim Corbett, Nena MacDonald, and Mary Kay Espinosa—were acquitted of all charges. The eleven Sanctuary workers were released on their own recognizance until sentencing and left the courtroom singing "We Shall Overcome"—a hymn that had become a hallmark of the civil rights and anti-Vietnam War movements.

Sentencing the Sanctuary Workers

What was the government supposed to do? . . . Was it supposed to look the other way? . . . Was the United States government supposed to turn their [sic] back and indicate to the public that because of the ostensible religious issues, the political issues in this case, that the United States government is faint of heart when it comes to enforcing the law with all persons?
    —Prosecutor Donald Reno (quoted in the *Washington Post*, May 2, 1986)

I think that if someone has a religious conviction to break the law, I think that's fine.

Break the law. But if you get caught, pay the price. Don't whine about it, the way the Sanctuary people did. When Martin Luther King violated the laws, he didn't whine about it, he did his time. And a matter of fact, he made a good point. Sanctuary didn't do this. They said: "Come get us, come get us, come get us." And we got 'em. Then they cried foul. They didn't play by their own rules. They didn't fess up to what they had done. They didn't say, "I'll take my punishment." They said: "Oh, the government cheated. Oh, they spied on us." They generally wimped out, I think.
                                              —INS official, Tucson (September, 1990)

Between May 1 and July 1, 1986, Judge Carroll received hundreds of letters requesting leniency for the Sanctuary workers. One came from forty-seven members of Congress (the majority of them Democrats) asking him to take into account the "underlying circumstances in Central America and the humanitarian motives of the defendants before passing sentence" (Crittenden 1988: 335). Denis DeConcinni, Democratic senator from Arizona, wrote Carroll asking that "in your deliberations you will consider the fine qualities of this man [John Fife] and grant him the ability to continue his work."[28] Other letters (which were also forwarded to Attorney General Edwin Meese III) flooded in from writers who identified themselves as nuns and priests, ministers, lawyers and law students, mothers, World War II veterans, university professors, concerned citizens, doctors and nurses, carpenters, Christians, and Americans:

> Dear Judge Carroll,
>   In 1868 my maternal grandparents left Austria to be welcomed in then-primitive Wisconsin. With wounds unhealed, and about to be called again for another military excursion of Emperor Franz Josef, husband, wife, and child left their homeland never to return. . . .
>   I am the progeny of their momentous step. And so it is with the great majority of us now calling ourselves U.S. natives. Our ancestors came in droves to escape religious, military, or economic oppression. Today, all too many of us fail to realize the glorious tradition of caring for others that so marked this nation's early colonization.
>   And so it is especially ironic that those being tried in an Arizona courtroom this month allegedly on the grounds of merely offering shelter, food, and rest to aliens fleeing from southern lands have been found guilty of transgressing our own U.S code of criminal justice.
>
> Dear Judge Carroll,
>   You and the prosecution may think that you have "won" the case against the Sanctuary defendants, but you really haven't.

You know you have simply participated in and contributed to a vast miscarriage of justice.

When I was about 14 years old, I saw a book on my grandmother's shelves entitled *The Diary of Anne Frank*. Since the girl on the cover looked something like me and we shared the same name, I picked the book up and started to read about the experiences of this extraordinary girl. Since that time, I vowed that I would never be like one of those "good Germans" who allowed what happened in Europe in the thirties and forties to happen here.

But it is happening here and it is happening now and it is not those "horrible Germans" who are the "bad guys" this time, it is us, the North Americans, particularly those who support Reagan's murderous policies in Central America. That includes most of the State Department, the INS, and, I am sorry to say, you yourself.

Dear Judge Carroll,

As our nation celebrates the renewal of the Statue of Liberty and its spirit of welcome to the tired and weary, it seems a bitter irony that earnest people working to give sanctuary to refugees from Central America be facing jail and fines for their efforts. I am a Christian minister, a member of the Presbyterian church, and I believe with all my heart in the Christian validity of the Sanctuary movement. I am also an American, and I believe equally as fervently that the Sanctuary movement is consistent with the spirit of freedom we boast.

I urge you to consider the religious roots of the Sanctuary movement and the motives of those who are being sentenced.

On July 1 and 2, 1986, Judge Carroll gave each of the defendants a suspended sentence of three to five years' probation, with the stipulation that if they were convicted again for similar offenses, the government could sentence them to jail for the original crime(s).[29] The suspended sentences surprised most of the defendants, who had made preparations to go to jail. (John Fife, for example, had been told by the national governing body of the Presbyterian Church U.S.A. that it would continue to support his family while he served his sentence, and the president of his Pittsburgh seminary pledged that he would make arrangements for Fife to begin doctoral studies while in prison.)[30] In statements made to the court before sentencing, the Sanctuary defendants were able to present their reasons for assisting undocumented Salvadorans and Guatemalans; many publicly declared their intention to continue Sanctuary work.

The Growth of Sanctuary

The Sanctuary movement did not immediately dwindle, as the government had hoped, with the convictions of eight Sanctuary workers; the courtroom drama in fact heightened public awareness of the Sanctuary ministry, and prompted several hundred churches, a few synagogues, and twenty-two city councils to declare themselves public sanctuaries for Central American refugees (see tables 3.3 and 3.4).[31] Sanctuary activities diversified and by 1987-88 there were three semiautonomous Sanctuary movements—in South Texas, southern Arizona, and southern California—funneling Central Americans northward. Each of these groups established its own independent network of church groups and funding resources and tended to operate in ignorance of the others' activities. Each region also developed its own style of Sanctuary. Texas, for example, never explicitly established an underground but maintained a "border ministry" of social services (including housing and transportation) for undocumented Central Americans. In addition, several Salvadorans formed their own Sanctuary communities (mainly in San Francisco and New York), many of which were coordinated through CARECEN (the Central American Refugee Center), headquartered in Washington, D.C.

The trial represented a rapid maturing moment for Sanctuary. As Sanctuary moved, metaphorically speaking, from childhood to adolescence through the "initiation rite" of the court, its internal difficulties also "matured." The posttrial period not only saw a widening of the chasm between the Chicago and Tucson sectors of the movement but also witnessed increasing criticism directed at the movement leadership. Some of these critical issues had emerged during the national conference held January 24-25, 1985. Several women in the movement, mainly from Chicago, resented the media's focus on the Anglo-male-clerical dimension of Sanctuary and were particularly disgruntled with the mythologizing of Fife and Corbett as the charismatics of the movement—which, they argued, failed to take into account the fact that Sanctuary was overwhelmingly run by women (see Lorentzn 1991; Golden 1986: 60). Others, such as William Sloane Coffin, were fearful of alienating low-income Americans from the movement and exhorted Sanctuary advocates to address domestic as well as foreign government policies. Also present at the conference were the critical voices of Central Americans who had become active in Sanctuary. Often relegated to the role of "telling" their horrible and tragic experiences to congregations, many Central Americans asked for a "true partnership" and more participation in the decision-making structures of the movement. Some asked for a clarification of the Sanc-

Table 3.3. Sanctuary sites by state

State	May 1985	June 1986	June 1987
Pacific Northwest/West Coast			
Oregon	5	7	9
Washington	8	11	13
Colorado	6	8	10
California	66	106	149
Total	85	132	181
Southwest			
Arizona	17	20	22
Nevada	1	1	1
Texas	6	9	9
Total	24	30	32
Central Plains			
Oklahoma	2	2	2
Kansas	1	1	1
Total	3	3	3
Midwest			
Missouri	1	2	3
Illinois	17	22	22
Indiana	2	4	6
Ohio	9	11	15
Iowa	4	3	5
Total	33	42	51
Upper Great Lakes			
Wisconsin	14	15	17
Minnesota	7	9	5
Michigan	5	6	7
Total	26	30	29
New England			
Connecticut	—	2	3
Massachusetts	5	9	12
Vermont	2	3	3
Maine	1	1	1
New Hampshire	1	1	2
Total	9	16	21
(continued)			

Table 3.3. Sanctuary sites by state (continued)

State	May 1985	June 1986	June 1987
Mid-Atlantic			
New York	14	19	24
Pennsylvania	6	14	18
New Jersey	1	2	3
Total	21	35	45
South			
Washington, D.C.	5	7	6
Maryland	5	5	6
Virginia	3	4	5
West Virginia	1	1	1
Georgia	2	3	4
Louisiana	1	1	1
Alabama	—	1	1
Florida	—	—	1
Total	17	22	25
Southeast			
North Carolina	1	2	2
South Carolina	—	—	1
Kentucky	1	1	1
Tennessee	—	—	1
Total	2	3	5
Unspecified	12	16	7
Total	226	329	399

Source: Data gathered by Sanctuary National Defense Fund, Chicago Religious Task Force on Central America, and published in *Basta! National Journal of the Chicago Religious Task Force* (May 1985, June 1986, June 1987).

tuary ministry, and, warning against paternalism, "declared their opposition to any attempts to make them mere objects of interest" (Bau 1985: 26):

> We need to understand that the structural situation of Sanctuary is paternalistic. The North Americans of Sanctuary congregation are the benefactors and the protectors. They have all the resources, all the answers, and all the control. The refugees enter the Sanctuary experience completely dependent on the largess of the North Americans. They are coming into an alien environment and culture, and usually they are coming out of a situation of suffering, of loss, of grief, of trauma. Suddenly they are surrounded by people who speak a different language, serve different foods, follow different customs. They are not

Table 3.4. Denominational breakdown

Denomination	April 1985	June 1986	June 1987
Catholic	39	49	64
Quaker	38	50	57
Unitarian Universalist	30	47	67
Presbyterian	23	29	26
United Church of Christ	14	14	11
Lutheran	9	9	11
Methodist	8	12	14
Brethren	7	7	9
Mennonite	7	12	13
Baptist	5	5	7
Episcopalian	5	4	6
Disciples of Christ	2	3	2
Jewish	3	18	37
Other Protestant/Ecumenical	21	30	30
Universities	10	12	16
Seminaries	1	1	1
City Councils	4	22	22[a]
New Jewish Agenda	—	5	6
Total	226	329	399
States	—		1

[a]Berkeley, West Hollywood, Santa Barbara, San Francisco, Sacramento, Davis, Santa Cruz in California; St. Paul, Duluth, and Minneapolis in Minnesota; Swarthmore, Pennsylvania; Rochester and Ithaca in New York; Cambridge and Brookline in Massachusetts; Madison, Wisconsin; Tacoma Park, Maryland; Olympia, Washington; Santa Fe, New Mexico; Seattle, Washington; Burlington, Vermont; East Lansing, Michigan. Governor Tony Anaya declared New Mexico a state sanctuary for Central American refugees in January 1986.

Source: Data gathered by Sanctuary National Defense Fund, Chicago Religious Task Force on Central America, and published in *Basta! National Journal of the Chicago Religious Task Force* (May 1985, June 1986, June 1987).

sure, initially, what behavior is acceptable, and what might prove offensive. And they have had little opportunity to observe quietly until they can figure it out. Instead, they often are thrust in front of hundreds of people, interviewed by the media, expected to describe in detail the ordeal they have experienced.

"A refugee woman was coming to speak to us and we heard that she'd been raped," a Sanctuary workshop participant told us, "but when she made her presentation, she didn't talk about it, so we didn't know whether or not it was true." Would this North American woman, if she were raped, be able to stand in front of a crowd of strangers and relate particulars of her pain and humiliation? (Malcolm 1987: 21-22)

While conference participants waded through the intellectual, theological, and organizational ramifications of Sanctuary, the more than three hundred church sanctuaries that had been declared by mid-1987 were dealing with problems of a different order. Many Sanctuary communities did not know how to handle some of the deep psychological problems refugee family members were manifesting as a result of torture, witnessing massacres, having family members "disappeared," or leaving children behind. Nor did they know how to respond to pervasive domestic violence within the Central American families. Complex political divisions between and among Salvadorans and Guatemalans had also come across the border, and in some instances severely divided the Central American communities in Sanctuary.

In Tucson, in the posttrial period, the movement not only experienced internal divisions along ideological lines—spawning a second underground movement called El Puente—but also a kind of organizational contraction. Some of the projects that had flourished in 1985 and 1986 saw the collapse of their funding base and were unable to support what had become a substantial paid staff. As a result, these projects were forced to concentrate their efforts on fund-raising; many social-service programs began to shrink, and eventually disappeared. Hence, although ideological issues eventually faded from Sanctuary discourse, practical problems of funding, different cultures, languages, politics, religion, and personalities continued to profoundly challenge the movement.

Sanctuary and the Construction of Church-State Culture

In many respects, the U.S. Sanctuary movement was the product of an intricate and mutual "church-making" and "state-making" process. The actions of both the state (the INS) and the church (Southside et al.) represent the efforts of two different ideological communities to constitute a form of self-identity—but always in relation to an opponent and, more specifically, in relation to establishing hegemony over the "other." Sanctuary as a statement about the church emerged as a response to the threat of state prosecution; thus the church-based movement, in important respects, was defined by the government. Yet Sanctuary, particularly as it evolved through the culture of the media, demanded that the state specify both the nature of its social role and the legitimate extent of its powers. In this sense, Southside and the other churches played a defining role in the articulation of state identity. Sanctuary's history is therefore a chronicle of a contentious process of creating a church-state culture—a process that was not resolved through the trial, even though eight of the defendants were found guilty.

The Sanctuary trial's powerful church-state subtext forced many people not only to ponder the proper relation of religion to politics, but also to critically reflect on the "sanctity" of state power in the areas of national security and foreign policy. Through Sanctuary, practicing "religion" became relevant to one's opinions on government foreign policy—arenas of power traditionally insulated from public influence in the United States. Sanctuary thus raised questions about religious identity that spanned a range of cultural identities—ultimately linking the individual conscience to the global identity of the American state.

In addition to raising challenging questions about the nature and scope of U.S. cultural identity, the Sanctuary movement put its own stamp on the long history of ecclesial asylum. Before exploring the "local culture" of Tucson's Sanctuary movement and how it articulated a set of disparate people into a group, we turn to the "roots" of church sanctuary in order to trace how it has been manipulated, as a tradition, by different social groups as they attempted to create church-state cultures. These roots go far back in history, to ancient Hebrew culture, medieval Europe, and precolonial New England, whose own varieties of eclesial sanctuary we will consider next.

Chapter 4

Sanctuary and the Judeo-Christian Tradition

Historically, sanctuaries in the Judeo-Christian tradition are cultural jurisdictions set off from the regular activities of everyday life. These jurisdictions are authoritative because of their sacred nature, a sanctity that is derived ultimately from a transcendent, omnipotent God. Over the history of sanctuary, this sacred authority has been associated with the holiness of a physical, geographic location (such as an altar or a church), the holiness of a particular community of believers (such as a covenant or a Levitical city), and the holiness of a religious specialist (such as a rabbi or a priest). In the next two chapters, we will examine the traditions of ancient Hebrew, medieval Christian, and contemporary U.S. church sanctuary, and will encounter various historical groups of people manipulating the sanctity of person, place, and community in the context of different religiopolitical cultures.

The Culture of Sanctuary

Liminality, Person, Place, and Community

Although sanctuaries are associated with the sacred, they can also be regarded as unique kinds of cultural spaces. They represent a physical and social jurisdiction that, in the words of anthropologist Victor Turner, is "liminal" or "betwixt and between" sacred and profane authorities. Sanctuary spaces always seem to be "between" cultural authorities, whether these be the covenant community and God (as in ancient Hebrew culture), Caesar and the pontiff (medieval Christian), or church and state (contemporary American).[1] As uniquely "liminal" spaces, sanctuaries can be viewed as points of church-state convergence, as institutions located in a "conflict zone" located "betwixt and between" the "sacred" and the "profane." As such, they not only highlight the distinctions made between church and state in the Judeo-Christian tradition but also offer a cultural lens through which to explore the formulation of these distinctions and their transformations throughout history.

In chapters 4 and 5, I analyze how the sacredness of person, place, and community was manipulated—as a liminal sanctuary space—within three different religiopolitical cultures. Although this history is brief and does not do justice to the complex political and economic forces undergirding church asylum, I attempt to demonstrate how shifts in medieval church-state relations shaped the practice of church sanctuary. In chapter 5, I return to the contemporary U.S. Sanctuary movement and explore how persons within this group, using some of these same cultural constructs, dehistoricized the sanctuary tradition and "reinvented" it.

Hebrew Sanctuaries

The practice of sanctuary among the ancient Hebrews originally emerged as a form of mitigation within a retaliatory blood-feud system (Bau 1985: 125).[2] In ancient Hebrew culture, when the blood of an innocent was spilled, the land became polluted or desecrated. In order to purge the land, the murder had to be expiated by the blood avenger, usually a male kinsman, who was duty-bound to kill the murderer (Cohn 1972a: 1117). According to some historians, sanctuary developed as a way of tempering revenge for a slaying by providing "space" and "time" for negotiations between the murderer and the offended party. Initially, sanctuary was a universal right for all murderers, but as the Hebraic criminal system developed a distinction between intentional murder (an uncommutable crime) and accidental homicide (manslaughter) (Milgrom 1972: 1118), only a person who killed another without premeditation—a special category of "criminal"—could take advantage of sanctuary:

> Whoever strikes a man so that he dies shall be put to death. But
> if he did not wait for him, but God let him fall into his hand,
> then I will appoint for you a place to which he may flee. But if a
> man willfully attacks another to kill him treacherously, you shall
> take him from my altar, that he may die. (Exod. 21:12-14)

Two types of sanctuaries seem to have existed among the ancient Hebrews: altar sanctuaries and communitarian sanctuaries. Altar sanctuaries, usually located in religious shrines, were asylums by virtue of their status as *holy places*. Desecrating these locales through violence or the spilling of blood meant committing a sin against God for which there was no compensation. (Exod. 21:12-14, just cited, mentions these altars, and in 1 Kings 1:50-53 and 1 Kings 2:28-29 Solomon both acknowledges the right of altar sanctuary and violates it.) Some scholars argue that as the cult of Yahweh worship centralized (into tribal groupings), so did many religious customs, including sanctuary. In accord with this centralizing trend, sanctuary shifted away from an association with many different shrines to a practice associated with specific cities. The former type of "altar sanctuary" persisted, but the latter "communitarian sanctuary" based in a city also became widely practiced.

In Deuteronomy—the fifth book of the Jewish and Christian Scriptures, which contains the Mosaic laws—Hebraic blood vengeance is divested of its private character and becomes part of a more public penal system based in city or communitarian sanctuaries. According to these laws, slayers of humans could no longer escape punishment by simply paying a penalty to a blood avenger; they now had to face punishment or, in the case of accidental homicide, seek sanctuary (exile) in one of six Levitical cities, each of which was linked with a former altar sanctuary:

> Then Moses set apart three cities in the east beyond Jordan, that the manslayer might flee there, who kills his neighbor unintentionally, without being at enmity with him in time past, and that by fleeing to one of these cities he might save his life: Bezer in the wilderness on the tableland for the Reubenites, and Ramoth in Gilead of the Gadites, and Golan in Bashan for the Manas'-sites. (Deut. 4:41-43)[3]

> But if any man hates his neighbor, and lies in wait for him, and attacks him, and wounds him mortally so that he dies, and the man flees into one of these cities, then the elders of his city shall send and fetch him from there, and hand him over to the avenger of blood, so that he may die. Your eye shall not pity him, but you shall purge the guilt of innocent blood from Israel, so that it may be well with you. (Deut. 19:11-13)

The slayer of a human, specified in the Scriptures as an Israelite or a sojourner among the Israelites, could be killed by the blood avenger only *before* the slayer reached the sanctuary city or if the fugitive strayed from its protective precincts. Once inside the city, though, sanctuary was not automatic: the malefactor had to establish absence of forethought before the city's council of elders. If the council granted asylum, the fugitive was permitted to work but could not engage in trades such as glassware, textile, or rope manufacture, for such occupations might draw the blood avenger into contact with the fugitive (Cohn 1972b: 592). If the high priest of the city died naturally during the fugitive's stay in sanctuary, the fugitive was free to return home with impunity since the high priest's death acted as atonement for the spilling of innocent blood (Milgrom 1972: 1118).

Hebraic communitarian sanctuaries can be seen as "liminal" institutions mainly because they represent a kind of exile (although fugitives technically remained part of the covenant community under God, they were not permitted to have normal membership in the human covenant so long as the spilling of human blood was unatoned for). Exile, then, was a kind of "betwixt and between" stage, a space where one was suspended between atonement and judgment.

Because the relationship between God and his human subjects was more of an "organic" one—than, for instance, the dichotomous church-state model that emerged in fourth-century Europe—the Hebrew sanctuaries were not sites of intense political conflict between competing sources of authority. If a sanctuary were violated, one (whether king or slave) simply had to face the wrath of God; there was no alternative secular system, as there was in the medieval period, challenging the right or efficacy of sanctuary.

Several themes inherent in Hebraic sanctuary were incorporated and modified in Christian sanctuary customs. The notion of sanctuary as a sacred place, imbued with special powers, was clearly adopted in many Christian asylums, and became the cultural foundation of church sanctuary in medieval Europe.[4] Christian sanctuaries also built upon the Hebraic idea that justice should recognize extenuating circumstances rather than pronounce an exact and identical punishment for every violation; crimes as well as the transgressor were to be "classified." Yet the communitarian or covenantal basis of sanctuary in the Hebraic tradition was not really adopted in medieval Christian practice, largely because the Christian cult of power shifted the epistemological basis of authority from the community to a clerical hierarchy. It appears that within ancient sectors of Hebrew culture, at least doctrinally, the punishment and forgiveness of crime was a corporate social responsibility, whereas medieval Christianity "hierarchized" the process of discipline and punishment. Through church sanctuary, clerics, as the official representatives of the church, became intercessors between individuals and civil justice, dispensing God's merciful judgment and obtaining reduced or limited punishments for fugitives. Jewish culture premised sanctuary more on the power of the community as a sacred population; medieval Christianity, as we shall see, underscored the sacred, intercessory role of the clerical person.

Christian Sanctuaries

Christian sanctuaries lingered in Western Europe for almost sixteen centuries. They began as intercessory institutions, places where a runaway slave or criminal could seek temporary asylum and, if the presiding cleric were sympathetic, obtain a diminishment of punishment. These institutions also served as "liminal" spaces, that is, as protective jurisdictions for fugitives who—caught betwixt and between ecclesial and imperial authority—sought temporary refuge from an abusive master. As they evolved, however, ecclesial sanctuaries became increasingly controlled by independent kings and eventually were transformed into holding pens for criminals pursued by the royal courts. Some historians have suggested that the shift to this penal function occurred as the Holy Roman Empire fragmented and as the medieval structure of church-state government crumbled under the rise of independent, divine-right kingships. As the church lost its hegemony in Western Europe, sanctuaries came to represent separate jurisdictions of authority under the church, and consequently were seen as a threat to the centralizing systems of kingly power.

The Political Economy of Christian Sanctuary: A Church and State Dialogic

Although church sanctuary has its roots in ancient Jewish culture, it is a cultural practice that is linked to the emergence of church-state culture within Western European Christianity. This emergence dates back to the fourth century when the Roman emperor Constantine converted to Christianity and made it the state religion. Under Constantine, ecclesial responsibilities in and authority over the earthly realm were formulated as part of a negotiated understanding of power with "Caesar." The medieval model of government for this earthly sphere established two jurisdictions of authority and two forms of government—the ecclesiastical and the civil—which, though distinct, were theoretically halves of the same governing enterprise.[5] The exact nature of this church-state relationship (what could be described as a kind of "dialogic") was contested, sometimes bitterly, by both emperor and ecclesiastic. In the perspective of some Christian emperors and kings, Europe was the "Roman body politic" and hence was rightly governed by an imperial authority whose power was to be sanctioned and supported by the church. Most pontiffs, however, took a different view: Europe (as "Christendom") was an embodiment of the "universal church" and should therefore ultimately be directed by the pope.[6]

For most of the Middle Ages, a powerful papal church (partner to a "weak state") forcefully inscribed its understanding of the church-state dialogic onto medieval culture; this understanding underscored the superior authority of the church in relation to the state and emphasized the intercessory power of the church. Ecclesial claims to power were, however, sometimes difficult to legitimate since even the sacred Scriptures—the medieval church's principal source of cultural authority—were ambiguous about the nature of church-state relations. In the scriptural passage from Mark 12 quoted at the beginning of this book, Jesus acknowledges a Caesar-God duality but offers little precise insight into what is to be rendered unto each. Moreover, the teaching is set within an attempted "entrapment" of Jesus by his detractors, thus rendering its meaning even more nebulous. Such biblical ambiguity—found throughout the Scriptures—set the stage for conflict, and the shifting power relations between ecclesial and civic authority are the basic context of power undergirding European sanctuary practices.

Before tracing the development of Judeo-Christian sanctuary, we need to note the important role that *classification* has played in history of ecclesial asylum. For both medieval civil and ecclesiastical governments, power was largely the ability to control the human subject—what might be broadly termed as the ability to maintain hegemony over the articulation of social identity. Within the dialogic of medieval power relations, church asylum seekers constituted a particularly problematic category for church and civil governments. As "criminals," they had violated laws and thus had to be punished in order to maintain social peace and order (the civil jurisdiction). Yet in the church's view, these fugitives were also "sinners," who, although they had transgressed laws and had to face punishment, were nonetheless independent subjects before God (the ecclesiastical jurisdiction). In the medieval cosmos, both church and civil government(s) possessed a legitimate jurisdiction over the social identity of the fugitive—yet whose jurisdiction was superior?

Early Christian Sanctuaries

There is little historical evidence to suggest that sanctuary was widely practiced by the early Christians under Roman rule. However, the rules and procedures governing sanctuary practices in the fourth and fifth centuries—after Christianity had become the religion of the empire—reflect some of the tensions inherent within the early church-state dialogic of power. Civil authority recognized ecclesial sanctuary as a separate jurisdiction under church control but nevertheless sought to restrict the right to church asylum by developing a classification of criminals who were to be exempted. The Theodosian Code of A.D. 392 (the first formal recognition of church sanctuary by the state) limited sanctuary in terms of the "nature of the crime and the character of the accused": public debtors, those who had embezzled money from the state, Jews, heretics, and apostates were excluded from the privilege (Bau 1985: 131).

Initially, sanctuary was limited to the altar of a church, but early in the fifth century the right of sanctuary was extended to include the houses of bishops and clergy as well as cloisters and cemeteries (Walsh and O'Neill 1987: 12; Bau 1985: 131). Justinian I's (482-565) *Corpus Juris Civilis*, which collected Roman laws under one code, also clarified the nature of church sanctuary: public debtors, tax officials, particular categories of criminals such as murderers, rapists, and adulterers, were all denied sanctuary protection.

Responding to these limitations of the sanctuary practice, church officials attempted to reassert their special status as the official representatives of God's will on earth. For them, church sanctuary—as a sacred institution—represented a cultural resource that buttressed the church's claim to superiority over the emperor. Pope Leo I, who reigned between A.D. 440 and 461, tried to counter some of these restrictions by arguing that the steward or advocate of the church had the right to examine all those seeking sanctuary. The papal decree reinforced the separate domain of church authority, but, more importantly, stressed that the church was the interpreter rather than a mere custodian of sanctuary—a distinction that reinforced the church's independent, discretionary understanding of its own power.

In the early days of ecclesial sanctuary, the church mainly assisted runaway and abused slaves. The pontiff authorized bishops to intervene on behalf of slaves who had fled disciplinary punishment from wrathful masters but who, in accepting sanctuary, became subject to the rule of the bishop—a feature of sanctuary that again stressed the superior and sacred nature of the cleric. If the bishop deemed the slave's complaint valid or misdemeanor pardonable, he could issue spiritual discipline to the fugitive and order the master to sell the slave to the church or to an individual. In the event of a reunification, the master had to take a sacred oath on the Gospels (*sacramentum impunitatis*) and swear not to punish the slave corporally; violation of this oath resulted in a fine and/or a payment of slaves to the church (Kirby 1989: 459; Riggs 1963: 23).

Although sanctuary churches probably were not popular among slave-owners, church asylum practices during this period did not seriously threaten church-state relations. One reason for this is perhaps related to the social status of the first church fugitives: slaves, the most common church asylees, were not "juridical persons" with rights and protections guaranteed in civil law. The civil government could therefore afford to ignore the church's discretionary protection of "marginal" or "oppressed" peoples—a protection that did not seriously jeopardize the institution of slavery and the socioeconomic system upon which it was based. As the clientele of church sanctuary shifted to citizens, debtors, and artisans, however, it appears that tensions between church and state over sanctuary intensified.

Church Sanctuaries in Medieval Christendom

The ecclesial sanctuaries of medieval Europe were engulfed by church-state tensions, and the contractions and expansions of the sanctuary privilege were often linked to fluctuating power relations between secular and ecclesial offices (Siebold 1934: 536). In the early medieval period, churches continued to practice the two main forms of Christian sanctuary (sanctuary based on place and sanctuary based on the holiness of the individual cleric), but official Christian pronouncements on church asylum tended to highlight the role of the church as an intercessory institution (Kirby 1989: 458).

In keeping with this pattern, church sanctuaries of the Anglo-Saxon kingdoms evolved as both sacred places and intercessory institutions. In A.D. 597, the first mention of ecclesial sanctuary in the Anglo-Saxon legal code was made by King Ethelbert, who established a penalty for the violation of the church's *fryth* or "peace."[7] A century later, King Ine of Wessex legislated sanctuary into the ancient and intricate Anglo-Saxon legal code on blood feud, but, like Ethelbert, he also regulated and restricted the sanctuary practice. Ine's code enabled sanctuary churches to collect compensation from those who violated the sanctuary right. More important from the church's perspective, the code acknowledged that ecclesial sanctuary was based in the sanctity of the intercessory cleric (Riggs 1963: 6).

In the eighth and ninth centuries, the Western Christian church consolidated some of its power under Emperor Charlemagne (768-814), who attempted a general revival of the Holy Roman Empire. Part of Charlemagne's strategy for the reunification of Western Europe was to Christianize the civic infrastructure of the empire and make ecclesiatics "officers" of the state.[8] Charlemagne and subsequent Carolingian emperors were wary of an autonomous ecclesial power, and the recodification of sanctuary laws under Charlemagne reflected this caution: church asylum seekers were not immune from prosecution by the secular courts and could only remain in the "peace" of the church until removed for trial before the civic courts (Siebold 1934: 535). Moreover, ecclesiatics became obliged to hand over the fugitive to civil officers (and not necessarily in exchange for a guarantee of immunity from corporal punishment).

Charlemagne's laws indicated that fugitives were first and foremost "criminals," subject to civil laws. Sanctuary, as one of the church's separate dominions of authority, was beginning to erode.

Sanctuaries in the Middle Medieval Period

Beginning in the ninth century, the rising influence of the landed nobility (though varying from region to region) began to threaten Europe's church-state governmental structure.[9] In the eleventh and twelfth centuries, this tension between civil and papal power intensified dramatically. Although the Roman church was losing ground in this period, prominent clerics attempted to reassert the "twin peaks" conception of power (and the Roman church's superior position within it). Pope Gregory VII (1073-85), for example, argued against the ascendancy of monarchical power by demanding an end to lay simony, the practice by which kings sold church offices to the highest bidder or to favored political allies (thereby drawing ecclesiastical allegiance away from the pope). In 1198, Pope Innocent II proclaimed that just as there are "two great lights" in the heavens, the sun and the moon, so are there two great earthly authorities, the church and the state; however, just as the moon is illuminated by the sun, so the state gets its authority from the church, the greater light and the greater power. Yet such metaphors were rapidly becoming anachronistic in Western Europe. The state was no longer a single, geographically concentrated entity but rather a series of political authorities spread across the empire. Moreover, the church itself was beginning to adopt the features of a dispersed configuration: by the end of the twelfth century, the church was fraught with internal schisms, and tensions between secular and clerical leaders had spread to England and France, where vigorous monarchs began to resist papal demands for military and fiscal support.

Amid these shifts in the medieval political landscape, sanctuary became a "loaded" institution, because ecclesial asylum underscored the independent nature of ecclesiastical power vis-à-vis the state. As I have suggested, because sanctuaries were institutions "set apart from the regulations of ordinary social intercourse" (Alles 1987), they represented "political spaces" through which the church could emphasize the autonomous nature of the individual's relation to God; in so doing, the church buttressed the basis of its own hegemony, particularly since clerics were the "brokers" of this individual bond. Because they called for a semi-independent realm of power for the Holy Roman church (thereby contradicting the movement toward monarchical consolidation of power), ecclesial sanctuaries were in many respects at the vortex of church-state tension in the late medieval period.[10] Throughout the Middle Ages and culminating in the sixteenth century, monarchs aggressively encroached upon the separate ecclesial jurisdiction that sanctuary represented and attempted to "secularize" church asylum. English kings, for example, increasingly restricted the general ecclesial sanctuary that had been available to a fugitive at every church for several centuries. In A.D. 887, Alfred the Great decreed that church officials administering sanctuary were to serve primarily as facilitators between two feuding parties (Riggs 1963: 34)—an interpretation of sanctuary that preserved its "intercessory" role but did not emphasize it as a separate jurisdiction of the church. The English kings also increasingly "bureaucratized" the procedures for claiming sanctuary, transforming the institution of sanctuary by swathing it in a complex set of rules and procedures. According to Alfred's laws, for example (which were linked to civil rules regarding compensation for murder), church sanctuary could be granted for three days to anyone accused of a crime; to a person fleeing enemies, sanctuary could be granted for seven days. (If a murderer did not make compensation within this period, the victim's family was permitted to invade the church [Walsh and O'Neill 1987: 13].) The church was not permitted to feed a fugitive who was fleeing enemies (hence limiting sanctuary stay by way of starvation), and thieves, whose crime was punishable by death, were automatically guaranteed a commutation of the death penalty if they entered sanctuary (Bau 1985: 139). At St. Cuthbert's in Durham, fugitives eventually were required to declare before "credible" witnesses why they were seeking sanctuary. Once admitted to the church, they were ordered to wear black gowns with yellow crosses on the left shoulder during their maximum thirty-seven days in sanctuary (Mazzinghi 1887: 25-28). At St. John's Church in Beverly, the fugitive had to take the following oath at the door of the sanctuary:

> Ye shall be true and faithful to the Archbishop of York, Lord of this, to the Provost of the same, to the Canons of this Church and all others its ministers.
> Ye shall bear good heart to the Baille and 12 Governors of this town, to all Burgesses and Commoners of the same.
> Ye shall bear no pointed weapon, dagger, knife, and no other weapon against the King's peace.
> Ye shall be ready at all your power if there be any debate or strife, or not so, then in the case of fire within the town to help to suppress it.
> Also ye shall be ready at the Obit of the King Aethelstone, at the Dirge, and the Messe, at such time as it is done at the warning of the belman of the towne, and do your good duty in

ringing and for to offer the Messe on the morrow, so help you
God and their Holy Evangelists. (ibid.: 32-33; also quoted in Bau
1985: 145)

The fugitive then kissed the "book" and, after paying the sheriff and
clerk a small fee, had his or her description (usually occupation) and
mode of crime entered in the register.[11] The fugitives were often guarded
during their stay and guards were fined if a refugee escaped during their
watch (Bau 1985: 146; Bellamy 1973: 108). Occasionally, the sanctuary
was violated by the king's officers, and in some circumstances pursuers of
the refugee set fire to the church to smoke out the fugitive (Bellamy 1973:
108; Walsh and O'Neill 1987: 12).[12]

The English kings also developed a new type of church asylum, which
removed the privilege even further from the sacred status of the cleric:
this was ecclesial sanctuary *by charter*. In this tradition, only certain
churches were permitted, by royal legislation, to offer sanctuary. St.
John's of Beverly, for example, was given the right of sanctuary through
the king's charter. Its sanctuary extended more than a mile in each direction from the church entrance, and its boundaries were marked by
wooden crosses. The sanctuary zone was divided into six concentric
rings, and fines for violation of sanctuary increased the closer one came
to the altar (Bau 1985: 139). This form of sanctuary foreshadowed the
process of secularization that began to threaten the ecclesial nature of
church sanctuaries: it located the legitimacy of sanctuary in the office of
the monarch by making the right of church asylum contingent upon the
prior consent of the king. In this respect, the eleventh-century English
kings were able to assume greater control over fugitives by making them
"total" subjects of the civil system, even to the extent that the king specified where they could seek church asylum.

Church Sanctuaries and the Late Middle Ages

Despite papal attempts to reassert power over civil rulers, the political,
social, and economic forces compelling European rulers toward consolidation of their own separate kingdoms ultimately proved unfavorable for
the political hegemony of the Roman church. As the largest landowner in
Western Europe, with access to considerable sources of revenue, and as
an important agent of socialization and administration, the Roman
church—no longer able to depend on the protection of its shattered pro-
tector, the Imperium—was a prime target of princes and kings. Anthropologist Mart Bax has suggested that, paradoxically, the church's pursuit
of an empire based on absolutist authority and territorial expansion generated the conditions for its own demise:

The expansion and consolidation of the ecclesiastical regime ultimately contributed to the very conditions that undermined its own powers. The religious orders opened up extensive tracts of virgin land and transformed them into settlements, which were attractive spoils for predatory princes. In the schools of churches and monasteries laymen were taught reading and writing, which was a necessary condition for the emergence of lay rival elites. The religious orders also contributed significantly to more pacified forms of trade. An extensive network of monasteries, which encompassed rapidly expanding lay settlements, offered safety and shelter to merchants and itinerant tradesmen. They were also attractive targets for power-hungry princes. (Bax 1991: 12)

Added to the political-economic currents undermining the absolutist and transcultural model of Christian authority was a gradual but substantial change in the intellectual life of medieval Europe. Renaissance ideas (which had begun to flourish in Italy around 1300) emphasized a revival of antiquity and a rebirth of learning through the classics (and hence exposure to Greek thought on government and democracy). Philosophy, social ethics, art, politics, and economic theory were gradually taken out of the church's control and pursued by princes, merchants, and bankers (i.e., laypersons) (Alhstrom 1972: 25). Anthropological travels had produced information on other cultures and civilizations; as the world expanded, Christianity began to be perceived by some intellectuals as one religion among many. Such developments did not strengthen the church's ideological hegemony.

Also contributing to the church's demise within Western Europe were internal disputes and despotism. A series of controversial papacies in France (where the Holy See had been transferred) and schisms undermined the moral and juridical supremacy of the apostolic church (among the more significant of these was the 1378 election of two popes in succession by factious cardinals). Dissent and dissatisfaction had also begun to spread among the episcopacy and lower clergy, who increasingly resented what they regarded as a corrupt papal mafia. In the early sixteenth century, discontent with the papal Curia prompted a theological reconsideration of what constituted "authentic faith" as well as sharp criticism of the church's structure. At the forefront of the dissenters was Martin Luther (1483-1546), an Augustinian priest and teacher at the University of Wittenberg, who radically (and, some historians argue, inadvertently) transformed Christianity. Luther declared that "faith" could not be authorized by clerics, but rather was a "gift" from God given to each person through biblical enlightenment. This notion that faith was sacred prop-

erty that all individuals could possess undermined the idea that only clerics, as the holy officers of God, could speak with authority on religious
matters. (Protestant culture was thus dispersing, not necessarily destroying, the cult of the sacred individual that underlay church sanctuary practices; as we shall see, this became particularly significant in the Vietnam
War church sanctuaries.) The implications of this waning of papal power
had profound ramifications for medieval church sanctuary, the privilege
of which was premised on a powerful, and centralized, church.

Changes in sanctuary practices in England during the late Middle Ages
occurred largely in concert with these processes of political-economic
consolidation and the disintegration of papal hegemony. The Plantagenet
kings (1154-1485), seeking to subject both secular lords and ecclesial authorities to royal jurisdiction, redefined traditional church-state relations
and attacked institutions that supported the old joint-trustee model.[13]
These kings progressively absorbed ecclesial sanctuary into the criminal
law system by bureaucratizing the procedure for claiming church asylum.
(This bureaucratization process, incidentally, strongly resembled the procedures for prosecuting and punishing a transgressor in the civil courts.)
By the fourteenth century, ecclesial sanctuary, which had begun as a way
to limit private revenge and temper the harshness of secular laws, was
subsumed by the civil criminal law system. Under fourteenth- and fif-
teenth-century English law, seeking sanctuary became identical to "abjuring the realm,"[14] and clerics, no longer intercessors on behalf of God,
became the facilitators of "the imposition of the sentence of banishment
without trial" (Bau 1985: 144). Under this system, when fugitives
reached sanctuary churches, a coroner was summoned to take the asylee's
confession before other witnesses.[15] The fugitive then had forty days to
decide whether to face the secular courts (and in all probability the death
sentence) or to abjure the realm. If she or he had not decided by the end
of forty days, the church had to stop giving food and thereby starve the
asylee out of sanctuary. (The fugitive was deemed automatically convicted of the original felony and prevented from abjuring the realm if he
or she did not make a decision within the forty-day limit.) If fugitives ab-
jured the realm, all their property was forfeited and they were sent, often
dressed like pilgrims and carrying a cross, to a port where they could
wade into the water up to their knees and hail a ship. If no ship picked
them up within forty days, they were returned to the sanctuary, presumably to try again a later date (Bellamy 1973: 112-13).[16] Sanctuary thus
became equivalent to "safe conduct" out of the realm, and church officials were enjoined to act "more as royal officers of justice rather than as
intercessors or mediators" (Bau 1985: 149-50).[17]

The Elimination of Church Sanctuary

Increasingly drawn into the orbit of kingly interests, ecclesial sanctuaries were virtually extinguished under the Tudor kings (Bellamy 1973: 111). With the Act of Supremacy in 1534, Henry VIII established an independent Church of England, making himself the supreme authority. Six years later, the English Royal Parliament limited sanctuary privileges to parish churches, cathedral churches, hospitals, collegiate churches, and dedicated chapels, and abolished the right for murderers, rapists, burglars and thieves, arsonists, and those guilty of sacrilege (Bau 1985: 154-55). Following these restrictions, Henry VIII established eight sanctuary cities (Wells, Westminster, Manchester, Northhampton, York, Derby, Launceston, and Norwich) where state-approved asylees had to remain on a permanent basis. (These sanctuaries became defunct during his son's reign.) Henry VIII also began to regulate church sanctuary on a national basis, and made the practice even more unattractive by decreeing in 1528 that all sanctuary seekers were to be branded with an "A" (abjurer) on the right thumb after their confession to the coroner. In addition, the king instituted strict rules for sanctuary inhabitants: all fugitives had to wear a badge on their upper arm (failure to do so resulted in loss of sanctuary); in some cases, they were not permitted to leave their lodging area between the hours of sunset and sunrise.

The deathblow to church sanctuary in England occurred in 1603, when Parliament repealed Elizabethan law and the sanctuary provisions along with it. Ecclesial sanctuary, however, was not officially abolished by statute until 1624:

> And Be it alsoe enacted by the authoritie of this present
> Parliament, that no Sanctuarie or Privilege of Sanctuary shalbe
> hereafter admitted or allowed in any case. (Mazzinghi 1887: 16)

The brief statute ended approximately eleven centuries of church sanctuary in England.[18]

The Catholic church endeavored, with little success, to retain the right of ecclesial asylum in the German, English and French kingdoms. Gregory XIV's bull *Cum Alias* (1591) declared that church buildings were inviolable and that fugitives were not to be removed from them without the permission of the rector; violation of this rule would result in excommunication. The Council of Trent, in its twenty-fifth session, declared that the church's right to provide sanctuary was divinely instituted, and in 1725 Pope Benedict XIII again threatened secular officials with excommunication for violation of the church sanctuary right. In 1919, canon 1179 reaffirmed the right of sanctuary but dropped the provision of fines if it were violated. Finally, in 1983 when Catholic canon law was revised, the canon on sanctuary was eliminated—despite strong recommendations that it be retained (Kirby 1989: 459).

Broad Features of the Sanctuary Tradition

What insights can be drawn from the long—and understudied—history of church sanctuary in Western Europe? Having examined the history and practice of European church sanctuary, let us sketch some of the broad features of the sanctuary tradition. Building on the Turnerian notion that church sanctuaries are "liminal" spaces, certain "traits," taken together, constitute a "profile" of church sanctuaries:

First, sanctuaries, as "liminal" spaces set off from the regular discourse of everyday life, are "authoritative" cultural spaces by virtue of their "sacred" nature, and derive their sanctity ultimately from a transcendent God. Throughout the history of church sanctuary, this authority of the sacred has been associated with the holiness of a physical, geographical location, the holiness of a particular community of believers, and the holiness of a religious specialist.

Second, church sanctuaries are unique kinds of "liminal" spaces in that they draw together different, conflicting streams of power into a particular discourse. European church sanctuaries drew "God" and "Caesar"—categories that corresponded to church and state jurisdictions of authority—into a dialogue about "shared power." As a forum of conflict, however, ecclesial sanctuaries are not neutral. They are clearly connected to church interests. Through sanctuary, the medieval church was able to make a claim to superior power over the state, a claim that was underscored by its being made on holy ground (in God's house) and through God's holy officers. In the late medieval period, sanctuary was one way the church resisted the homogenizing thrust of civil power; the sanctuary privilege both grew out of and sustained the medieval twin-peaks model of political power, and, by extension, supported the church's special authority within this dual structure of government.

Third, much of the controversy sparked by church sanctuaries seems to be linked to the social status of the subjects within them. Medieval church asylum seekers, as "criminals" and "sinners," were simultaneously "subjects" of both church and state. As asylum seekers, however, they invited conflict between the two powers since, once in sanctuary, they demanded clarification (between church and state) of the extent of religious intercessory power. In the late medieval era, the ramifications of controlling this "controversial subject" were far-reaching for both the church and the civil government, for, in many respects, the ability to define social identity was commensurate with power. Church sanctuaries were a jurisdiction in which the church could flex its "classificatory" muscles around a human subject.

This brief history of medieval ecclesial asylum suggests that the nature of the sanctuary space was transformed by Europe's shifting political economy over nine centuries, and that Christian clerics attempted to manipulate the cult of the sacred individual and the sacred place as a means of perpetuating not only church sanctuary but also their special status as holy persons—their source of power—within the medieval cosmos.

We now leave medieval Europe and jump ahead several centuries to explore how the sacredness of place, person, and community was creatively manipulated in the church sanctuaries of the United States.

Chapter 5

Separation and Covenant: Church Sanctuary in the U.S. Tradition

Informal sanctuary practices in North America date back to the colonial era, but the explicit use of sanctuary is relatively recent in U.S. history. Church sanctuary was first declared publicly in the United States on October 16, 1967, by the Arlington Street Unitarian Church in Boston, Massachusetts, when it claimed asylum for nearly three hundred Vietnam War draft resisters.[1] Although they bore some structural similarities to those of medieval Europe, the sanctuaries of this post-World War II period adopted a unique character—one that was rooted in the peculiar culture of church-state relations in the United States. In chapter 4 we saw that church sanctuaries were located at a vortex of cultural power because they drew together two principal sources of authority and social identity, the Sacerdotium and the Imperium, into a discourse about the human subject—a discourse that, while focused on the classification of "sinner" and "criminal," also dealt with "power." Like their European antecedents, U.S. church sanctuaries are located at a vortex of cultural power. Their principal dialogue partners are "God" and "the Republic"—important sources of social identity in the United States—and their subject of discourse is essentially cultural power. Yet although this culture of power recognizes a distinction between church and state, it is quite different from that of medieval Europe. Unlike the joint-trusteeship paradigm characterizing medieval European government, the religiopolitical culture of the United States reflects two central models of church-state relations. These models were based on seemingly contradictory traditions of "separation" and "fusion" between religion and politics. The religiopolitical traditions of separation and fusion seem to reflect two irreconcilable visions of nationhood and are characterized, as historian Harry Stout suggests, by tension between America as a "chosen nation" and as a "godless republic":

> These tensions reflect . . . two conflicting "realities" or points of departure: the one political and constitutional, which explicitly separate[s] church and state and [leaves] God out of the formulation; and the other rhetorical and religious, in which "America" inherited New England's colonial covenant and where God orchestrate[s] a sacred union of church and state for his redemptive purposes. (Stout 1990: 63)

These dichotomous images, Stout argues, have produced "a paradox of conflicting speech over the meaning of America," and, one could add, paradoxical models of the place of religion in U.S. society.

Church and State in U.S. Culture: Historical Roots

This religiopolitical "paradox" has its historical and cultural roots in the questions regarding collective identity that surfaced during the constitutional debates of the late eighteenth century. For many colonists, the issue of cultural identity entailed not only the overall configuration of the nation but also the role that Christianity would play in the new federation of states. Yet not all colonial groups, though Christian in orientation, shared the same vision regarding government and the integration of religion and politics within it. Each of the three Protestant geographical and "ecclesial" blocks—in the South, New England, and the Middle colonies—adopted different interpretations of religion and cultural identity; they also fluctuated between governmental models in which church and state were fused or were clearly disengaged.

In many of the southern colonies, for example, the Church of England dominated colonial life with a direct and often heavy hand: fines were levied against those who did not meet church obligations; Catholics, Quakers, and Puritans were generally unwelcome; and Methodists and Baptists were frequently imprisoned for disturbing the peace by speaking against the established church. (The Carolinas were similarly dominated by members of the Church of England, but its Constitution of 1670, attributed to John Locke, showed a somewhat greater toleration toward non-Anglicans—it included Amerindians while excluding atheists.) In this model of colonial government, religion pervaded public and private life, and ecclesial bodies set clear limits on the nature and extent of religious practice.

Contrasting this pattern was the relatively "tolerant" attitude of the Middle colonies (New York, New Jersey, Delaware, and Pennsylvania) toward religious dissenters. Settlers in this region imported Anabaptist, Congregationalist, and Baptist traditions that separated political and ecclesiastical authority; many communities advocated a "gathered church" that was voluntary in nature, in which religion was conducted as a private affair between the individual and God. (Strangely enough, these sectarian Protestants—whose separation of church and state was based on a distrust of civil intrusion into religious life—became the unexpected bedfellows of "Enlightenment-spawned" rationalists. Among this latter group, the impetus for a separation of church and state was based on an opposite concern—fear of church interference in political-economic affairs.)

The New England states, often cited as "theocratic colonies," show a distinct pattern of church-state relations. The Massachusetts Bay Colony established what some scholars have called a "Bible state" or a "holy commonwealth"—a model of society and government in which the whole community had a sacred covenant with God (Miller 1961: 322-68). Under the civil covenant, church and state assumed different responsibilities, but, as one historian notes, these responsibilities were complementary: in the churches, the word of God "was preached," and in the courts, it "was enforced" (Hughey 1983: 74). Hence, in the colonial period, Puritan orthodoxy was buttressed by strict legal codes and penal discipline: persons were fined for nonattendance at church and the 1646 Act Against Heresy listed punishments for those who would not accept Puritan religious dogma. Quakers were occasionally executed when they refused to obey expulsion orders, and in some communities the Christmas festival was forbidden as a "manifestation of popery." Church and state, in this context, though "separate in theory, . . . were married in fact as pillars of the City of God" (ibid.).

In these colonial forms of government one discovers the tension between Stout's "godless republic" and "chosen nation" manifest inchoately in distinctions drawn between church and state jurisdictions of the social world. One also finds the preliminary architectural plans, as it were, for the two frames for religious identity: one trend, spearheaded by the Middle colonies, favored "separation" of religion and politics; another, led by the Puritans, advanced a fusion of religion and politics based in a "covenantal" paradigm. The haphazard nature of colonial settlement established a pattern of semi-isolation among the colonies and permitted each to pursue its own paradigm of Christian government. This situation was radically altered by the American Revolution and the rise of a new, largely Christian, nationalist ideology.

Revolutionary Ideology and Church-State Relations

The American Revolution (1775-83) dramatically transformed both patterns of religious symbolism and images of church and state within what became the United States of America. As historian Ruth Bloch notes, diverse religious and political terminology fused during the American Revolution as the colonies attempted to create a sacred national identity (Bloch 1990). The Revolution provided an opportunity for the colonies to fashion a collective identity and articulate it as a national enterprise. Because one aspect of this identity was antimonarchical, it was critical of the privileges that the Church of England (the royal church) enjoyed in some of the colonies. Consequently, the covenantal and self-righteous imagery of the Puritans often was seized upon as an alternative nationalist ideology (Stout 1986: 302). In the emergent national theology, "liberty" was sacred not only because of its intimate symbolic relation to grace but also because it was part of God's divine plan for his "chosen people"—Christianized liberty was to be a mainstay of the New Zion.

The Christian nationalism that developed during the American Revolution pushed the colonies toward a unified sovereignty, "one nation under God." Yet this broad nationalism or inclination toward "covenant" was repeatedly contradicted by an orientation toward fragmentary sovereignty or "separation," a position represented by states' rights advocates. Churches in the states wanted a jurisdiction independent of the national body, a place where they could practice religion free from government intervention and interference. At the end of the American revolutionary war, ten of the thirteen colonies still had, and desired to maintain, some form of "established church" (Rhode Island, Pennsylvania, and Delaware were the three exceptions). Several states required religious qualifications for state office, some demanded belief in heaven and hell, and one state permitted freedom of religion only to Protestants. At the same time, approximately "six different value systems competed for the allegiance of Americans . . . Calvinist orthodoxy, Anglican moralism, civic humanism, classical liberalism, Tom Paine radicalism, and Scottish moral sense and common sense philosophy" (Murrin 1990: 27). A powerful, embryonic nationalism, however, based largely in Christian symbolism, had blurred ideological and religious differences and had planted the seeds of a federal patriotism.

As the United States moved toward confederation, the two seemingly contradictory modes of being religious—separation and covenant—began to take shape. One model sought an unequivocal disassociation between the federal government and religious experience, thereby underscoring religion as a local and private practice. The other tended to view the state as a religiously motivated enterprise and the culmination of sacred values that all American colonists theoretically shared. Within the dialectic of these two postures we see a movement toward and a movement away from the state. In this regard, "religion," particularly for the federalists, was a volatile issue; it embodied the potential both to blow the nation apart and to fuel the fires of national unity.

Fashioning the Wall of Separation

"Separation" of church and state eventually was incorporated into and protected by the American constitutional documents. In the First Amendment on individual liberties (1791)—a clause outlining the civil privileges that are considered the "rights" of all U.S. citizens—the federal government is prohibited from intervening in the religious affairs of the local states. The First Amendment protects local state regulation of religion from federal interference:

> Congress shall make no law respecting an establishment of religion, or prohibiting the free exercise thereof; or abridging the freedom of speech, or of the press; or the right of the people peaceably to assemble, and to petition the Government for a redress of grievances.

The amendment declares that the *federal* government cannot "establish" one religion over another, it cannot institute articles of religious faith and practice, and it cannot interfere with state provisions on the relation between religion and government (Semonche 1986: 22-27).[2]

Under the Fourteenth Amendment (1866), however, the responsibility for enforcing "separation" of church and state in local affairs became a federal power. The amendment (part of the abolitionist platform to protect blacks against local state slavery legislation by giving them federally protected civil rights) reads in part:

> No State shall make or enforce any law which shall abridge the privileges or immunities of citizens of the United States; nor shall any State deprive any person of life, liberty, or property without due process of law; nor deny to any person within its jurisdiction the equal protection of the laws.

The Fourteenth Amendment gave the Supreme Court "supervisory power" over the state legislatures (Edel 1987: 100) and eventually became the legal instrument by which the federal government made the religious clauses of the First Amendment applicable to the regional states.

Under the Fourteenth Amendment, no state could interfere with a person's religious practices.[3] The amendment also enabled the federal government to assume control of the protection and enforcement of church-state "separation," and to interpret in a binding fashion the circumstances in which "separation" applied.[4]

This separationist construction of a church-state paradigm is quite distinct from the "twin-peaks" model of government that characterized medieval Europe. Although church and state are given separate jurisdictions in the American constitutional framework, the state is clearly the interpreter and enforcer of the divide between religion and politics.

American Religious Culture: Separation and Covenant

The traditions of separation articulate American religious identity within a set of "symbolic boundaries" that represent *paradigms* for—not *definitions* of—religious expression and experience. These paradigms are dominant cultural "frames" that shape both the experience of and discourse about religion in the United States. Both of these frames underlie cultural distinctions and connections made between "religion" and "politics"—"God" and "Caesar"—and both are premised on cultural assumptions about the sacredness of the *person* and of the *community* in U.S. culture, values that we have already seen operative in the sanctuaries of ancient Hebrew and medieval Christian cultures.

Separation

The *separationist frame* allows for a constitutional disengagement of church and state, and celebrates religious diversity. Religion, in this paradigm, is largely a local, private, and personal activity far removed from politics. The Supreme Court—acting as the state's guardian of "separation"—is the ultimate interpreter of the church-state wall paradigm within American society, and has specified legal contexts or boundaries that separate religious behavior from the rest of the social world.[5] Supreme Court rulings involving religious freedom or separation have generally emphasized church and state as disengaged spheres of experience—an approach most commonly adopted in decisions on education and religion, and in particular in rulings regarding religious activities in public schools.[6] The Court's separationist rulings have prescribed a social and symbolic domain for religion, in which religion is depicted as largely a private, localized affair, whose proper context is the home, the family, the denominational school, the place of worship, and the individual conscience. The concept of "conscience" is particularly powerful within the separationist frame and derives historically from a Protestant emphasis on a direct, intimate, and personal link with God. Protestant, particularly Calivinist, cultures stress that the conscience—as the inner psychic and holy meeting place of God and the individual—is the primary medium through which God instructs the individual. Protestant groups tend to stress that each person has to rely upon his or her own judgment/conscience in religious matters—a concept that counters, for example, the Catholic emphasis on a hierarchy of interpreters and obedience to ecclesiatical authority. The Supreme Court recognizes "conscience" as the principal construct of "separation" and as a cultural authority that is independent of the state.

Despite the Supreme Court's upholding of the curtain between religious individuals and the government, however, it does not recognize a strict, inviolable, and permanent separation between religion and the state. In many instances, the Court has restricted an individual's right to practice religion "freely" by forcing religious groups to follow social regulations regarding compulsory vaccinations, education, and emergency medical services, and has prohibited the use of narcotics, snakes, or poisonous substances in some religious ceremonies.[7] Significantly, Supreme Court restrictions on religious liberty frequently have been imposed on individuals during times of war: conscientious objection to military service (the refusal to bear arms owing to personal religious convictions), for example, has not been readily allowed by the state.[8]

The Supreme Court is not the only body that has attempted to define the parameters of church-state separation. Many mainline Protestant groups, for example, have historically advocated a strict separation of church and state in an effort to prevent Catholics, Jews, and antiwhite minority groups (such as the Black Muslims) from obtaining "undue" influence in government. Minority churches, too, have manipulated the separation to maintain the integrity and privileges of their minority status, a recent example of this being the formation of the Coalition for Religious Freedom in 1984, which felt that the government's prosecution of Rev. Sun Myung Moon for tax fraud constituted gross state interference in religious affairs (see Wuthnow 1988: 100). These examples suggest that the paradigm for religion as a distinct, local, and state-free realm of experience exists as a kind of ideological weapon, deftly wielded by state and religious groups according to differing political goals.

Covenant

Although the wall metaphor is pervasive in American discourse about religion and politics, there is another predominant cultural frame for religious belief and practice in the United States. It is one that appropriates the notion of an individual-personal contract with God and translates it into a civil *covenant*. This paradigm, many historians argue, springs largely from colonial religious symbolism, and collectivizes religious experience in terms of a national project or a sacred community.

In the post-World War II era, U.S. sociologists wrote extensively about this nation-based frame of religious experience. Among the more influential ideas to emerge was Robert Bellah's concept of "civil religion":

> [There are] certain common elements of religious orientation that the great majority of Americans share. These have played a critical role in the development of America's institutions and still provide a religious dimension for the whole fabric of American life, including the political sphere. This public, religious dimension is expressed in a set of beliefs, symbols and rituals that I am calling the American civil religion. (Bellah 1970: 171)

According to Bellah, civil religion is not the religion of denominations. Rather, it is religion that emerges from the life of the "folk"; it manifests itself as the basic ideas and values expressed in everyday life. Bellah claimed that this notion of a national religion originated in the Puritan tradition (particularly in their notion of the holy Christian commonwealth in which government is "enlightened" and directed by Christianity) and is manifested in modern societies through the sacralization of certain figures and events, for example, in presidential addresses and during national holidays (see also Warner 1961; Hammond 1974). The concept of American civil religion generated voluminous literature on how the civil cult rearticulated religious, ethnic, and racial identity (discourses about "difference") into a national ideological community (e.g., Herberg 1956; Lenski 1963) and thereby promoted social cohesion through an all-embracing value system. Anthony Wallace referred to this as a distinct "religiopolitical cult" (1966: 77); Sidney Mead termed it the "religion of the Republic" (1975: 30).

The observation that there is a unique kind of national-political culture that is connected, oftentimes ambiguously, to religious identity in the United States is interesting but problematic. It is important to recognize that Bellah's civil religion does not exist in the singular: there are, and always have been, a plurality of national-religious cults within U.S. political culture. These manifestations of civil religion range from those represented in the liberal Protestant tradition (e.g., the social gospel movements associated with Walter Rauschenbusch) and black sectarian radical activism (e.g., Martin Luther King's vision of an integrated society based in a redemptive civil religion), to the conservative agenda of Southern, white, evangelical churches (e.g., the civil religion of Jerry Falwell and Pat Robertson's "spontaneously God-oriented" America). Moreover, Bellah's concept implies that all Americans, regardless of race, class, ethnic identity, or gender, have equal access to and participation in the national cult—but women and Native Americans, for example, have had a very different experience of civil religion than have dominant groups.[9]

It is perhaps more helpful to regard civil religion not as a "thing" that all Americans possess as a normative feature of their culture, as some of the sociological literature implies, but rather as a particular cultural frame for religious expression and experience that is creatively manipulated (both in hegemonic and resistant ways) by different individuals and groups. Unlike the *separationist* frame (which underlines a distinction between religion and politics), this frame fuses religion and politics, and celebrates the "sacredness of community" in light of a specific political goal. I am suggesting that this frame is based in a *covenantal* metaphor—covenant referring to a community that has cohesion and purpose by virtue of its sacred mission as a group—in which religious experience is articulated as a collective enterprise. In this covenantal frame, church and state possess a rhetorical fusion and religion is regarded as a public, corporate practice that encompasses and is encompassed by collective identity.

The individual within U.S. culture possesses a paradoxical role vis-à-vis these frames: theoretically, one can practice religion in a private, constitutionally unfettered manner, yet one can also practice religion as part of the public, rhetorically religious national discourse. These *separationist* and *covenantal* frames are experienced and manipulated differently by various groups (Anglo Protestants, for example, have greater access to national covenantal ideology than Hispanic Catholics, and minorities have greater linkage with separationist ideology than dominant groups), but taken together, as paradigms of cultural experience, they constitute a kind of "structure of religious identity." Although the frames exist as ideological tools and can be wielded in hegemonic and counterhegemonic ways, they also exist as a set of ideological conditions that shape religious identity. Both frames are thus "articulating principles" within broader cultural discourses about religious identity and practice. Consequently, one can expect that the articulation of religious identity within U.S. culture—particularly when it involves a church-state conflict—will occur within the vocabulary and constraints of these frames. The church sanctuaries that emerged during the 1960s and the 1980s are significant historical instances of the relation of religion to politics being contested in the fluid language and imagery of these separationist and covenantal frames.

The church sanctuaries of the 1960s and the 1980s were premised on themes of separation and covenant, and those that manipulated these frames ultimately created an alternative "political space" betwixt and between Caesar's authority and God's commandments. In the sanctuary space, Americans opposed to the Vietnam War or U.S. foreign policy in Central America were able to challenge dominant interpretations of the proper relation of religion to national identity and explored new perceptions of themselves, the wider faith community, government, and the linkage among them. In the remainder of this chapter, I contrast the sanctuaries of the Vietnam War era with those that emerged in response to Central American refugees. I stress separation and covenant as a set of ideological conditions—a kind of cultural vocabulary—which shaped the development of the sanctuaries and gave U.S. ecclesial asylum a distinctive stamp.

Sanctuaries in the Vietnam War Era

The tumultuous cultural context of the anti-Vietnam War church sanctuaries was the 1960s, a decade of dramatic economic, demographic, political, and social change, a time when, as historian Sidney Ahlstrom notes, "the old grounds of national confidence, patriotic idealism, moral traditionalism, and even historic Judeo-Christian theism, were awash" (1978: 446). In this period, the United States experienced radical transformation in social attitudes toward race, gender, and sexual morality; it saw the rise of black power, women's liberation, and the antiwar movement; it lived through the Cuban missile crisis; and it witnessed assassinations of prominent national figures—John F. Kennedy, Malcolm X, Martin Luther King Jr., and Robert Kennedy. The decade also marked the construction of the Berlin Wall and a revival of the ideological struggle between East and West superpowers—the entrenchment of which rekindled a zealous rejection of communism in U.S. culture.

The 1960s were also a period of tremendous turmoil for many churches. Protestant hegemony in the United States had given way to a pluralism "that extended well beyond the Protestant-Catholic-Jewish mainstream" (Wilson and Drakeman 1987: 223). This was accompanied by fundamental shifts in American moral and religious attitudes. In the wake of Nazi extermination camps, the bombing of Hiroshima, and increasing tension between the nuclear superpowers, intellectuals were reflecting on the destructive and violent dimensions of humanity. Some seriously questioned the relevance and future of religion in "modern" society; others—resisting "secularizing" trends that insisted religion had become moribund—were acknowledging that religion in America had reached a crisis point. These writers recognized that the churches had to adopt new self-critical directions and strategies, an attitude exemplified, as Sidney Ahlstrom notes, in the writings of Martin Marty in *The Second Chance for American Protestants* (1963), Catholic social historian Thomas O'Dea in *The Catholic Crisis* (1968), and Rabbi Richard Rubenstein in *After Auschwitz* (1966).[10] Yet, despite this self-critical attitude and the churches' efforts to respond to contemporary issues, the 1960s saw a dramatic decline in church attendance and an exodus of young, largely Anglo, college-educated people from the churches. This defection was accompanied by the rapid growth of new "alternative" and "experimental" religions.

U.S. involvement in the Vietnam "conflict" (1961-75) cost the lives of over fifty-five thousand U.S. military personnel and upwards of 1.5 million Vietnamese. The protracted conflict sparked widespread discussion of nationalism, religious and cultural values, and the legitimate authority and purview of state power. In 1967, the same year that Arlington Street Unitarian Church declared sanctuary, Gen. William Westmoreland assured Congress that the allied forces were winning the war in Vietnam, but President Johnson in his State-of-the-Union address warned of a long struggle and asked for a 6 percent, two-year surcharge on personal and corporate income taxes in order to sustain the war effort. As U.S. involvement escalated—in 1965 there were two hundred thousand troops in Vietnam; by 1969 the figure had reached almost half a million—public opposition mounted, creating not only severe division between supporters and critics of the war but also cynicism toward a government whose military interests, many believed, were setting U.S. priorities.[11]

As opposition to the Vietnam War swelled, it coalesced around an antidraft movement. By 1966, this movement had assembled an unusual coalition of groups opposed to the war, including many churches and church-based organizations, some of which adopted sanctuary as a way to publicize their opposition to the war.[12]

The sermon for the first invocation of U.S. church sanctuary was given by Rev. William Sloane Coffin Jr., then chaplain at Yale University. Coffin appropriated the notion of a sacred place for his invocation of church asylum, but he also attempted to give it a uniquely American twist by emphasizing a separationist religious frame. He accomplished this by aligning church sanctuary with the sanctity of conscience:

> Now if in the Middle Ages churches could offer sanctuary to the most common of criminals, could they not today do the same for the most conscientious among us? And if in the Middle Ages

they could offer forty days to a man who had committed a sin and a crime, could they not today offer an indefinite period to one who had committed no sin?

The churches must not shrink from their responsibility in deciding whether or not a man's objection is conscientious. But should a church declare itself as "sanctuary for conscience" this should be considered less a means to shield a man, more as a means to expose a church, an effort to make a church really a church.

For if the state should decide that the arm of the law was long enough to reach inside a church there would be little church members could do to prevent an arrest. But the members could point out what they had already dramatically demonstrated, that the sanctity of conscience was being violated.[13]

Churches in several cities (San Francisco, New York, Detroit, Providence, and Marin City, California) declared themselves sanctuaries for draft resisters and most, like Coffin, attempted to justify sanctuary by citing the primacy of the individual conscience.[14] Unlike medieval church sanctuary, which celebrated the sanctity of the cleric, U.S. sanctuaries claimed a sanctity or holiness for every individual—something the Constitution ostensibly had acknowledged in its protection of religious freedom. These claims for ecclesial asylum, then, were built upon powerful and widely recognized cultural traditions within U.S. society.

Many sanctuaries, however, were "penetrated" by the state. Coffin, Dr. Benjamin Spock, and three others were arrested for "conspiring to 'counsel, aid and abet' young men who were prepared to refuse induction into the army" (Weber 1978: 271). All of the defendants, except one, were found guilty in June 1968 and sentenced to two years in prison; Coffin also received a five-thousand-dollar fine.[15] In May 1968, twenty-one-year-old Robert Talmanson, whose appeal to overturn a conviction for draft resistance had been rejected by the Supreme Court, took sanctuary in St. Andrew United Presbyterian Church of Marin City. Three days later, U.S. marshals, armed with Mace and clubs, pushed their way through a group of supporters, arrested Talmanson at the pulpit, and dragged him away. In June, the FBI broke through a locked door of the Unitarian Universalist Church of the Mediator in Providence, Rhode Island, and arrested two draft resisters and nine protesters. The same month, Donlad C. Baty, 22, was arrested in the sanctuary of the Washington Square United Methodist Church in Greenwich Village in New York City; he was sentenced to four years in prison (see Bau 1985: 162-69).[16]

Conflicting Paradigms

The conflict between dissenting churches and the state over Vietnam was articulated within the powerful religious imagery of separation and covenant, and both groups wielded these frames according to different ideological agendas. Under President Lyndon B. Johnson, for example, the state utilized the *separationist* paradigm as part of a strategy to mobilize the male population into a military force. During the war, the state's version of the separationist frame recognized the individual as a "sacredly free" entity with an autonomous conscience, but it was an individual whose conscience compelled him to bear arms on behalf of the nation. In this version, patriotism, as gauged by the readiness to accept military service, flourished in the individual conscience (a locus that was free of state influence) but was manifestly identical with state interests and goals. The state thus recognized "conscience" as a cultural institution, but only within a certain context of actions and structure of ideological goals. The government often "Americanized" the conscience by placing it within a covenantal framework in which the individual became linked to the military mission of a nation. In his speeches defending U.S. involvement in Vietnam, Johnson frequently referred to this civil covenant, which was implicitly linked to America's sacred duty to keep the earth "free," "capitalist," and "saved" from the clutches of a voracious socialism and godless communism.[17]

The anti-Vietnam War sanctuary churches also appropriated these separationist and covenantal paradigms as "frames of resistance" to the state. Church activists wielded the *separationist* frame in order to emphasize first, the sanctity of the conscience as a holy place that was both independent of the state and universally possessed, and second, their right to practice what their conscience dictated. By taking their antiwar agenda into the churches, anti-Vietnam War protesters attempted to establish a parallel between their individual consciences and God's will, and then collapse this distinction in God's holy house. Using the church as a symbolic frame, sanctuary participants claimed that the conscience—like the church—was a sacred "house" of God, a "place" where one experienced a more intimate and forceful link with God. In the church, one was, as it were, "closer" to God, and through their closer proximity to God in the church, sanctuary participants claimed a more direct connection to God's desires concerning the war.

The *covenantal* frame was also manipulated in sanctuary churches, particularly in the emphasis placed on communitarian sanctuary—a concept that, like the Puritan notion of a civil covenant, emphasized sanctuary as a cultural jurisdiction based in a believing community. During the

Vietnam War, the covenantal theme was dramatized both in the actual practice of sanctuary (supporters, forming a protective ring, often slept with the draft resisters in the church and blocked the entrance of military personnel intent upon arresting the resisters) and in the rhetoric of church leaders accusing the U.S. government of corruption and betrayal of "American values." In this respect, the consciences of the *separationist* frame formed a moral community—a covenant—in the context of a church.

Although their presence in the United States was short-lived, the church sanctuaries of the 1960s and early 1970s, as suggested earlier, became alternative political spaces—liminal moments in the traditional structure of church-state relations. Within these liminal spaces, cultural paradigms of religion and national identity were reexamined, reconstituted, and finally proffered as an option to those paradigms constructed by the state. Because the sanctuary process occurred in a "space" outside of the hegemony of the Supreme Court, it threatened the state's authority to define ideologies of religion and politics and, by extension, the nature of individual and collective cultural identity. The questions about religious and national identity raised by church sanctuary during the Vietnam War period were not, however, directly addressed in the courts. Those arrested in sanctuaries, for example, did not attempt to legitimize or legalize church sanctuary as a cultural practice. This may explain why ecclesial asylum never became a significant public issue in the 1960s. Some scholars have suggested that the anti-Vietnam War church asylums were primarily a symbolic medium through which liberal church groups dramatized and expressed their opposition to the war, and that this is what distinguishes them from the sanctuary churches of the 1980s and early 1990s whose scope and objectives extend far beyond this symbolic dimension. Like their predecessors in the 1960s, however, the later generation of sanctuary activists found themselves not only redrawing the traditional cultural boundaries surrounding, separating, and linking church and state, but also delineating a new concept of "church," one that entailed novel separationist and covenantal frames of religious identity.

Ecclesial Sanctuary for Central Americans

When church sanctuary reappeared in the 1980s, it did so in a political and religious climate that—though also in a state of flux—was markedly different from that of the 1960s. Religion was not only making a comeback as a political force—in a 1986 survey, the *Nation* estimated that of those active in social movements, two-thirds were religiously motivated;

it also had become a deeply divisive issue. Unlike the period between 1973 and 1980, which generally had been a time of consolidation among the churches (Wuthnow 1988: 164), the 1980s witnessed the rise and spread of evangelical fundamentalism and the consequent polarization of churches into two mutually hostile "liberal" and "conservative" camps.[18]

During this period (and continuing into the present), the churches on the "right" consisted mainly of a Protestant fundamentalist coalition, as well as a smaller number of neoconservative Catholics and Protestants. Foremost on the agenda of these groups has been an antiabortion campaign, an agenda that the Republicans incorporated into their party platform in 1976. The Christian right also decried the teaching of what it referred to as "secular humanist" values and "evolutionism," arguing that creationism (the biblical account of human origins, which presumed a belief in God) should replace scientific explanations in the schools; many fundamentalist groups wanted prayer and Bible study to be part of school curricula. Commonly associated with "traditional family values" (encompassing antihomosexuality and antipornography stances), the right-wing churches evinced a stridently pro-free-market and anticommunist political orientation.

The agenda of the Christian "left" was considerably different from that of conservative churches, and focused on three main areas. First, in the area of civil rights and "liberation" struggles, many of these church groups supported affirmative action and equal opportunity legislation for blacks, Hispanics, and the poor.[19] Second, they developed critical attitudes toward capitalism, which, many argued, created economic dislocation and unemployment, particularly in the industrial sector. (This "economic" critique has been concomitant with an interest in corporate America, especially in relation to corporate investments in South Africa and First World economic policies in the Third World.) Third, left-leaning church groups condemned the nuclear arms buildup and focused on issues of U.S. foreign policy.[20]

Although the specific agendas of the right and left wings of U.S. churches demonstrate the profound political differences dividing America's "people of faith" during the 1980s, the two groups share one important feature. Both reject a model of strict separation in which religion and politics remain distinct jurisdictions.[21] Consequently, both the right and the left wings of the church, despite their political differences, have opted for a "marriage" between religion and politics, and have advocated two distinct visions of what is, in fundamental respects, a similar paradigm of church-state relations. For both factions, the main issue is not whether religion and politics *should* be merged, but *how* they are to be merged.

Both groups endorse a fusion of religion and politics that, while taking different directions, has profoundly challenged the traditional boundary between private and collective morality in the United States.

Separation and Covenant in Sanctuary for Central Americans

Sanctuary theologies of the 1980s both build upon the traditions of separation and covenant and incorporate novel prophetic elements (influenced largely by Latin American liberation theology). Hence they have significant cultural continuity with U.S. religious culture as well as some important departures from it.

These theologies generally utilized the sanctity of place (a church) as a starting point, and, as the statements of the INS and the Border Patrol attest, this was a place that, given the powerful cultural authority that a church, as a separate jurisdiction, commanded, the state was extremely reluctant to penetrate.[22] State "violation" of the sanctuary space meant crossing the sacred divide, the wall of separation, existing between church and state.

As the movement matured, spokespersons generally did not—in contrast to the Vietnam sanctuary participants—celebrate the "conscience" as a treasured democratic institution in and of itself. Rather, they emphasized the conscience as an individual's ability, in the face of potential persecution, to choose *a specific ideological direction*—which then was articulated into a "covenant community." Following Latin American liberationist rhetoric, this choice was articulated within a social-justice framework—a framework that stressed resistance to oppressive economic, political, and social structures and advocated a "preferential option for the poor."

In the U.S. Sanctuary movement, the "conscience," the principal component of the separationist frame, was transformed into a specific kind of consciousness and activism, one that grew out of traditional liberal values of individualism but also was based in the selection of a specific "way of being" in the world. In keeping with liberationist themes, this "way of being" focused on *structures of oppression* and looked to the *experience of the poor* as a guiding principle. It did not recognize the barriers separating religion and politics in the United States and advocated instead an epistemological melding of the two—a melding centered in the ideological mandate to "stand with the oppressed." The result was a novel paradigm of covenant in which individual consciences did not stand "alone" for their beliefs but were articulated through a community of believers or a sacred population mobilized around "solidarity with the oppressed." In this sacred community, church affiliation ceased to be the guiding principle of membership; more important was one's attitude toward "faith" and one's understanding of "being faithful" (Lernoux 1989: 277).

Significantly, although the covenantal theology of Sanctuary endeavored to meld "different experiences of national culture, regional church and denominational community" (Tabb 1986: xv), it refused to become a "civil religion" built on a state-linked nationalism—a central feature of the civil covenant of the New Christian Right. Particularly after the indictments and the 1985-86 trial, Sanctuary communities developed a forceful anti-U.S. state posture and advocated a model of community that was explicitly transnational or global in scope:

> Authentic solidarity goes beyond remembering the suffering of our brothers and sisters. It embodies the biblical call to universal brotherhood and sisterhood. It lays upon us a new sense of kinship. We as North Americans are called to claim our family to the south.
>
> That means that Maria Elizabeth, the 55-year-old woman who goes every day to the San Salvador morgue carrying pictures of her disappeared son, is our mother. Cristina, the 17-year-old university student raped by the National Guard is our sister. Roberto, a Nicaraguan delegate of the Word, his throat slit by *contras* attacking Jalapa, is our brother. Filiberto, a Mayan Indian from Quiche, who now sits in a clandestine jail in Guatemala City, is our father.
>
> When people ask what they can do to help the people of Central America, our response is: What would you do if your sister were being raped, your brother killed, your father disappeared and your mother mourning daily? We do as much as we can at the deepest level of our lives. ("Statement of Faith," Chicago Religious Task Force, January 1985)

Members of the Tucson community expressed this concept as a "covenant ecumenism," arguing that a "church" could only find its true meaning and purpose if it stood as "protective community" in solidarity with the poor (Nichols 1988: 247). Like the Chicago version, this covenant ecumenism, because its doctrinal requirement consisted solely of a "commitment to the poor," was international in scope and engulfed all faiths—Jews, Christians, Muslims—as well as nonbelievers.

Establishing Authority: Creating an Alternative "Space"

In the language of separation and (principally) covenant, the participants of the 1980 Sanctuary movement attempted to create an "alternative political space" in which the relation of religion to politics was contested and reconstituted. The creation of this space was, to a large degree, a response to state prosecution—which forced those aiding undocumented Central Americans to establish both a context and a tradition for their actions. Reaching deep into the wells of history, sanctuary workers not only claimed ecclesial asylum as a cultural resource but profoundly transformed it. This transformation or reconstitution of tradition occurred within the cultural vocabulary of sanctity of place, person, and community, and in the context of separation and covenant.

U.S. church sanctuaries became cultural spaces that drew "God" and "Caesar" together into a discourse about power, and, more specifically, into a highly charged discussion about the proper mixture of religion and politics in society. Like the *criminal/sinner* of medieval church asylum and the *conscientious objector/soldier* of the anti-Vietnam War sanctuaries, the Central American *refugee/illegal alien* invited church-state conflict. The Central American fugitives were a particularly volatile issue given that "God" claimed them as fugitives from persecution, and Caesar depicted them as a threat to economic and national security.

Unlike medieval sanctuary, however, U.S. church sanctuaries in the 1980s drew upon the Hebraic concept of sanctuary as a communitarian institution, advocating a religious practice that was premised more in the sanctity of a community than in the holiness of an individual's conscience. These sanctuaries were also distinct from those in Vietnam period, particularly in light of liberationist themes that shifted the sanctity of conscience away from *individual rights* (the free exercise of religion) toward sacred communities focused on *collective rights* (those of the oppressed). U.S. church sanctuaries, moreover, were not, like their medieval counterparts, *disappearing* but *appearing* in the face of centralizing and dominating state power. These sanctuaries, therefore, cannot be regarded, like their European antecedents, as the lingering remains of a church that was losing much of its power. They speak more of an ascendant church endeavoring to assert its cultural power in a political context that recognized the importance and relevance of "religion" for "politics."

Chapter 6
Creating "Social Space": Sanctuary and the Reconstitution of "Church"

Although Sanctuary coalesced around Central American refugees and U.S. foreign policy, the movement involved much more than resistance to government immigration practices. Sanctuary bonded people together in a novel social group by recasting the way in which they perceived and experienced themselves as a "church." In redefining what a "church" was, the participants of the Sanctuary movement profoundly reconstituted their social reality and their place within it. This process of "articulation" altered the ways in which individuals identified themselves vis-à-vis their families/kin groups, their denominational churches, their nation/government, and, ultimately, the international community.

This chapter explores Sanctuary as a process of articulation that created distinct cultural "spaces" and social identities. First, I examine the ideologies of social organization undergirding Tucson's Sanctuary community, as well as patterns of participation within the movement. Second, I analyze how a network of participants talked about their involvement in the Sanctuary movement, and attempt to illustrate how their discourse, as a genre for organizing experience, became part of the Sanctuary "space." Third, I look at the ideology/theology of two Sanctuary churches—particularly in comparison to Latin American liberation theology—and focus on how it restructured the cultural links between the individual and the family, the worshiping community, and the nation. In this chapter, we return to the steps of Sanctuary—not to mark the passing of the Border Patrol car (as we did in chapter 1), but to enter the Sanctuary "space" itself.

North Americans and the Sanctuary Network

"Personal Networks"

One of the first tasks I faced—as did any newcomer to Tucson's Sanctuary movement—was how to plug into the Sanctuary network. My initial strategy was twofold: to identify and visit with key figures in the movement, and to attend as many Sanctuary-related activities as possible. Not realizing that the organizational ideology undergirding Tucson's Sanctuary movement rejected hierarchical or centralized models in favor of a segmented model, I found the first two months of fieldwork extremely trying, mainly because I could not find anyone who could provide me with a "snapshot" view of Sanctuary. People seemed to know bits and pieces about what was going on in the overall network, and they shared information about the various activity "cells," but no one person seemed able to provide a complete picture—what I hoped would be at least a rough map of Sanctuary's contours. What each person did possess, however, was a network of personal relations that they had developed within a field of church-linked activities (see table 6.1). Although the majority of people circulating in the Sanctuary network were based in one of three religious communities—Southside Presbyterian Church, Desert Pilgrims (Catholic), and the Saguaro Friends (Quaker)—it was rare to find any two people who shared an identical network. In order to enter into the Sanctuary community and to survey its dimensions, I had to develop my own personal network.

Developing such a network is not premised on geographical location; one cannot establish membership in the Sanctuary community simply by living or hanging out in a particular neighborhood. The Tucson Sanctuary networks are not based on residency—that is, these networks, and even the churches to which they are tied, are no longer "neighborhood" phenomena. Many of the Native American, black, and Hispanic congregants who belong to the Sanctuary community historically descend from an older model of a "minority" or "barrio" church. Their involvement in the network is articulated mainly through Southside, and their affiliation with the church stems from Southside's days as a mission church in which the congregation reflected the neighborhood's class, ethnic, and kin composition. As Southside became an Anglo, middle-class, educated congregation, however, the neighborhood—as well as class, ethnic, and racial—base of the church changed dramatically. Currently, the majority of Southside's congregants drive to Southside from neighborhoods all over the city and its suburbs. Similarly, the Desert Pilgrims

Table 6.1. Tucson's Sanctuary network: principal churches and activity cells

Level 1: Worship services

Southside Church (Presbyterian)	Desert Pilgrims (Catholic)	Saguaro Friends (Quaker)	St. Luke's[a] (Episcopalian)

Level 2: Church activities
- Choir • Youth/Children's group
- Bible study/Discussion groups • Prayer groups
- Study groups • Pastoral outreach
- Religious education • Building committee
- Business meetings
- Other committees/Meetings

Level 3: Church activities: refugee-related

A. Coordinated through TEC task force and Southside Church	B. Coordinated through Desert Pilgrims	C. Coordinated through Saguaro Friends	
• Language study	• Weekly vigil	• Refugee concerns	
• Social services	• Weekly refugee		
• Sanctuary placement	Mass conducted		
• Volunteer placement	by a Catholic priest		
• Public education	and held in a		
• Legal services	Protestant church		
• Central American			
• Cultural outreach			

Level 4: Underground activities

• trsg (the underground) (The majority of members are from Southside.)		• Desert Rescue (run principally by Saguaro Friends)	• El Puente (a splinter underground)

[a]St. Luke's is linked to a splinter Sanctuary community within Tucson. Owing to conflict among underground members in the posttrial period, a group of Sanctuary participants established their own underground. (See chapter 8.)

community consists of middle-class, educated Anglos, many of whom drive twenty to thirty-five miles to worship.

Involvement in the Tucson Sanctuary network is based largely upon establishing "membership" in one of the Sanctuary churches/synagogues.[1] Membership provides access to information about what activities are going on, although figuring out how to participate in them involves more work. Gaining entry into the network is ultimately premised on establishing trust in a small cell of people with whom one usually has no kin or neighborhood bonds.

Since Sanctuary encompasses several different kinds of activities— from doing border crossings to joining the church choir—each of the groups listed in figure 6.1 represents a "node of access" or point of entry into the overall community. Not all of these nodes, however, are *equally* accessible. Southside Presbyterian Church and its resident TEC task force are central access nodes in the spectrum of "cells" that make up the Sanctuary network. In theory, any North American can become part of Sanctuary by showing up at the Southside Church for worship on Sunday (level 1) and joining one of the church's affiliated groups (level 2). This is probably the easiest and most direct way of becoming involved. The hardest node to access (for both Central Americans and North Americans) is the underground (level 4); a variety of informal screening processes are in place to filter membership into this category.

Anglo or North American entrance into Tucson's Sanctuary movement depends principally on the degree to which one is known in the Sanctuary community, how long one has been around and active, and how much free time one has. Central Americans (and their families) usually enter into the network either as previously "approved refugees" or as individuals who, on their own, have been able to make their way to Southside Church. (In some instances, Central Americans have been dropped off at Southside Church by the Border Patrol after being arrested and released on their own recognizance.) As a result, Central Americans are primarily involved in the network through level 3 as *recipients* of services. Although a few refugees are involved in the coordination and management of the services, and a handful attend the principal religious services (level 1), none are involved in the underground (level 4). North Americans who come with a trusted recommendation are quickly absorbed into the network at level 3, and possibly level 4. Mission volunteers who join Sanctuary, for example, usually have been recommended and sponsored by another Sanctuary church (or a church sympathetic to the movement), which has done an initial screening.

An anthropologist's entry into the network is uniquely problematic. The profile of an anthropologist is not unlike that of a government spy: both have plenty of free time, both are eager to participate in community activities (particularly the underground), both ask a lot of questions, and both (albeit for different ends) are intent on "recording" information. (I quickly learned not to refer to Sanctuary participants as field "informants"!) Moreover, many in the movement were critical of the academic voyeurism and political neutrality so often associated with ethnographic research. As a result, building trust and confidence, being clear about my objectives, and being respectful of any boundaries Sanctuary workers might set around my presence were critical elements in my anthropological participation.

Table 6.2. Membership of Desert Pilgrims

Age distribution		Percentage of total
Under 15	1	3.6
30-40	5	17.8
50-65	11	39.3
65-75	11	39.3
Ethnic distribution		Percentage of total
Hispanic	2	7.1
Native American	1	3.6
White/Anglo	25	89.3
Gender distribution		Percentage of total
Female	16	57.1
Male	12	42.9

Total active members: 28
Married units: 7

Source: Data collected May-November 1990

For newcomers, then, participation in the network can be difficult. Participation usually begins with initiating membership in one of the Sanctuary worship communities—I, for example, ended up attending three to four religious services each weekend. A second, fairly simple way of becoming part of the Sanctuary network—without having to establish religious affiliation—is to attend the weekly Vigil protesting U.S. foreign policy in Central America. This event is open to anyone who wishes to attend. The Desert Pilgrims, another primary Sanctuary church, is not an "open" faith community like Southside Church in that its location for worship is not an urban church but a small, sequestered chapel, and the weekend service is sometimes held at different locations; its members have deliberately tried to keep the group small and maintain a fair degree of ideological uniformity.[2]

As mentioned, both Southside Presbyterian and Desert Pilgrims are predominantly middle-class faith communities (see tables 6.2 and 6.3). To some extent, because of the emphasis on secondary activities held out-side of weekend church services, "full" participation in these communi-ties requires traditionally middle-class resources: spare time for voluntary (nonrenumerative) activities and "wheels" (a readily available vehicle). The latter is particularly important since Tucson's public-transit system is limited both in size and hours of operation. (Poorer families, as well as the majority of Central Americans in Tucson, are largely dependent on

Table 6.3. Membership of Southside Presbyterian Church

Age distribution		Percentage of total
Under 25	7	4.3
26–45	80	49.0
46–55	28	17.1
56–65	18	11.0
Over 65	30	18.4

Ethnic distribution		Percentage of total
African American	11	6.7
Hispanic	25	15.3
Native American	16	9.8
White/Anglo	109	66.9
Other	2	1.2

Gender distribution		Percentage of total
Female	107	65.6
Male	56	34.4

Total active members: 163[a]
Married units: 25

[a]This figure does not include children in the congregation.
Including children, Southside's membership is approximately 225.

Source: Session Annual Statistical Report, Presbyterian
Church U.S.A., year ending December 31, 1990.

public transportation. Although some of these families do have cars, there is usually only one per household.)

Women in Tucson's Sanctuary Network

A salient feature of Tucson's Sanctuary network (and of Sanctuary communities across the United States) is the prominence of women. Women are far more active in the movement than men and participate more fully in the full range of activities that constitute giving Sanctuary. Women occupy positions of leadership and authority within the Tucson community, although not generally on a public level. Tucson's public profile has been, and remains, dominated by men (namely, Rev. John Fife, Jim Corbett, and other male church leaders). The reasons for the continued presence of a male-dominated public leadership are complex: both Fife and Corbett have played critical roles in getting the movement off the ground and shaping its direction, and their role as leaders is consistent with their historical importance for Sanctuary. Yet, as a church movement, Sanctuary inherited a male-dominated (clerical) structure, which privileged men in authority roles and gave them greater opportunities for public leadership. Media agents also tended to approach men as spokespersons of the movement and focused on cults of male personality in portraying Sanctuary to the rest of the country. Members of the Tucson community, too, both men and women, have colluded with this process of male privilege—many have found the issue of gender and public leadership explosive or disruptive.

Despite a general reluctance among female Sanctuary workers to openly criticize Fife or Corbett, or to make male-dominated leadership a central issue, gender issues were frequently raised in their discourse. Most of these references, however, were made in relation to their families and the difficulties that Sanctuary involvement imposed on them as wives and mothers. Consequently, many wives and mothers in Tucson's Sanctuary network expressed strong tension between *faith-community* and *family-based* paradigms for their social identity as women:

> I really got involved in Sanctuary. It was just something that I had to do. I had to help these people who were so desperate. My—for want of a better word—my conscience told me to do it. In doing Sanctuary work, however, I was neglecting what my husband perceived to be my household duties. The laundry would pile up, the kids would get up in the morning and nobody would have any underwear or any socks. Half the time there wasn't any dinner because I was at a meeting. There was a lot of that stuff. The regular household routine really began to collapse. I was probably going to a meeting four or five times [a week]. . . . So things got chaotic. And my husband got pissed off because things were not running the way they should.

The tension that this Sanctuary worker describes reflects a contradiction that is inherent in Sanctuary activities for many women: Sanctuary activities are both continuous with traditional ideologies about women's work and disruptive of them.

The continuity with traditional women's roles is related both to the ideology of "church space" in U.S. culture and to the specific nature of Sanctuary work. First, the church, like the home, is continuous with the "inside and private" domains that Sylvia Yanigisako (1977) suggests are linked to women in American culture. Recurrent references in Sanctuary discourse to the "church" as a loving and merciful "mother," in particular, underscore a special association between church and women. Similarly, the notion of sanctuary as a jurisdiction removed from the cruel demands of the "outside," "secular" domain corresponds to the concept of the home as a "haven" from the male-dominated, public arena. Second, many of the secondary activities of these churches, like those of the home, are nonremunerative and fall into the category of "social reproduction." A great number of Sanctuary activities—finding homes, providing food and clothing, obtaining medical care, arranging schooling, taking care of children, and so on—can be classified under the rubric of social reproduction and are fulfilled primarily by women. (One tends to encounter a stronger male presence in legal and fund-raising activities, and to a somewhat lesser degree in the educational and underground subgroups.) In this sense, participation in Sanctuary can be said to have strong continuities with women's traditional activities within their homes.

Yet Sanctuary also involves planning runs, assisting undocumented aliens across the border, participating in demonstrations, and the risk of being arrested. Beyond the time commitment that women make to Sanctuary (which in itself can disrupt the household routine), these activities threaten women's traditional responsibilities as mothers and wives, and many women find it difficult to balance both roles:

> Now that the kids are gone, I could leave all of this [gestures to the house and furniture]. I could give it up tomorrow. If it weren't for my husband, I know I would be more involved in Sanctuary. I think my husband lives in mortal fear that I will do something—like getting arrested—that shames him, that jeopardizes the family.

Hence, although many of the tasks women perform in their homes are transferred into Sanctuary, participation in the movement also rearticulates women's identities in powerful ways: they become individuals who are willing to take risks that often have major consequences for their households; they adopt a set of priorities that transcends their immediate responsibilities to their families; and, in relation to their husbands, they acquire prominent roles in the public sphere. Sanctuary, therefore, is an alternative source of cultural identity for women, and can serve as a counterweight to the hegemony of the traditional family group.[3]

Some, but not all, women are able to satisfactorily resolve the tensions that arise from their participation in Sanctuary, and several (particularly those with young children) avoid activities that involve potential arrest and prison sentences (indeed, they are often advised to do so). Women with younger families who are active in underground activities often tell stories of long and painful transition periods in which husbands and children had to adjust to their new roles. Women without families (usually unmarried, widowed, divorced, or retired) are much more active in Sanctuary's controversial practices and, because of the nature of their work, achieve special stature within the Sanctuary network. Consequently, there is a division of labor among Tucson's women participants that is linked to their status as wives and mothers.

Sanctuary, then, both extends women's traditional roles *and* redefines them; participation in Sanctuary exposes women to a complex set of contradictions. Women maneuver creatively within these contradictions— taking advantage of the new identities that Sanctuary offers—and articulate their roles in a variety of ways, so their participation in Sanctuary has multiple meanings and considerable flexibility.

Ideologies of Organization: Sanctuary as a "Base" Community

How are people in Tucson's Sanctuary network linked to one another? Neighborhood and kinship ties are not salient principles of membership for the North Americans in either Southside Church or Desert Pilgrims. For the most part, people get involved in the secondary cell groups as individuals, not as married couples or members of a particular family. (The one exception to this is the Vigil, where several married, mostly retired, couples are present.) When I came to Tucson to conduct fieldwork, the fact that I had no neighborhood or kin ties to anyone in the community was not unusual.

As we saw in chapter 3, there are no explicit governing bodies or official leaders of Tucson's Sanctuary movement. In contrast to other Sanctuary communities, Tucson purposely resisted forming a centralized policy-making body with elected representatives, and chose instead to accentuate the local autonomy of each Sanctuary cluster. The personal networks structuring Sanctuary are an outgrowth of this ideology—and represent a unique experiment in the organization of religious culture.

Within each of the three religious groups outlined in figure 6.1, the unofficial (though still influential) spokepersons of the movement—a Presbyterian pastor, a Catholic priest, and a Friend (Quaker)—have advocated paradigms of "church" that reflect noncentralizing, acephalous principles. While the three versions of this paradigm are informed by different Christian traditions, each position is influenced by Latin American liberation theology, and in particular the concept of *comunidades de base*—basic Christian communities (BCCs).

Latin American BCCs are a product of the late 1950s and are linked to broader theological and political shifts within the Latin American church. These faith communities are small groups of people (usually twenty to thirty family units) who, typically under lay leadership, come together to study the Bible, reflect on their social, political, and economic conditions, develop strategies for social change, and celebrate the Catholic liturgy.[4] The BCCs are viewed as the building blocks of a larger process referred to as "liberation," a term that encompasses (1) an acknowledgment of the social, economic, and political injustices that create and perpetuate poverty in Latin America and (2) the expression (through action) of a commitment both "to the life, cause and struggle of millions of debased and marginalized human beings" and "to ending . . . historical inequity" (Boff and Boff 1988: 3).[5] The first dimension is accomplished primarily through "conscientization"—a term coined by Brazilian educator Paulo Freire, who insisted, as a result of his work among the illiterate poor, that learning should always be linked to the social and political context of the learner (Freire 1972). This methodology rejects the traditional pattern of church teaching—indoctrination—in favor of small-group reflection on Christian Scripture. The second dimension of liberation—solidarity—entails *action* on behalf of the poor. This "action of solidarity" (orthopraxis), many liberation theologians have argued, is more important than "correct thinking" (orthodoxy), or even theological reflection:

> Theology is reflection, a critical attitude. Theology *follows*; it is the second step. . . . The pastoral activity of the church does not flow as a conclusion from theological premises. Theology does not produce pastoral activity; rather it reflects upon it. . . . The theology of liberation attempts to reflect on the experience and meaning of faith based in on the commitment to abolish injustice and to build a new society; this theology must be verified by the practice of that commitment, by active, effective participation in the struggle which the exploited social classes have undertaken against their oppressors. (Gutiérrez 1973: 11, 307)

In liberationist ideology, these worshiping communities are said to be the principal units of the "church" because they constitute the *base* of society—the poor, or those who, in the Latin American context, constitute the vast majority. The operational principle of the BCCs is to keep *articulation of the faith* at the base throughout these local, semiautonomous communities.[6]

Appropriating Liberation Models

Many in the Quaker contingent of Tucson's Sanctuary community appropriated the BCC concept to promulgate a paradigm of church that resonated with these liberationist themes. In Jim Corbett's model, for example, the base is defined in terms of an *interfaith* group committed to solidarity with the oppressed. Because the U.S. Sanctuary context—

unlike that of Latin America—is not based on a relatively homogeneous religious tradition, one of the prime problems for Sanctuary leaders was how to establish a base that incorporated different Christian and Jewish traditions. Building on the Quaker belief that all persons (regardless of social status) can be vehicles of God's grace, Corbett resolved this problem by underscoring the *ecumenical* nature of the BCC Sanctuary church:

> Latin America's Covenant ecumenism is truly catholic. In contrast to "the European ecumenical agenda" of corporate mergers and homogenized beliefs, it is integrative rather than assimilative, delighting in the unreduced diversity of those who unite in the service to the Kingdom. Yet, when we compare the Christian communities formed by the poor in Latin America with the communities now formed from the practice of sanctuary in the United States, we see distinctive ways that this . . . is uniting us here in Anglo America. First, our joint practice is grafting the people that is the church into the people that is Israel; we are— Christian and Jew—affirming in practice that we are formed by the same Covenant. Second, unbelievers are being fully incorporated into Covenant-formed base communities. Third, Sanctuary is the needle's eye through which congregations composed of the beneficiaries of violence are entering into active community with the violated. (Corbett 1986: 152)

In Corbett's writings, this ecumenical church, like the BCCs, had to remain autonomous and nonhierarchical to be effective.

Coming from a Protestant tradition, Southside members appropriated the BCC concept and attempted to "Americanize" it. John Fife's contextualization of the BCC, for example, was built on the Protestant "congregational" model in which a small group of believers selects a minister to lead the worshiping community. In the congregational model, the minister is always accountable to the faith community and his leadership is always guided by the concerns of the group:

> We were trying to figure out a BCC style of organization, not the North American electoral, representative style that we had previously adopted, and we wanted to know how liberation theology could inform this style of organization as opposed to a North American hierarchical organization that elects a representative body that informs policy and then develops spokespersons. It was clear that if there was an analogue to the BCC of Latin America, it was probably the small congregation in North America, and so we said that in order to be a Sanctuary congregation you have to be grounded in a community model. . . . So we said, we're going to use the congregation as an analogue

to the BCC and that it's going to be a broad-based, grass-roots community that doesn't depend on church hierarchy in order to go ahead. And it's not going to create its own hierarchy in terms of imposing a set of policies or a set of directions on the whole Sanctuary movement. We were going to depend on each of those communities to devise its own theology and to give its own ministry a sense of direction, so that the power is always with the base and not migrating toward a smaller and smaller kind of hierarchical organization. (John Fife, interview, July 1990)

Fife, too, was attracted by the acephalous organizational principles of the BCCs, largely because he felt that these kinds of groups are better able to maintain a popular basis and have substantive political "staying power" since they are much more difficult for the state (or other hierarchical institutions) to crush:

Hierarchical models are extremely susceptible because leadership can be tied up in legal battles for two or three years and this can destroy the whole movement. Or sometimes [leaders] get killed. And what happens is that this devastates the rest of the organization that has become dependent upon one or two people or a small group of people at the top for direction and policy. And the government has become expert at knocking off social reform movements in precisely that way. We don't understand how vulnerable they are, and this is why the Christian base community movement has survived in Latin America even through murder and torture. Their viability continues because it is not dependent upon anybody except God. (Ibid.)

Father Ricardo Elford, a Catholic priest deeply involved in Sanctuary, was also influenced by the BCC model, but his uniquely Catholic analogue was based on the faith communities of the early church and a desire to return to "Galilean roots." Elford's vision of a church rejected church hierarchy or a "pyramid church with a throne room on top and the poor multitudes at the bottom." Instead he advocated a church symbolized by "disciples gathered in a circle"—the kind of church, he argued, that characterized early Christianity. Elford's work with the Desert Pilgrims was part of his effort to reject hierarchical models of Catholicism in which faith was decreed by clerics at the top of a huge institutional structure.

All of these paradigms of church—Catholic, Presbyterian, and Quaker—appropriated the Latin American BCC model, and all strove to retain the articulating power of the base. The confusing array of personal networks that I encountered in Tucson—an American counterpart to the acephalous, nonhierarchical base of the Latin American *iglesia popular*—was a manifestation of an "Americanized" BCC ideology.[7]

The Articulating "Base" of Sanctuary

Given that the general organizational ideology of the Tucson Sanctuary movement is one that avoids centralization while striving to give the power of articulation to the base, who are the individuals that constitute this base, and how is Sanctuary an articulating experience for them?

Out of the Sanctuary community (of roughly 168 persons) in which I circulated, I formed a core network of twenty people. All of these individuals had their own networks of fifteen to twenty people (with considerable overlap). Within this core group, I was able to conduct intensive life-history interviews with fifteen Sanctuary workers. In these tape-recorded interviews, I individually asked them to tell me about their involvement in the movement by recounting the history of their "religious development." We began with their childhoods and their earliest memories of religion and religious education, and moved progressively through the life cycle—grade school, high school, college (where applicable), marriage/divorce, children, work, retirement, and so on—to the point where they became active in Sanctuary. I kept my questions broad and endeavored to let my informants dictate what *they* thought was significant about their past in relation to their eventual participation in Sanctuary. In these interviews (and more than fifty other informal interviews), I also asked subjects to describe their conceptions of God and faith, and their understanding of key terms within Sanctuary discourse: community, liberation theology, the poor, the church, and so on. I asked these second kinds of questions in the hopes of collecting a Sanctuary *theology of the base* that I could compare with the versions I was hearing from the pulpit during weekend worship services. Table 6.4 is a profile of the fifteen members from my Sanctuary cell.

All fifteen members of this group are middle-class whites ("Anglos" in local terminology). In this group, five attended the Desert Pilgrims' Saturday worship, eight the Sunday service at Southside Church, three the Vigil, and thirteen worked with the underground. Disposable time management within this group varied depending on age and the nature of the income source. Three retired members had an adequate and stable income base, largely from pensions and investment returns, and consequently had considerable amounts of free time for work with Central American refugees. Two members in the 50-60 age bracket were directly employed by a Sanctuary church and worked full-time with Central Americans. Three members in the 50-60 age bracket, and one man in the

Table 6.4. Profile of Sanctuary cell

Religion	Gender	Age	Education	Occupation	Marital status
Catholic	F	70	college	military/retired	married
Catholic	M	72	college	military/retired	married
Catholic	F	68	prof. school	medical/retired	married
Presbyterian	F	55	high school	clerical	divorced
Catholic	F	50	college+	social services	divorced
Catholic	F	50	college+	social services	single
Presbyterian	F	50	college+	social services	divorced
Jewish	F	46	college+	housewife/student	married
Catholic	M	29	college+	mission volunteer	single
Presbyterian	F	29	college+	mission volunteer	single
Presbyterian	M	27	college+	mission volunteer	single
Presbyterian	M	27	college+	social services	married
Presbyterian	M	27	college	mission volunteer	single
Presbyterian	M	26	college+	mission volunteer	single
Quaker	F	24	college	mission volunteer	single

24-29 age bracket, were employed outside of the Sanctuary network, and had the least amount of free time available. The majority of the younger people in this cell were "mission volunteers" who were able to work full-time on refugee-related activities within the Sanctuary community; their stipends ranged from six to ten thousand dollars per year. (On several occasions, these members have had to find part-time work to make ends meet.)[8] All members of the group are U.S. citizens; one male was born in Canada but moved to the United States as a young child. Only one is a "local," born and raised in the Tucson-Phoenix region.

Thirteen of the people I interviewed were core members of the underground. They formed a kind of "inner sanctum" and were regarded as the people who did the "real" work of the movement, that is, as those who were taking the greatest risks on behalf of the cause. As a result, age distribution is an important feature of my Sanctuary cell. The members of this cell tended to be either under 30 or over 50—a salient feature of the underground group. People within the 30-45 age bracket (those most likely to have dependent children) tended, in general, not to be involved in underground activities because of the risks of imprisonment and its potentially disastrous effect on young families dependent upon two income earners.

Several excerpts from the fifteen interviews I conducted between May and November of 1990 and March and July of 1991 are presented here. My first step in organizing these interviews was to transcribe them, and then to locate unifying motifs in the telling of these life stories—a sense of pattern that was not immediately apparent to me owing to the "surface" diversity in the individuals' religious history. As I listened to the interviews, I isolated instances in which individuals used ancedotes from their pasts to illustrate a point about their religious development, and then identified "organizing principles" in these selections. Among the religious traditions represented are conservative Catholicism, evangelical and fundamentalist Christianity, liberal Presbyterianism, Reform Judaism, unprogrammed Quakerism, and agnosticism.

Despite this diversity, there were certain themes running through each of the discourses, which, following the insights of Susan Harding, represent a "bundle of strategies—symbolic, narrative, poetic and rhetorical" that act as "a mode of organizing and interpreting experience" (Harding 1987: 167). By identifying these themes and tracing their development, I was able to discern what linked these separate discourses together, and to observe how, taken as a whole, participation in Sanctuary (for these Anglos) is very much a process of reconstituting not only the self but also the social environment (the family, church, nation) in which the self is contextualized. In short, these interviews were representative of the *articulating base* of Tucson's Sanctuary churches.

A recurring motif in these interviews was "liminality." In chapter 5 I delineated sanctuary as a uniquely liminal space, always located *between* competing cultural authorities, whether Caesar and the pontiff or church and state. The liminality of these interviews refers to the location of the individual in a world that continually spawned contradictory messages about how to behave. Liminality was therefore conveyed as a sense of being "betwixt and between" conflicting cultural discourses, of being caught between the conflicting moral messages that traditional and conventional authority (parents, relatives, teachers, church, government) taught the individual. These conflicting messages instructed individuals that all people are created equal *but* blacks are not welcome in a white church; that men and women are equal before the eyes of God *but* women's participation in the church is secondary; that the individual conscience is sacrosanct *but* children must always obey their parents, and so on. In each of the interviews, what emerged to resolve the conflicting messages was the *voice of the conscience*.

The archetypal liminal experiences of Sanctuary have been well documented and mythologized in Sanctuary literature. One celebrated story has both John Fife and Jim Corbett finding themselves caught between what the INS termed the law and their understandings of Christian morality. The resolution of these conflicting discourses occurred for these archetypal subjects through the voice of the conscience and in the Sanctuary community—a cultural space, as I have argued, that has historically drawn together conflicting discourses about power.

In a fashion similar to the organization of the dominant "myths" in Sanctuary, the discourse of the Tucson Sanctuary workers reveals patterned experiences of liminality, discernible in stories of confrontation with parental and church authority, as well as conventional attitudes toward race, gender, Jewish-Christian relations, and government authority. Each of the excerpted discourses presented here conveys the sense of people organizing their past experience in order to construct, and make sense of, new experiences and relationships in the present. Although these stories shifted between two types of conversion narratives—immediate and gradual—the organizing motif was contradiction and conflict, and making a *choice*. In the transcripts, I isolated sequences in the principal anecdotes that not only recurred throughout but also structured the interviews. These sequences capture the sense of conflict and liminality— the "betwixt and between."

Reactions to Church Authority

By far the most common theme in these interviews was (negative) reactions to religious sources of authority. Many stories revolving around religious experience were told in an indignant, can-you-believe-this? tone. Motifs of feeling caught, trapped, or alienated by narrow-minded or hypocritical religious authorities recurred frequently:

When I was a teenager we went to a church. It was a huge church and very wealthy. The minister drove a Cadillac and wore cashmere sweaters and stuff. There was an assistant pastor—we called him Holly—in religious education. We had these really neat discussions. We'd met in his little hovel, this little shingled house with the door hanging off. Here is this stone mansion of the minister with his wife, with the Cadillac parked in the drive. Here is the church. And here is Holly's house. And he's got four kids and his wife is pregnant. And he had books! Everywhere! We could go in whenever we wanted and talk. And we had these neat discussions and stuff. He would get so excited about ideas he would forget to shave and often he had B.O., body odor. Which was a great sin in the fifties. In other words he was an embarrassment. And apparently he made the mistake of saying in response to one of the kids' questions about the Trinity, that perhaps there wasn't . . . that perhaps it didn't matter. Well, that got back to the kid's parents. And a special session was called and he was fired, with his wife pregnant with their fifth child. And they were gone like that [snaps fingers]. And then the minister tried to have a meeting—and they got in a new guy who was a pompous asshole.

—Shelly (50-60 age bracket)

My husband and I are both strongly—you know—anti-Zionist. If there is such a thing. We have a lot of trouble with the concept of Israel. So it's real important to me not to get involved in a congregation that's going to instill that stuff. So many congregations focus on a lot of problems that are specifically Jewish. And that's a real problem for me. When we tried to bring our children to temple, this congregation embodied all that I found distasteful in the religion. You know, there it was. Complete with the old men sound asleep in their chairs. And the rabbi up there droning on and on and people kind of wandering around. That if you put in your time, everything would be OK. And tomorrow you can go back to your business. It was a real sadness to me that, at least as I perceived it, that Jews as a group didn't have a sense of social responsibility to "others"—other than themselves.

—Rachel (40-50 age bracket)

As an adolescent, fourteen or fifteen years old, I had these really terrible nightmares, blood and guts and everything. Almost every night for four years. I just thought that there was some nasty force trying to get me. I just thought that the devil was trying to make me a bad person, that devils were trying to make me insane and I just could not stop them. I had nightmares all the time. And I really thought there was some great cosmic battle over my soul. I imagined, at least when I was younger, that God had a fixed image. But the devil could be whatever it wanted. And that it could be nice things. So the devil was trying to trick me by pretending to be nice things. This all came from Uncle Jack, [who] was really the only steady religious influence in my childhood. He was hard-core evangelical. Born again, walking with the Lord, tow the line or—you know, very much fire and brimstone. He scared the shit out of me. If I pull anything out of my childhood, it's that. Which took a long time to get rid of. You know, just fears because you have to accept Jesus as your personal Lord and savior, and be born again and saved in the blood of the lamb and all that type of stuff. And, yeah, I remember thinking in high school, Wow, what about these others? Here's Sara and she's one of my best friends and she's Jewish. I never really bought into it, though. I think that's what got me questioning. Uncle Jack made it so hard to be loved by God. It was a task, that you had to do a lot to get God's love. And I think that the Christian message through Christ is that,

*no, you don't. You don't have to do all that much. You just have
to ask.*

—Paul (20-30 age bracket)

Women in my interview pool frequently expressed a strong awareness
of and resentment toward patriarchal hegemony within their previous religious communities:

*I was nun and a teacher for a good part of my life. And [after
Vatican II] I remember a pastor coming over and reprimanding
me, so to speak, because I had allowed another teacher to use a
magazine in her classroom; it was a magazine that was put out
by some scholastic company and this priest didn't like it. He
thought it was radical or something. It turned out she wasn't
even using it. So it took two weeks to straighten that out.
Then the next thing, he was over because in the religion
books there was a song by Peter, Paul, and Mary, "If I Had
a Hammer." And that was a communist song. And then the
next thing was that they had pictures of angels as humans. In
this case he wound up taking all the books out of the seventh
and eighth grades and telling me that they could never come
out as long as he was there. It was a constant battle between the
old and new theology. In fact, one of the hardest things for me
was to stay within the school system, where the final voice
was—in terms of everything you did—the pastor. If he said
"I want the children to walk up the aisle backwards for
communion this year," you did it. So no matter what was
happening to me theologically, there was so much turmoil
created every time I turned around. I was just constantly kicking
against the good.*

—Susan (50-60 age bracket)

*To give you an example of something that occurred to us—and
this happened before my husband [who was Protestant at the
time] became a Catholic. Our son was to go to a party. It was
Friday. They were going to have hot dogs and so forth—
marshmallows, etc. And there was a priest who stopped off to
visit us and was having dinner with us that evening. I always
kept Friday—I didn't serve meat. But supposedly, being in the
military you were exempt from this, and I thought it wouldn't
affect our son at this party. So I thought we were exempt but as
it turned out, my husband had to be the Catholic; only as long
as it was the man who was the Catholic, then we were exempt.
You could see how ridiculous it was. It made me so angry. I
guess I was responding to sexism in the church but I didn't know*

*it. Now I see it! How did I live with this? I don't know. I guess I
was so busy rearing children.*

—Louise (60-70 age bracket)

Several Sanctuary workers focused on experiences of racism and elitism
in their religious communities:

*I attended a Presbyterian church and the only black there was a
janitor. I was in my—gee—I must have been 22 or 23. The man
was cleaning while we were cooking supper [in the church
kitchen] and came in and said that the children—some of the
children who were playing out there where he was cleaning—one
had called him a nigger. And he said: "I know these children
hear it at home." Well, he was fired the next week. I didn't
believe this was happening. A lot of the women at the church
said that he spoke out of turn. I didn't say anything. I couldn't
believe that this was happening. And then I happened to be in
the presence of the minister and his wife and they were talking
about the situation, and he just kind of shrugged it off like it was
no big deal. And I thought: they have black people clean their
houses for them, take care of their children, but they don't
worship with them. And I thought "No."*

—Betty (50-60 age bracket)

*[In college] I applied to go to Nigeria with Inter-Varsity and I
went. And we did door-to-door evangelism. It was a real mixed
area. I think it might have been 40 percent animist, 40 percent
Muslim, and 20 percent Christian. I started to feel real strange
about evangelism. In meeting Muslims I think that was one of
the key things. I finally came to believe that Christians didn't
have a monopoly on truth. I would get into these very technical
arguments about Scripture and I realized that these guys knew
what they were talking about and that they were absolutely
sincere. It just seemed really beautiful to me. And the other
Christians around would make fun of these silly calls to prayer
and bowing down to face one direction. They just thought it was
silly and I thought it was beautiful. Because of my own conflict
with my own sexuality I was beginning to become more and
more uncomfortable with mainline Christianity. And I came back
from Nigeria and broke down spiritually and didn't want to have
anything to do with organized Christianity.*

—Tim (20-30 age bracket)

Throughout the interviews, these stories of church/religious authority
seemed to serve both as an exposé of how bad things had been in the individual's religious pasts and as an explanation behind his or her current
participation in the Sanctuary community; all those interviewed indicated

that they had, often after painful periods of alienation and guilt, rejected this kind of church authority. Feeling trapped, isolated, and alienated in these religious contexts was a strong feature of their rhetoric about previous religious experience. They emphasized that they had made a deliberate choice to find something else.

Reactions to State Authority

Because Sanctuary activities are strongly linked to a critique of the state and its foreign policy in Central America, I was prepared to hear anecdotes conveying a sense of alienation from the government. Indeed, several individuals recounted stories of conflict with the government, particularly its military orientation:

Even back in World War II, I was aware that the war was not just fought for the poor Jewish people who were over there. That it was brought on—our government had really caused Hitler to come into power. He couldn't have come in to power without us. I felt strongly that way. I know that I told my husband and he didn't feel that way at all. I knew it after World War I. I knew that that treaty was one that would definitely cause further problems. The treaty contributed to the German people getting a man such as Hitler in. Then, as we know now, those who were Nazis after the war—we welcomed them into this country!
—Louise (60-70 age bracket)

After my retirement, we began to read about Latin America and liberation theology; until that time I did not question my faith with regard to being in the military or to the support of the military. I worked in the same office with a Catholic chaplain. I never saw any dichotomy in Christian faiths and the support of the military. [During the Vietnam War] I was strongly anticommunistic and [I believed that] we [the United States] were just honoring our Southeast Asia Treaty Organization commitments when we went to Vietnam. We were fighting communism. Even after retiring, I didn't throw out any [of these] opinions until the Sanctuary trial. We became avid trial watchers. We went to the library and began to dig out books on the history of Latin America and we began to read these. They told history in a way that I had never seen. And I began to believe her [my wife]. It was really that which turned me around. It opened my eyes. I had been deceived. I had bought the party line about why we were in Vietnam, in Korea. About why we fought World War II.
—George (60-70 age bracket)

After college, I went to Europe with a friend to meet people in the European peace movement. We traveled around a lot, and in Germany I met this commander on a base [we were protesting at]. And he took a very antagonistic approach to me: "Who are you? Why are you on that side of the fence? Where's your patriotism? You should be supporting us and you should be on the side of the fence supporting military buildup." And I would talk to him about what I believed in and that I didn't believe that that [what he was doing] was right, and that I really believed that it was wrong to kill and that my faith said no. So we did a lot of Bible battling between the two of us. But the first day that I had met him he had told me just ruthlessly how many communists he had killed in Korea and the Vietnam War, women and children, that kind of stuff. He was just a very cold, ruthless kind of person and I left him crying because I had never met someone that able to kill like that. And I really struggled with that. What did that mean? How great evil is and where does evil come from? And why does it exist? I remember thinking and crying because someone could push a button and the world could blow up.

—Joyce (20-30 age bracket)

Consistent with these experiences was an inclination among interviewees to collapse the distinction between state, government, and nation and convey a rejection of and/or ambiguity toward any state-aligned identity:

I'm mostly ashamed [to be an American]. I have no faith in our political process. None. Basically [the situation is] hopeless in terms of the ability of our government to make any kind of decision that is truly for a just world order and because it cares about people. I think we've sold out on the values we said we had when we started this country. I think that capitalism can't work. It always depends on taking advantage of somebody somewhere. If we're not fucking the Indians, we're going to fuck the European sweatshops. And if we're not fucking them, we're going to fuck people in the maquiladoras *for $2.50 a day. It always, always depends on somebody having something less than somebody else. I'm ashamed of the system. I'm ashamed of our national value system. And I'm mostly ashamed to talk with my Latin American brothers and sisters.*

—Luke (20-30 age bracket)

Reactions to Parental Authority

In these interviews, negative or alienated reactions to parental author-

ity were usually linked to the way in which parents communicated or enforced social or religious values:

> *I was always a rebel. I was a rebel against my parents. They*
> *were suspicious of the unknown. I wanted to know blacks, what*
> *we called Negroes back then. By the time I got into nurse's*
> *training, there was one black student, my classmate, the first in*
> *that school. Well, I wanted to bring her home and my mother*
> *told me no. [She said,] "You should be nice to her but you don't*
> *need to associate with her." I think she was afraid of what she*
> *didn't know. If she had known her, she would have been fine.*
> *Well, I couldn't be that way.*
>
> —Jackie (60-70 age bracket)

> *I went to a traditional, convent Catholic school. I was always*
> *the one who questioned what we were being taught. Like you*
> *were always being told God will take care of you if you are*
> *good, and if you follow these commandments all the time and*
> *[do] acts of mercy. And it always seemed that where we lived in*
> *the community, it was very contrary to what the nuns would tell*
> *us during the day in school. Twice a year the gypsies would come*
> *to our area and I was always told [by my parents] that they were*
> *very bad people, that they were very poor and they would steal*
> *from us. And my dad had a drugstore and oftentimes I would*
> *say, "Couldn't you just give those kids a candy bar?" And he*
> *would say, "Watch out! Close the door! Cause they'll steal our*
> *candy bars." And I said, "But if they're so poor, can't you just*
> *give them a candy bar?" But he said "No." But when the nuns*
> *and the priests would come, they got to have the candy bars*
> *[free] and I thought, "But they don't need the candy bars!*
> *They're not so poor that they couldn't buy them."*
>
> —Sarah (50-60 age bracket)

> *I grew up in a Catholic home, in a Catholic town. I mean it was*
> *very Catholic. Ninety-five percent of everyone who lived in this*
> *town was Catholic. My particular family, even more so than my*
> *friends, was fanatically Catholic, meaning you said the rosary*
> *every day. You went to church all the time, you had all kinds of*
> *litanies to say at special times of the month, prayers to say. But I*
> *think my earliest memories were quite negative—dealing with the*
> *way my parents presented what I would call this negative and*
> *punishing God. I was very much against the God of my parents.*
> *And very angry toward them and toward their faith. And it was*
> *only by force that they got me to go the [second] Catholic*
> *sacrament after baptism—meaning communion—and then first*
> *confession. As soon as I had choice, when I was sixteen, I did*
> *not get confirmed. I was the only one out of a class of fifty-two*

to not do it. Most of my friends just went along. So, my religious upbringing was in many ways an act of my parents' will over mine. . . . Some of my teachers ran around crazy trying to prove to me that there was a God. If I didn't believe, I was either wrong or evil, going to hell or something terrible. I mean there was no process of a journey. You either accepted and were good and OK and everything was fine, [or] if you rejected it, then something was wrong with you. And that was not my style. I didn't really have a choice. It was either you live at home and do these things, or you don't live at home. The choice was either leave or stay. And there was no way at fourteen or fifteen that I was ready to leave home. For me those issues were so important that if I made a decision that I was not going to church, period, that would be the same as saying I'm leaving this house.
—Matthew (20-30 age bracket)

Although these taped interviews spanned many hours and many topics, themes of alienation from major cultural institutions surfaced repeatedly. Contradictory messages from dominant cultural authorities (such as parents, the church, teachers, the government, and social convention) were a recurring theme in the discourse of these Sanctuary participants. The anecdotes of feeling caught betwixt and between these messages built up—like a crescendo in a symphony—as individuals recounted their life histories. Their involvement in Sanctuary was described as a choice to "do the right thing" in the midst of these contradictory messages and experiences, a choice often made without the approval of their parents, friends, church leaders, and government.

As articulations of Sanctuary's base, these liminal narratives are a particular genre of organizing personal experience. Yet they are also paradigmatic in that the anecdotes are not mere recollections or interpretations of the past. They represent a model of membership, based on shared kinds of experience, for a particular group of people who are bonded to one another through their involvement in the Sanctuary movement. For those whom I interviewed, Sanctuary became the arena in which these stories could be drawn together, addressed, and redirected.

The Sanctuary Space: Rearticulating Liminality

Southside Presbyterian Church and the Desert Pilgrims—as worshiping centers of Tucson's Sanctuary movement—are cultural spaces in which liminal discourses surrounding a person's social identity are brought together and resolved. As a congregant in these two faith groups, one learns how to articulate past and present experiences into a series of *conflicted moments* so that the choice to be part of the Sanctuary group *makes sense*. This process of rearticulation involves fundamental changes in the way a person views the world and a Christian's place in it.

Southside Presbyterian is a congregation of 163 adult members and fifty-five children who meet every Sunday at 9:30 A.M. for a two-and-a-half-hour worship service and one hour of socializing following the service. Sunday mornings around 9 A.M. people begin to arrive at the church and collect a program at the door before entering. Inside, chairs are arranged in horseshoe fashion around a slightly raised platform at the front of the church's main room. As is typical in Protestant churches, no pictures of saints and no statues adorn the wall of Southside's plain, austere, and rather worn interior. At the very front of the church is a simple eight-foot cross on the platform, placed just behind the pulpit. A few stones encircle the cross at the base, and a plain, striped "campesino" blanket is draped across its arms. Southside is not a wealthy church and those who attend it dress simply—one does not see much gold jewelry, fancy hats, ties, or high heels. The pastor, usually dressed in a long white robe and wearing a Central American stole, enters through a side door at the front of the church. At the end of the service, he strides the full length of the church to the bell rope near the front doors, where, usually with a child in his arms, he rings Southside's sonorous bells and announces the return of his renewed and revivified congregation to the world outside.[9]

Desert Pilgrims, in contrast, is a small Catholic community of twenty-eight who, under the leadership of Father Ricardo, meet twice a month for an hour-long Mass. (They alternate Mass with base community-like meetings in a member's home.) The Mass is held in a small, isolated chapel with one large window facing out onto the desert. Inside the chapel are various mostly abstract pictures of Christ and Mary on the walls, and the priest who celebrates Mass often places a religious icon on a low table slightly in front and to the left of the altar. The chairs are arranged in a circle around the altar and the members, by their own vote, remain seated for the entire liturgy. Fifteen to twenty-two people usually attend.

Liturgically, Southside and Desert Pilgrims are not "radical" churches; both build on traditional models of worship. Noticeably untraditional elements in Southside's liturgy are the children's sermon (usually a very amusing event at the beginning of the service and in front of all the adults), the mixture of music (staid Protestant hymns and vibrant black gospel music), and the seating arrangement. (The horseshoe pattern de-emphasizes the power of the pastor and underscores the nature of the church as communal body.) Also rather unorthodox is the mixture of announcements heard at the end of the service; typically, one is not only invited to join the youth group, the Christmas Fund, and the choir, but also notified about upcoming protests against military aid to El Salvador or how to get information on tax resistance. During the prayers of intention, when people publicly ask others to pray over a specific problem, congregants sometimes request blessings for those on a "picnic" or taking a short "trip" to Mexico—veiled references to underground members who are doing a border crossing.

Desert Pilgrims follows the standard format of a Catholic Mass. Untraditional elements within Desert Pilgrims are its size, the regular presence of women at the altar (particularly as readers of the Gospel), its circular seating arrangement, and the communal distribution of the Eucharist (a basket containing the hosts is passed from person to person rather than distributed to each individual by the priest). The priest of this community also seats himself as frequently as possible within the circle, thereby de-emphasizing the distinction between cleric and layperson. Announcement time at the Desert Pilgrim Mass is also typically an occasion when members update each other on activities and events surrounding protest against U.S. aid to El Salvador and human rights abuses in Central America.[10]

Perhaps the most distinctive feature of these faith communities is what one hears from the pulpit. John Fife is a masterful preacher who, for twenty to thirty minutes every Sunday, deftly integrates personal experience, humor, and biblical exegesis to make his point. Father Ricardo, in homilies of similar duration, adopts a more informal and conversational style. Both leaders use biblical readings as the basis for their sermons, but as points of departure for talking about themes we saw in interview excerpts: contradictory messages about class, gender, race, religious and political identity. Their sermons are clearly a public mode of organizing and interpreting experience, and as a result these religious leaders exert tremendous influence on their congregations.

In the sermons of the Reverend Fife and Father Ricardo, conflict in moral messages about the social world are first highlighted, and then subsumed into a larger dichotomy between "the wealthy" and "the poor." Congregants are challenged to make a paradigmatic choice about who God calls them to be: a church reflecting the values of the dominant culture and wealthy classes or a church advocating the rights of the dispossessed. Fife explored this theme in a sermon delivered on October 7, 1990. In his usual fashion, he illustrated his point through reference to his own personal experience:

[My wife] Marianne and I went to Phoenix the other night. My cousin and his wife had called. They were at a conference in

Phoenix . . . and invited us to come and have dinner with them at their hotel in Phoenix. It was lovely. (Long pause.) It's called the Phoenician.[11] (Laughter.) It's located right at the base of Camelback Mountain within eyeshot of Barry Goldwater's house and the establishment of Phoenix. And it is gorgeous. We pulled into the parking garage and, unlike most parking garages, this had a lobby encased in glass and with marble floors that led to a battery of elevators complete with flowers and sculpture. In the parking garage! As you entered the [hotel] lobby, there were these gorgeous fountains and individual sculptures, and the entire floor was in Italian marble with various beautiful mosaics.

And we went out onto the terrace for dinner. And it was a full moon. The lights of Phoenix below. And terraced down from the lobby of the hotel were a series of swimming pools of various configurations and beauty. Some in marble. Some with lights arrayed around the pool and various beautiful sculptures. The last one was the crowning jewel of the Phoenician. It is a swimming pool finished entirely in mother-of-pearl. (Congregation gasps.)

[The evening was] a glimpse of—a vision of what wealth and privilege can buy in the world today. But there was another vision there, however, that was not as apparent. It was the vision of tens of thousands of people who were bilked out of their money to build the Phoenician. Who poured their life savings into the promises of Charlie Keating so that he could build his monument to greed. Folks who believed that they would get a return on their investment. Folks who are now despairing. . . . You couldn't see that vision from the mother-of-pearl swimming pool. But if you had an eye for the world in which we live today, it was enough to ruin a lovely dinner.

It's a parable about a vision of the world in which we live.

It's the difference between seeing beauty, and privilege, and reward for one's efforts when you go the Phoenician, and seeing the human suffering that that kind of greed produces. You don't have to go to the Phoenician, though. Just drive around the streets of this city. Just look at what people think is theirs, what belongs to them. That they believe they deserve as a reward for their labors. And then drive through the fence at Nogales and look at the suffering. Look at the hungry children in the face.

Folks, it's the choice we have to make.

In struggling with this choice, this disjuncture between two interpretations, congregants are invited to "resolve" and "rearticulate" the kinds of conflicts expressed in the interviews. Within a dichotomy that polarizes the interests of the wealthy (the oppressor) against the rights of the dispossessed (the oppressed), Matthew's experience of conflict regarding parental and church authority, Sarah and Rachel's efforts to make sense of religious exclusivism, George and Joyce's conflict with state authority, Louise and Susan's experiences with church sexism, and Jackie and Betty's accounts of racism are translated into moments of oppressor versus oppressed. Framed in this way, these experiences become, for Sanctuary participants, moments of "choice."

These experiences contain examples of *archetypal* moments for making a choice between the two positions. The Reverend Fife and Father Ricardo highlight racial, gender, class, and religious differences as points of conflict—as crucial moments of choice—between the two proffered paradigms. The cultural forces surrounding those choices are state authority, parental hegemony, cultural convention, and religious/church orthodoxy. The individual conscience becomes the arbiter of the conflict and, directed by a "theology of the oppressed," makes a choice. This choice is usually an unpopular one, which, often taking elements of traditional values, exposes the hypocrisy of cultural hegemony, state power, and church authority. Such an ideology undergirds the Tucson community's claim that the U.S. government is violating its own laws regarding freedom of religious expression and its treatment of refugees. Thus it is the conscience, informed by a specific theology, that resolves "liminality."

Choosing a Religious Identity

What is both interesting and puzzling about Tucson's theology of choice is that, despite overwhelmingly negative experiences with traditional religion, Sanctuary participants continue to choose religion as a predominant form of individual and group identity. How are variables of class, race, ethnicity, and gender part of this identity and why have they assumed a secondary position in relation to religion? Part of the answer lies with the unique problems such variables present for these Sanctuary communities.

Sanctuary is ultimately an iconoclastic or countercultural identity; by participating in it, individuals reject the status quo and adopt the posture of *resisters*. As a result, Sanctuary participants view themselves as marginalized in a political sense and much of their discourse revolves around the rhetoric of marginality and resistance. Subsequently, identification with (1) the dominant culture or (2) social variables that can cut across community unity becomes highly problematic. In both cases, class, race, ethnicity, and gender are troublesome.

First, as a predominantly Anglo, educated, and moderately affluent congregation, Sanctuary participants share strong class, race, and ethnic ties to the dominant culture; marginality or resistance expressed in these terms, therefore, does not effectively distinguish them from the groups they are challenging. Class, race, and ethnicity are particularly vexatious for North Americans who adopt a liberationist orientation since liberation theologies (such as the one appropriated in Sanctuary) emerge from a Third World context in which the vast majority of participants are poor and nonwhite, and liberation is expressed as resistance to a dominant white, wealthy culture. Such identities are obviously not easily available to the majority of North American Sanctuary participants, so solidarity with the liberation struggle has to be expressed in other terms.

Second, Southside's historic church identity is based on ethnic, racial, and class marginality; the church's iconoclastic ministry was originally identified with poor blacks, Hispanics, and Native Americans. These distinctions persist between older and newer families in the church, and indeed there is some resentment on behalf of the Hispanic and Native American families toward the new Anglo population that now dominates their church (a change that occurred after the arrival of John Fife and in conjunction with Sanctuary activities). In this sense, class, race, and ethnicity are potentially disruptive rather than unifying variables for the Southside community.[12]

Gender, too, is potentially divisive for these communities, and its disruptive potential is linked to larger divisions with the national Sanctuary network. In the mid-1980s, when the movement divided into two general directions (labeled Chicago and Tucson wings), many who adopted a critical stance toward Tucson based their criticism on what they perceived as a patriarchal domination of the movement by "macho males." John Fife and Jim Corbett were identified as particularly baneful examples of this machismo. As anthropologist Robin Lorentzn notes in her study of women in Chicago sanctuaries, gender for these groups became a rallying point around which female Sanctuary participants articulated themselves as an underclass. By isolating gender as a political issue within the movement, these women sought to seize authority and get proper credit for their shaping role in Sanctuary (see Lorentzn 1991). Gender is thus an issue that distinguishes two general Sanctuary orientations. In the Tucson communities—with the exception of a splinter group that allied itself with Chicago-based Sanctuary—women and men were critical of male domination in a general sense, but, for the most part, did not raise it (particularly in a public way) in relation to Sanctuary's power structure. I concluded that, for these Tucson communities, the rhetoric regarding gender was so associated with an anti-Tucson critique that it had become a "loaded" topic for Southside and Desert Pilgrims, with the (perceived) potential to seriously divide the community along pro- and anti-Tucson lines. (Moreover, these congregations had adopted a consensus model as a paradigm for decision making and were generally adverse to confrontational politics within their own group.) As a result, gender issues and analyses were incorporated into Tucson's Sanctuary space, but in such a way that potentially long-lasting gender-based divisions within the congregation were avoided.

It is perhaps for some of these reasons, among the Tucson communities, that class, race, ethnicity, and gender are subsumed within a predominantly religious discourse. Each variable possesses a unique place within the ideological structure of Tucson's Sanctuary movement, and each variable possesses a unique historical legacy or "loadedness" that has shaped its incorporation into the congregation.

"Community": Refashioning the Individual vis-à-vis the Group

If I went to prison, I'd get letters.

—Sanctuary worker

The religious identity of Tucson's Sanctuary, while incorporating issues of class, race, and gender inequality, is often expressed in the rhetoric of one central concept: *community*. Based on the frequency with which this word surfaced in conversations with Sanctuary participants, I concluded that community is a principal motif organizing and defining Tucson's Sanctuary networks, and can be thought of as both a physical and an ideological context in which Sanctuary members are bonded together.

In Tucson's Sanctuary networks, ideologies of Western individualism—which emphasize that each person is a discrete, integral, and fully operational unit unto itself—are rejected in favor of a corporate identity. The ideology of Sanctuary avoids identifying people *primarily* as individuals, as men or women, as family or ethnic groups, or as a denominational church body. As one Sanctuary worker implied, these social identities are viewed as important but *secondary* attributes; people are first and foremost regarded as a "People of God":[13]

> A real community is a place where people are not related by family but by faith and struggle. My community isn't a city but a pueblo—the people. The true church community is one that has many faiths; you are not going to be asked if you are a

Methodist or a Catholic, but you are a community struggling together as a People of God.

In Sanctuary ideology, a person's family, race, ethnic, and denominational identities are gathered together and reconstructed as a structure of interdependence and mutual obligation. Ideally, membership in the Sanctuary community automatically entails primary responsibilities toward *all* others in the faith group, without regard to kin ties, class, ethnic, gender, age status, or denominational affiliation. One enters into the community with the expectation that others will regard you in the same way:

> *I mean, by community, people I know I can depend on for anything. It means when I go on a run, if I get into trouble, there is a huge group of people who are mobilized, immediately starting with the core group of people around me. They have a shared sense of humor, a shared sense of purpose, and a shared sense of faith. A shared sense of values, just in terms of caring about human life and protecting it. Sometimes this is stifling, like we were talking about the obligatory gatherings. But I wouldn't trade it for anything . . . it's what a church should be.*

> *Recognizing interdependence is the cornerstone of the whole thing to it all. That this whole society is individualistic, make it on your own, if you work hard enough you can do anything you want. And it doesn't work that way. We are so supported and guided by models that tell us to go out and do your own thing. And I think women always, through the whole world, have recognized that interdependency among people, among children and parents, and between people and nature. I think those are basic feminist values.*

For the individuals who make up the Sanctuary network, the process of *creating community* entails relationships that extend beyond the weekly worship services, and, to some extent, there is an expectation that one will participate in the extrachurch activities. In this respect, the Sanctuary understanding of community somewhat resembles the New Christian Right concept of a "total Christian lifestyle." (Lacking the same financial resources, however, extraworship contacts among Sanctuary participants tend to be in low-budget, secondary church activities: Bible study groups, the choir, refugee-related programs, the Vigil, and so on, and not in schools, universities, and the workplace.)

The model of community that seems to characterize Tucson's Sanctuary networks—while based on principles of class, racial, and gender inclusivity and the mutuality of obligation—has its own boundaries of membership. Sanctuary is clearly not a freewheeling community in which "anything goes."

In the two Sanctuary communities I studied, group membership is built on the assumption that individuals within the group share a common bond of "faith." This faith, however, is not typically or simply a statement of orthodox beliefs, or even a belief in God. Nor is it premised, as it is in many New Christian Right cults, on strict ritual orthodoxy (accepting Jesus as your Savior through baptism and becoming "saved"). Sanctuary congregants are generally Christo-centric but have a fairly flexible understanding of faith, ranging from simple, unshakable belief in the existence of God to an agnostic inclination toward "social justice." Yet, although the Sanctuary community is flexible about the orthodoxy of "faith," it is also a "covenant" community in that the groups making up the overall network are united by a common set of ideological assumptions about the world, how it has evolved historically, and how it should be transformed. The Sanctuary communities are quick to embrace class, race, gender, and denominational differences, but they do not easily absorb diverse "political" orientations. Even though the Sanctuary network theoretically is open to anyone, it would be extremely difficult to get through either Southside or Desert Pilgrim's services if one's politics were "conservative." Another factor, then, that distinguishes these Sanctuary communities from other Christian churches in the United States is the specific political or *liberationist* orientation of their religiopolitical cult.[14]

Both Southside's and Desert Pilgrim's Sanctuary theologies are strongly influenced by Latin American liberation theology and begin theological reflection with the question, "Why is there poverty?" (not, as in Latin America, "Why am *I* poor?").[15] These communities reject traditional Christian arguments that poverty is God's will or judgment on the sinful, and examine the unique implication of North Americans, as a privileged class, in the production and maintenance of poverty. As a result, Sanctuary participants (and not just its preachers) often use liberationist motifs to explain the terms of membership in these communities:[16]

> To me there is no such thing—and this may sound judgmental
> —as a Christian community that does not have at its core a
> concrete, visible option for the poor. [There has to be] something
> that is ongoing and provokes a deepening of our faith. It's not
> something where you say, "Ah, I'll pull out my checkbook and
> give it to St. Alban's Society and they can send it to the missions
> in Africa." That's not a group commitment. That's bullshit,
> period. I'm talking about where their lives are personally touched
> by the poor. My interpretation is that Christ incorporated the

outcast into his life and I see it as the work of God to bring in those people who have been excluded.

I think that God is with the poor and the only hope that we have as people of this culture who have grown up with so much in terms of possessions and things, the only hope we have to understand God is to unite ourselves with the poor. To make a conscious decision to let go of our stuff and be with people who have less. . . . A person of faith? It means that I am a person of moral conviction. And I surround myself with people of like moral convictions. That's my community of faith . . . to try and bring everything in my life into some kind of line with what I believe. Which is why there ought to be some kind of equity in this world. That there ought not to be people who drive around with three cars while other people who are making those cars in the Ford plant in Hermosillo [Mexico] can't feed their kids. . . . I don't believe that faithful people say "I believe this" and then do nothing about it.

This ideology of membership—again, following Latin American liberation theology—is strongly action- or praxis-centered. This has important implications for North American Sanctuary participants, who, as we have noted, are mainly white and middle class and are themselves associated (by virtue of these traits) with dominant cultures. Through actions on behalf of the poor, Sanctuary participants can redefine who they are and redeem their privileged status. Although individuals within these faith groups express different interpretations about this orientation toward the poor, Sanctuary participants generally described the ideal faith community in terms of praxis-centered, liberationist motifs:

[I]n order to bring about the kingdom of God, we as Christians are called to work for peace and for justice, so that any type of oppression is deterring the kingdom of God, the kingdom coming in its full glory, whatever that is. And I can't really define what I think that is. I think it's when everything is just wonderful. There's a psalm, I forget which one it is, but it talks about love and justice being the two pillars of the universe, that hold the entire universe in place. And when there is not justice, you are rocking the entire balance of the cosmos, and everything is completely out of whack. And so in order to have the kingdom of the God—which is all of the universe and cosmos—intact and peaceful and loving and everything, you have to work for justice. So it's liberating, it's spiritual liberation as well as a political liberation. I was reading this pamphlet, and it said, "What good is it to say God loves you when this person is hungry, is

oppressed? Do something about it." It's not waiting in your
room for God to come and save you. It's active responsibility
. . . it's active, it's getting up and fulfilling your role to help make
that base stronger so that the universe and the cosmos can be
balanced again.

Community versus State Authority

The characterization of a "God of the poor" in Sanctuary cosmology
is part of a larger rejection of a wholly transcendent God (far removed
from the human world) in favor of a God who is directly in the human
world, even to the extent that God suffers alongside of the dispossessed.[17] In the North American context, this liberationist theme under-
cuts the affiliation between Christianity and the state (an association frequently promoted by groups of the New Christian Right and in
Protestant Reformation traditions, which view governments as "agents
of God" that are to be obeyed).

Because of their experience with government infiltration and prosecution, Tucson's Sanctuary communities find the whole issue of state power
and allegiance to the state highly problematic. For many, the Christian
Scriptures complicate the issue, because they offer a variety of interpretations on this subject—swathing the individual in ambiguous messages
about authority. How does one render unto Caesar what is Caesar's and
unto God what is God's—especially in a situation where the state has become the focus of resistance? On the other hand, how does one maintain
resistance to the state when Sunday readings emphasize obedience to civil
authorities?

Fife's sermons often focus on this topic and demonstrate a principal
way in which Tucson's Sanctuary ideology has resolved the conflict. In
one sermon, for example, Fife presented a unique interpretation of a passage from Rom. 13:1-10, in which Saint Paul tells Christians to "obey all
authorities." Fife took issue with the association between *God's author-*
ity and *government,* and relocated it (following liberationist themes) in
the *community of the poor.* He argued that Christians have a duty to
obey "authority," but only authority based on justice for the oppressed:

> When we're talking about how the community life should be run,
> it is the responsibility of governments to provide for the common
> good and to care for the welfare of the people. And governments
> should be the embodiment of Torah, the law, which is summed
> up as "you shall love your neighbor as yourself." . . . The
> authorities are given that godly authority to carry out that godly
> responsibility to the people. And when the authorities fulfill their
> responsibility, we should fulfill our responsibility toward them—

the order which cares for and protects the weakest members of the community and does justice. . . . But when the authorities do not fulfill this obligation, what do we do? We still are obligated to the people, to the godly authority to love your neighbor as yourself. . . . For God is in the midst of the community, and God is amongst the weakest of that community. That is where we find God. And that is where the authority of the community resides. That's where matters of conscience are, where matters of what it means to love and care are, and that's the presence of God. And authority is to be found in the midst of the vulnerable and the weakest and the most despised.

As Fife's sermon illustrates, Sanctuary participants have adopted an ideology of authority that establishes a distinct locus of power—one that resides in the church group and is expressed (and justified) by the actions of that group. Such a relocation can either undercut or complement the authority base of other loci of power in an individual's social field (e.g., the kin group, the workplace, local and national governments). These other sources of authority may remain relevant for an individual, but ultimately they become secondary (in either a complementary or a contradictory way) to the authority of the worshiping group. An individual consequently finds, consummate power and authority through commitment to the liberationist struggle, which, as Fife defines it, is really God's ultimate struggle.

Not surprisingly, the pervasive critique of the authority of the state and the concomitant relocation of God's authority in the *community of the poor* prompted many Sanctuary participants to reexamine their social identity vis-à-vis not only their families and church, but also their government. Sanctuary participants tend to express their American identity not in cultural terms, but almost exclusively in relation to their government and its policies. Their experience with the INS and its treatment of Central American fugitives, and their encounter with the state in the courtroom, have resulted in widespread ambiguity toward (and in some cases, a rejection of) their identity as American citizens:

Sometimes I am ashamed of myself as an American . . . it almost seems that I could easily give that up and go live in Central America. I think I could. But I don't know if I really could. That's a question I put off in the back of my mind . . . when I bring it forward, I'm just as responsible as the next morning. My patriotic sense is very much in the background.

When I'm in Central America I'm very aware of [being an American]. You can't help but feel guilty about what your nation

*is doing. . . . But I'm a Christian before I'm an American, I'm a
human being before I'm an American, so I'm not going to bog
myself down. It's not my fault that I was born in this country.
I'm in this because of my faith. I've always had this cosmic
attachment to Ben Franklin, Abraham Lincoln. But the
[American] Revolution, I have mixed feelings about it. The
American Revolution was solely an economic revolution. The
British didn't have death squads that were coming and killing
them or anything. It was like, "We don't like your taxes too
much, King George." . . . What I always come back to is, How
can we justify that revolution and then condemn this
[Nicaraguan] revolution? How can we have any sense of
patriotism? We should love what the Revolution stood for. And
if we love what the Revolution stands for, how can we condemn
this [Nicaraguan] revolution for what it stands for—let's be
honest—so much more?*

*I think the things I'd love to own have been sold out. I'd love to
own and talk about the civil rights movement and really believe
in that. Except that it's the 1990s and we're still screwing up the
blacks, the African-Americans in this country. I think this
country has been ground-breaking in terms of how women
should be treated. And I'm proud of that. But I'm still ashamed
of all of the goddamn men in this country who continue to—and
women, too—who bought the lies for so long that they just
won't let them go.*

As these excerpts suggest, Sanctuary participants are inclined to reject
a broad-based, state-aligned social identity. Yet Sanctuary ideology does
not entirely jettison notions of a collective identity that, like nationalism,
articulates individuals into larger, more abstract groupings in which
members of different groups, though they may never meet or know each
other personally, are nevertheless linked. Sanctuary participants frequently replace a sense of national identity with the notion of a "global
Christianity"—a tendency I noted after the fifth time I was told by Sanctuary workers, "We are Christians first, not Americans." In keeping with
some of the *community* themes outlined earlier, Sanctuary participants
define their Christian globalism by an association with a "globally oppressed" class; just as the poor are global, so too are the Christians who
define themselves by advocacy on their behalf. Consequently, Christians
are defined by values and goals that transcend specific ties to the nation-
state (or indeed any kind of nonglobal government), but that are based in
the social justice ideology of international liberation. Within the theology
of Sanctuary, then, one's adoption of a Christian identity has important

implications for one's social role vis-à-vis the state's economic and political policies; the global community basis to Sanctuary not only allows, but also compels Christians to criticize all oppression no matter what its source.

In this chapter, I attempted to depict Sanctuary as a process of "articulation," one that created a distinct kind of cultural "space." I examined both the ideologies of social organization undergirding Tucson's Sanctuary community and elements of its unique liberationist theologies. I also explored how a network of participants talked about their involvement in the Sanctuary movement, and how their "liminal" discourse played a constitutive role in creating the Sanctuary space—a space that ultimately redefined the individual in relation to his or her family, church group, national government, and international community.

I have emphasized some of the general trends within two Sanctuary communities, and have offered a glimpse into some of the chief characteristics of the Tucson-based Sanctuary movement. Undoubtedly, the Sanctuary groups across the United States both share and depart from some of the characteristics I have outlined; each group reflects a specific history that has shaped issues of class, race, ethnicity, gender, and religion in its community (see Lorentzn 1991; Coutin 1993). Nevertheless, from conversations and interviews that I have had with members of non-Tucson Sanctuary groups, I have concluded that issues of liminality, theologies of choice, and the various liberationist motifs seem to be widespread in U.S. Sanctuary. Also widespread in these groups is conflict—for example, between women and men, Anglos and Central Americans—which, though distinct in each context, also reveals some structural patterns.

In the next chapter, I endeavor to shed light on this sense of conflict within Sanctuary by discussing the "articulation" of Central Americans in Tucson's Sanctuary movement. By analyzing how Central American experiences of, and participation in, Tucson's Sanctuary movement differed from those of North Americans, we will see how Sanctuary reflects a process not only of resistance, but also of hegemony.

Chapter 7

Sanctuary and the Central American Odyssey

Central American journeys into Sanctuary are usually bitter tales—difficult to relate, painful to remember, and distressing to hear.

The trek through El Salvador and Guatemala is a perilous one, and the passage through Mexico poses its own dangers. Central Americans follow several different routes to the United States. Most cross the Guatemalan border into the Mexican state of Chiapas. One common crossing point is at Tecún Umán at the base of Guatemala's western border with Mexico.[1] Not far from this town is Mexico's dreary and garbage-strewn Tapachula, where coyotes can be hired from seven to fifteen hundred dollars per capita for the long trip north. Central Americans heading to California, Washington, or British Columbia travel up the Pacific Coast, sometimes using fishing boats to get to Baja California. From there, they cross into the United States through Tijuana. Others take the route through the Mexican states of Veracruz and Tamaulipas along the Gulf of Mexico, and cross the Texas-Mexico border at Matamoros or Nuevo Laredo. Still others head into Mexico City, trek north to Chihuahua, and then cross at Juárez-El Paso or try to get into the United States through one of the smaller border towns, such as Agua Prieta or Nogales.

Many Central Americans in the United States have fled horrific experiences: torture in prison, the burning of villages, the death of family members. Yet exodus does not end the danger. From the moment they begin their journey north, Central Americans become the targets of extortion and physical abuse. In Mexico, immigration officials (*la migra*), federal judicial police, municipal police, military officers, and bus drivers are potential abusers; each group regularly extorts *mordidas* ("bites" or bribe payments) from Central Americans (see Ross 1987). Women often suffer the severest abuse, and are routinely raped or forced into prostitution by corrupt Mexican police. (Social workers at Southside told me that in six years they had met only a handful of Central American women who had not been raped either in their own countries or in Mexico.) In addition, individuals who appear to be Central American or from the south (i.e., short, indigenous, or rural-looking in dress and accent) are often targeted by gangs of thieves. Coyotes, too, are untrustworthy and exploitative, and have been known to take money and then abandon their "cargo."[2] If Central Americans do make it to the U.S.-Mexico border, they are by no means safe from police violence. They also become subject to an immigration service that views them mainly as "economic migrants" and seems intent on deporting them as quickly as possible.[3]

For Central Americans, then, the journey to Sanctuary involves experiences that are strikingly different from those of North Americans. The nightmares they suffer are often submerged in the discourse of everyday life in Tucson, but they pervade the air like a noisome odor that will not go away.

This chapter explores several Central American experiences of Sanctuary in Tucson. Although these experiences are by no means representative of all Central Americans involved in Sanctuary, and although Tucson is only one example out of several hundred in the United States, they are not unusual in light of what I have learned from other Sanctuary communities in the northeastern United States. In these communities as well, issues of language, class, cultural, religious, and political differences have profoundly structured the ways in which Sanctuary has "articulated" Central Americans into the movement.

Central Americans in Tucson

In the ideology of Tucson's Sanctuary churches, Central American refugees are the focus of spiritual reflection and community action.[4] Refugees are not merely regarded as *members* of Sanctuary's inclusive community—they have a special status within it. Central Americans are said to be the "spiritual guides" of the movement, the ones who fundamentally challenge North Americans to rearticulate who they are and what it means to be a Christian. Rhetorically and ideologically, refugees are depicted as leaders of the movement, yet in 1990 and 1991, almost ten years after the movement had started, the Central American presence in Tucson's Sanctuary community was markedly circumscribed.

Social workers and INS officials estimate that there are four to five thousand Central Americans in Tucson, yet fewer than a hundred seem to have retained sustained contact with the Sanctuary community. Within this group, twenty to thirty are "closely" connected to Southside and its services; this network is based primarily on two extended families (one Guatemalan, the other Salvadoran), with secondary families making up the other tributaries of the network. Only one Salvadoran family is officially a member of Southside Presbyterian Church, and it appears to have limited interaction with the larger Central American community in Tucson's Sanctuary network.[5] A separate, weekly Mass (conducted in Spanish and in a Protestant church) is attended by twenty-five Central Americans and three, sometimes five, North Americans. In nine months of fieldwork in Tucson, I saw Central Americans speak spontaneously at Southside's services only twice.

Formal kinds of interaction between Central Americans and North Americans are often related to educational and fund-raising events such as concerts in church halls and information seminars on Central America. Predominant images of Central Americans in these situations are of (1) women cooking traditional foods in church kitchens, (2) Central American musicians performing on stage, and (3) Central Americans giving "testimonials" through a translator to small groups of Anglos who want to learn more about the border.[6] Sanctuary's Anglo and Central American populations seem to interact most frequently in an informal way— for example, during the birthday parties usually held for Central Americans. During these gatherings (replete with gifts and a huge cake), nevertheless, Central American and North American divisions remain pronounced, all the more so in that most of the North Americans do not speak Spanish and most of the Central Americans do not speak English.

Other important areas of interaction between the two groups are in home sanctuaries, the homes of Anglo families who often shelter refugees for long periods of time. Home sanctuary has, in several cases, produced deeper and more sustained kinds of contact between Anglos and Central Americans—to the extent that some refugees, after they have left Tucson, will return to visit their Sanctuary family.

The limited involvement of Guatemalans and Salvadorans in Tucson's Sanctuary movement is partly defined by the transitory nature of the Central American population in the Southwest. This transience is framed both by the extremely limited kinds of government assistance available to refugees and by the dearth of jobs in the area. Central Americans who are successful in finding jobs in Tucson usually end up working in the restaurant/hotel and construction/landscaping industries. (Some women have successfully started their own housecleaning businesses.) The vast majority of Central Americans, however, merely pass through Tucson and move on to better job opportunities in the informal economies of Los Angeles, Chicago, Boston, and New York.

The Ideology of Asylum: "Refugees" and the Sanctuary Space

Although economic opportunities and linguistic, class, cultural, and political differences are important variables undergirding Anglo-Central American interaction in Tucson's Sanctuary community, the ideology of the Sanctuary space itself structures refugee social identity and participation in ways that are profoundly different from those of North Americans. As suggested in chapter 4, the asylee is often the least empowered of those occupying the Sanctuary space; historically, sanctuaries have been places of refuge for individuals who flee one cultural authority only to place themselves in the hands of another. In ancient Jewish cultures, the "murderer" fled the avenging community and became an exile under the protection of a merciful God. In medieval Europe, the "criminal" who sought asylum found himself or herself under the thumb of the intercessory church but (at least until the sixteenth century) beyond the tentacles of the king. Similarly, Central American refugees, once in Sanctuary, become dependent on the authority of the church as it attempts to assert its autonomy from the state.

Although North American Sanctuary participants are also betwixt and between competing cultural authorities, they have experienced Sanctuary as a moment of "defiance," as a moment of self-articulation based on asserting the voice of the conscience. For the anti-Vietnam War movement, for example, Sanctuary expressed resistance to the draft and the state's war-making authority. For the contemporary movement, Sanctuary counters the hegemony of the INS and defies the brutality of U.S. foreign policy toward Central American nations. In contrast, Central Americans often have experienced church asylum much in the same way that ancient Hebrew and medieval Christian subjects did—as Victor Turner's "declassified liminal subject" or as the relatively disempowered object of competing authorities. Unlike North American participants, Central American refugees cannot use their "liminality"—defined here as the "betwixt and between" of cultural authority—as a resource for articulating a new social identity. Although Central Americans both resist and take advantage of the "cultural repackaging" that goes on in Sanctuary, ultimately their social identity is the product of either a compromise between two powers or the triumph of one authority over the other. The uniquely North American ideology of Sanctuary as dissent (based on the constitutionally enshrined right of the conscience) does not extend to Central American refugees, who are really "objects" rather than empowered "subjects" of Sanctuary. Consequently, the framework of power that structures Central American entrance into Sanctuary is primarily one of dependency. This "ideological" dependency is reinforced by a "material" dependency as refugees become the recipients of the social services of food, clothing, and shelter that the Sanctuary movement provides.[7]

Tensions over "Participation"

Since the Sanctuary movement's inception, Central American and North American participants have faced pronounced cultural, economic, and political differences between the two communities. The year 1986, however, seems to have been decisive for Anglo-Central American relations in Tucson. Throughout 1985, as Central Americans began to organize themselves into political-action committees and scriptural reflection groups, tensions over political alliances and representative leadership had begun to surface within both the Central American and the North American communities. Some Central Americans began to question why they were not being represented in decision-making structures and to criticize what they perceived to be the inherent condescension of the Sanctuary movement toward refugees. Some Anglo participants, recalling this period, emphasized that the conflict was not just between North and Central Americans, but was a feature that characterized the Central American population as a whole:

> The Central Americans said that the North American community
> was . . . excluding them from decision making and full
> participation in different aspects of the Sanctuary movement.
> And there was frustration on the part of the North American
> community because there was a lot of conflict within the Central
> American community. Finally, the Salvadoran community was
> asked to attend the task force meetings and they were asked to
> [send] representatives. And there was this jockeying about who it
> was going to be. . . . I mean it was stupid to think it was going
> to work in the first place. They thought: "Well, we'll have a
> Salvadoran representative and a Guatemalan representative."
> There was all this jockeying for who's the voice of the
> Salvadoran community, who's the voice of the Guatemalan
> community. They are never going to agree on that. So there was
> all this wrangling. Also about this time, a number of families
> who were involved in Sanctuary became very resentful about the
> North American Sanctuary community. And the whole thing
> finally blew up when a Salvadoran man organized a . . . series of
> meetings for airing this issue . . . and they were very conflictive
> meetings and they went very badly.

Around the same time that these meetings were taking place, a thirteen-year-old Guatemalan boy was dropped off at Southside by what had become a splinter underground movement. The boy was interviewed by John Fife and a Guatemalan man who was working for the Sanctuary movement. These interviews revealed that the boy was not a political refugee but had run away from home because of conflicts with his parents. Fife and the Guatemalan social worker discussed several options with him; it was decided that he would go home to Guatemala on a bus. The Central American community was deeply distressed by this decision; one individual organized a petition among Guatemalans and Salvadorans condemning Southside Church and the North American Sanctuary community for having deported a Central American "back to death." At the same time, a Salvadoran man stood up in church and stated that he and many other Central Americans resented the paternalism of Sanctuary and that refugees felt "used" because they were not allowed to participate in decision making. Again, in the view of Anglo participants, Sanctuary subsequently opened meetings to Guatemalans and Salvadorans but, as a result of problems *internal* to the Central American population, little changed:

> So, after the petition came out . . . the task force said, "Let's have refugees on the task force." We had this public meeting; all these different viewpoints were presented by Central Americans. Some of the very politicized talked about participating in decision making. Others were saying that no, the problem was [that] we need security to participate in these meetings, it was hard to be involved when struggling to feed family and keep one's head above water. It was a big powwow. The task force said: "OK, we'll open the meetings up." Right after that, the whole thing sort of died. I guess a lot of Central Americans didn't trust members of the community, and added to this was the fact that as soon as this thing erupted, the Central American community just split apart. They became more afraid of one person among them having more power than another.

Several Central Americans remember this period differently. One man, for example, saw the event more as a "moment" when North Americans "shut the door" on an autonomous Latino voice:

> In 1986, to be exact, there was a movement of Central Americans against some people in Sanctuary (three Anglos and one Guatemalan man). And we wanted to write a letter . . . all of this was over a situation with a Guatemalan child. This child of thirteen years had no family, he had nothing here. They asked him, "What would you rather do? Do you want to live here with an Anglo family or go back to Guatemala?" And they would put him on either a plane or a bus. The child said he wanted to go to

Guatemala. And that's where the problem began. That's what Sanctuary told us happened. But the Central Americans said the opposite. They said Sanctuary had deported him. . . . Essentially, I feel that there is a need for Central Americans in the movement. Because we are familiar with the customs, and the language, and they will have more trust in telling a Latino things than a gringo. . . . Essentially, there needs to be Central Americans in the movement. One or two persons. . . . Right now there aren't really any [Central American] families in the movement.

As these excerpts suggest, Central Americans and North Americans frequently have very different viewpoints on Sanctuary, particularly in terms of the nature and extent of refugee participation. Because Sanctuary's ideology emphasizes inclusivity and underscores the unique role of the refugee in the movement, the paucity of Central Americans involved in the movement is a difficult topic for many North American Sanctuary workers. Some Anglo Sanctuary workers acknowledge that "things are not great" with the Central American population, and that their objective of moving from a relationship of "hospitality" to "partnership with" Central Americans has yet to be achieved. They suggest that class differences between Anglos and Latinos, as well as internal political problems among Central Americans, account for this separation, and offer different reasons for why so few Central Americans are involved (again, many of these "reasons" made the problematic of participation inherent to the Central American community):

The first wave of refugees were politically active. They were union leaders and catechists. Now the refugees are more campesinos, and just are not likely to become activists. Also, a lot of those leaders have moved on to other cities.

One family talks to a lot of groups. But they are not really involved in any meaningful way in the decision-making bodies. I think we talked to one woman about becoming involved. But she felt that she couldn't waste time needed for earning a living. In the end, though, I think most of the refugees didn't have the resources and the freedom to be involved.

Our relationship is not great. I'm very critical. There's a lot we're fighting against. It's just a fact that it's very difficult to treat someone as an equal when they can't get a job better than gardening, even though they have a very good education. It's just very hard to find a way to treat that person as your equal. . . . It's hard to feel connected to people who come through the church and they're gone in two days or even three months. . . .

*In Tucson, there just isn't a whole lot of organizing work done
by Central Americans and Anglos together. The reality is that the
gringos organize. And in other communities, not in Tucson, the
Central Americans organize. In Tucson, I think the community is
too transient. . . . I think it's been very hard for the two groups
to work together. Obviously, it is paternalistic. Refugees come to
the church, we get them food, we try and find them work.
They're helpless. In any sense of the word, they are helpless. . . .
It's not what I like. . . . I think that it is impossible, and I'll say
it, that it's going to be impossible to escape our racism and
classism in dealing with Central Americans. . . . We can always
walk away . . . that makes us inherently different [from them].*

Central Americans also acknowledge the divide that separates Anglos
and Latinos in the movement, but are reluctant to discuss the topic (particularly with an Anglo). Most Guatemalans and Salvadorans I spoke
with expressed gratitude for North American assistance; many felt strong
bonds of affection for individual Anglos. They felt "guilty" for having
criticisms and seemed silenced into an acquiescent thankfulness by their
experiences of Anglo Sanctuary hospitality. Yet Central American im-
pressions of Tucson's Sanctuary movement point to the ways in which
differences of language, class, religion, culture, and politics simmer beneath the inclusive ideology of Sanctuary, creating a structure of exclusion that Central Americans experience in unique ways. In the following
section, I analyze the comments of fifteen Central Americans who permitted me to interview them about their experiences in the Sanctuary
movement. Of this group, only a few are still involved in Sanctuary: nine
are women between the ages of 26 and 60, and six are men between the
ages of 25 and 65; eight are Salvadoran, and seven are Guatemalan. With
one or two exceptions, these Central Americans are from moderate to
large urban centers, and all are Ladino. Most became involved in Sanctuary in the mid-1980s through Southside Church, where they resided after entering the United States by themselves or after being transported
into the country by members of the underground. Because many of these
Central Americans were reluctant to discuss their feelings regarding Sanctuary and did so only with assurances that I would not reveal their identity, I do not identify any by age or nationality. Female subjects are indicated by a / and males by ?.

Language and Cultural Identity

In order to keep the power of the base, you need free access to open lines of com-

*munication that are constantly ongoing. And anybody should be able to access
these lines of communication.*

—Anglo Sanctuary worker

In Tucson's Sanctuary movement, perhaps the most substantial variable
isolating Central Americans and North Americans from one another is
language. Throughout my fieldwork I recorded low levels of Spanish-
English bilingualism within both populations. The majority of Central
Americans, even if they understand quite a bit of English, are able to generate only a few phrases. Among Anglo Sanctuary workers the incidence
of bilingualism is higher; most of the mission volunteers, for example, are
fluent in Spanish, and contact between the Central American and Anglo
groups is filtered through a dozen or so Spanish-speaking Anglos, most of
whom occupy important positions in Sanctuary's decision-making structures. Both non-Spanish-speaking Anglos and non-English-speaking Central Americans use this bilingual group as a convenient go-between,
thereby colluding in a pattern that forces neither side to learn the other's
language.

The primary places in which Sanctuary members congregate—their religious services and cell groups—are, as might be expected, English contexts. Although the Sanctuary movement, in its first six years of operation, endeavored to make some of its meetings and worship services
bilingual contexts, the effort generally failed. Because the loci of Sanctuary activities have remained English, the majority of Central Americans
have little or no access to Sanctuary's dominant form of discourse and are
highly dependent (even among those who have lived in Tucson for six or
more years) on interpreters to express their viewpoints to the larger Anglo community.

Perhaps the most problematic *linguistic* arena within Tucson's Sanctuary movement is its focal point: Southside Presbyterian Church. The
church is both the principal locus of the Anglo Sanctuary cadre and the
focus of Central American activities by virtue of being the physical place
where Central Americans officially become "refugees." The two claims
on the church—one Anglo, the other Central American—have divided
Southside into two Sanctuary spaces, occupied separately by both groups
over the course of a week. From Monday to Saturday, Southside is pretty
much Central American space: the central and largest church room, as
well as its rear quarters, is utilized by Central Americans as a living space;
they sleep, eat, study English, arrange for transportation or meetings with
lawyers and immigration officials, and hang out.[8] These spaces are "off-
limits" (without permission) to visitors during the week, and (following
an unspoken rule) volunteers usually report to the TEC "office," a tiny

and cramped room (roughly 12′ × 11′) staffed by two overworked, under-paid social workers (one of whom is bilingual). From Monday to Friday, the "zone of interface" between non-English-speaking Central Americans and non-Spanish-speaking Anglos is primarily this office, which, already problematic for the two workers by virtue of its small size, is not inviting to visitors. In addition, conversations occurring between Anglos and Central Americans are mostly filtered through the bilingual Sanctuary worker, who is often doing sundry other things at the same time.[9]

On Sunday, Southside becomes an Anglo space: the chairs are pulled out of storage and arranged in the sanctuary, the church is filled with English-speakers, and the service is conducted in English.[10] Central Americans in Sanctuary often retreat to the back rooms or sit on the outside steps during the Sunday service. Many of the handful who remain for the service cluster in the upper left-hand corner of the church, near a door that leads to the refugees' communal kitchen—an area that remains off-limits to Anglos even on Sundays. The presence of these Central Americans in the church's corner visually emphasizes their isolation from the Anglo community. Many of Southside's English-speaking community feel awkward about interacting with Central Americans:

> At church I see a lot of refugees who seem shiftless, just restless. And I never know what to say. I sort of avoid them because I don't know what to say. And I only know how to say a couple of things. And I don't want to spend time with them without being able to talk because I feel uncomfortable about being with someone and not being able to talk.

Central Americans, of course, experience this same alienation.

The kinds of jobs that Central Americans are able to find in Tucson—mostly in the service sector, where there is limited contact with English-speakers—are one of the prime reasons why English is not quickly learned by Central American adults. The problem is particularly acute for Central American women, who most often get work as maids in hotels or as domestic workers who move from house to house. These women learn a limited and specialized English vocabulary related to their work, but for most of their day they interact with other Spanish-speakers. Central American men, who are more likely to get jobs in restaurants or factories, seem able to learn more English because of their more concentrated interaction with Anglos. (Most of the Central Americans I interviewed felt that they had neither the time nor the financial resources to take English classes. Television viewing, many claimed, has enabled them to understand English, but they do not often get the chance to speak it.)

For some of those in Tucson's Central American Sanctuary community, learning English is a "culturally loaded" process—that is, it is linked
to "gaining" linguistic facility (and possibly a better job), but at the "ex-
pense" of losing one's cultural identity. Many Central Americans have
conflicting attitudes toward North Americans, and a deep distrust of
"gringos" that, although mitigated by their experience of Sanctuary, remains pronounced.[11] Moreover, learning English is perceived by some
Central Americans as a sellout to American culture; those who do learn
English can find themselves harshly criticized by fellow Guatemalans or
Salvadorans. In one case, a Guatemalan teenager recounted his troubles
at his high school, where a gang of Guatemalan youths was continually
trying to beat him up, simply because he was learning English, and therefore becoming, in their eyes, "Americanized."[12]

Sanctuary and Religious Culture

In addition to being an "English space," Tucson's Sanctuary movement is
a uniquely "religious space." The majority of the Central Americans who
have passed through Tucson are Catholic, yet they have found sanctuary
in a Protestant church. For some Central Americans, the fact that Southside is Presbyterian was perplexing; for others it presented no problem. In
my sample, however, the absence of religious statues or devotional objects in Southside's austere interior was troubling for Catholic Central
Americans, especially those whose religiosity is tied to the saints.[13]

Discomfort over the lack of saints in Sanctuary churches is not just an
issue of familiar surroundings for many Central Americans; saints are
an important source of power in Latin American Catholicism. In both
Ladino and Indígena cultures, God's wishes are frequently channeled
through a series of intercessory figures (saints) who are known to be resident in heaven and capable of performing miracles. The absence of saints
(as well as of a statue of Christ) in Southside can make the church seem
stark and barren, or simply unchurchlike, to the Latin American Catholic, whose own church is usually filled with saints, holy pictures, and a
statue of a prone Christ bleeding from the wounds of the Crucifixion.
These saints are central to Latin American Catholic spirituality, partly because God is conceptualized as a transcendent being whose exact contours are a mystery, and hence God can be approached only through an
intercessor (i.e., the saints):

/ *When my family had problems in Guatemala, when my*
husband was kidnapped, I felt that God was angry at me. I
prayed each moment, I went to many masses, I prayed to the

*saints. . . . I was brought up to believe that God was a pure
spirit, a perfect spirit. And I had no idea about what he looked
like—whether like the priest or my father. And we would see him
on Judgment Day, but we could not see him until then. . . . In
Guatemala, there are many saints in the church. It is very
traditional. And the church [usually] has been there for a long
time. [In the church] there are great windows and a ceiling.
Everything. And there are stages of the life of Jesus when he
suffered on the cross. And also there is Saint Paul, Saint John,
the Virgin. And we go to, for example, the Virgin, the Virgin of
desperate causes. And many times we go up to this Virgin and
pray to her. My mother gave me this Virgin and I have it here
with me. It is our custom that when you have a grave problem—
if, for example, your husband is kidnapped—you go to her and
pray. . . . Saint Anthony is for protecting animals so they don't
get lost. Each saint has its own history. . . . I prefer my church in
Guatemala. But I can continue my customs here. I go to the
church here but there are no saints. But I can go to other places
where there are saints and I keep some in my house. There are
also lots of Catholic festivals. It is a little strange here because
they do not celebrate them. . . . Always, in Guatemala, when you
pass in front of a Catholic church you cross yourself out of
respect. Or if there is a funeral procession. Here they do not
do that.*

Beyond the intercessory role that saints play in human contact with an
unknown God, there are also ways in which individuals can relate to God
in a personal way and attempt to shape the course of their own salvation
(Gudeman 1988: 30).[14] Although salvation, for Catholics, is a transcendent process, encompassing all those baptized in the church, individuals
still wish to experience salvation in a personal way: as, for example, in
the curing of a sick relative, the landing of a job, or the safe passage of a
family member into the United States. The saints, who arrange these
things for individuals, are a source of self-empowerment for Central
American Catholics, a way in which they attempt to exert control over
their lives. Consequently, their absence in Southside is sometimes felt
acutely by those have already been severely displaced from their culture.

The non-Catholic basis of Tucson's Sanctuary is also problematic for
some Central Americans in light of their experience with Protestantism
(usually in the form of evangelical churches) in their own countries.[15] For
some, attending a Protestant church is akin to converting:

*/ One refugee man, who spent time working in the church,
changed his religion to Presbyterian. For some of us, we feel that*

to attend the services at Southside would be like changing our religion. For example, if they invite me, I'll go to Southside. And I don't understand much of the sermon, because of the language. Because if I go to the service, I won't be able to understand the pastor. I won't be able to take anything with me, nothing. And so we think that if we go to this religion, it is like losing our own, like being converted. Religion is a gift, it is my origin. I am not going to change.

Others have experienced Protestantism as a highly divisive force within their own countries and as a potentially dangerous affiliation.[16] In Guatemala, for example, particularly during the regime of General José Efraín Ríos Montt (1982-83), Protestantism became associated with state policies and a legitimization of violence and repression.[17] In contrast, Catholicism became associated with subversion and communism.[18] Several of the Central Americans I interviewed acknowledged (and even admired) the differences between the Protestant churches in Central America and those in the United States, but many retained a wariness of Protestant culture:

? I want to tell you something. The members of the churches here, they are more open when they come together. It doesn't matter what church it is. . . . It's the same God, right? The people here are not fanatics. On the other hand, in my country, there is hatred between the different churches. Especially the evangelical [churches]. There is hatred toward the Catholics. There is fanaticism.

? I think that the church here is more mature, more professional. Because here there is no dispute. I doubt that there is a dispute, or a struggle. For the Anglos there is not the dispute and struggle that has come to Salvador. A struggle, for example . . . between the Protestants and Catholics that has come to the comunidades of Salvador. By Protestant, I mean evangelicals. The Protestant churches have waged war against the Catholic church. . . . They are saying that the Catholic church . . . is demonic. That is what is happening there. They are very different churches. [The attacking] is not so much on the part of the Catholics, but the Protestants. . . . And here I have not seen that. There is more harmony here.

Cultural and Political Divisions

Divisions *within* the Central American community are among the most tenacious cultural differences that play into the broader cultural differences separating Anglos and Latinos in Sanctuary. In my interview

pool, only one Central American suggested that cultural differences between Guatemalans and Salvadorans are minimized once a person enters
the United States. The majority expressed a distrust of and/or disinterest
in members of a Central American country different from their own:

? *Me, I don't have a lot to do with the Guatemalans. Because,
in the first place, our paths don't cross. We talk with each other
[at] the church but practically we are very different. We are from
different countries. We are all Central Americans, but are
different. We are brought up differently. And because of this, we
don't really have relations.*

This distrust was often articulated in terms of perceived favoritism on the
part of Anglo Sanctuary workers:

? *We will never be against Sanctuary because we respect them
and what they are doing. We have a lot of respect for Sanctuary
workers but have not always been in agreement with their
actions. . . . In some cases, we feel that Salvadorans, specifically,
have been treated poorly. They [the Anglos] have said
Salvadorans can't stay in Sanctuary . . . that they must go. And I
have heard in two cases that there is preference for Guatemalans.
I see how they treat the Guatemalans. [They say] "Yes you can
stay . . . whatever you like." And they find them places to stay.
But they don't treat Salvadorans equally. . . . And it is not only
me who says this; others say the same thing.*

/ *There are differences toward nationalities. . . . I know of
cases . . . where Guatemalans have not been permitted to stay
more than one night, and the next night [at Southside Church]
they kick them out. On the other hand, people [Salvadorans] can
stay two to three months or more. This we have seen. We have
proof. We have not wanted to say anything because they won't
agree with us.*

For the most part, and with the exception of those Central Americans
who live in Southside Church, the Guatemalan and Salvadoran communities tied to the Sanctuary movement function independently from one
another; they do not invite each other to their birthday parties (although
they invite the same group of Anglos) and, during the weekly refugee
Mass, they usually sit on opposite sides of the church in a formal liturgical setting that, spatially, does not evoke unified "community."

As we have noted, political cleavages within both Salvadoran and
Guatemalan groups have fractured the Central American community.
These political divisions—adding to the daily strain of interacting with
people one does not know or, possibly, does not trust—occur not only

along the fault lines of conservative versus revolutionary political parties, but also within highly fragmented, and often fratricidal, leftist sectors.[19] Some Central Americans argue that an all-consuming fear of deportation, as well as differing educational levels, divide and weaken the Central American population in Tucson. Others note how Central Americans quickly become absorbed into U.S. culture and lose a sense of themselves as a distinct group:

> ? It is an interesting thing that we [Central Americans] are disunited. I have observed in the majority of Central Americans who come to this country, maybe 90 percent are people who haven't made it to the third or fourth grade. And they are rural workers. They have spent most of their lives working and they couldn't study. And so when these people come to this country, they come with an idea that they will find work, to make money, so they can send it to their family [back home]. And they come thinking this. On the other hand, the other 10 percent like organizations. They like meetings, gatherings . . . but they stay here for a couple of weeks and go to other states. And they don't stay here. But the few of us here are people who have distinct ideas. . . . Some think of sports only. Others think of having a club where there are games and where they can dance. And because of this we can't come together. . . . The first thing is unity, and later we can see the differences. United we can be one voice to say: "We are Central Americans and this is our culture."

> ? You have all kinds of people here, like ex-police, ex-soldiers, people who were in the revolutionary movement and unions. So you have all that mixture of people. And I think that it is hard to have a community. For instance, when we talk about communities in Guatemala, we talk about GAM, the mutual support group.[20] There is a goal and a purpose. But when we talk about a community here, it is hard [because] people come from different backgrounds. Sometimes when people come here, and they don't know what was going on, they get caught up in the culture here. They see the media and the VCRs and they want those things. Sometimes a Latino, for example, doesn't even know he has an identity as a Latino. So he comes to this country and is easily absorbed by the system because he doesn't have a sense of who he is and what the situation is in his homeland. And therefore [you] come here and the system really absorbs you.

As these excerpts intimate, the Sanctuary space itself is not "safe" for Central American political organization since virtually anyone—from union organizers to ex-members of the military—is offered lodging at

Southside Church, as long as she or he does not drink or use drugs. Consequently, those staying in Sanctuary cannot freely discuss their histories without fear of reprisals (particularly against their families in Central America):

> ? *Staying in Southside was really weird. Because there were*
> *people at that time who had a clear idea about what was going*
> *on in El Salvador and Guatemala. Also there were Central*
> *Americans who didn't have any idea of what was going on. And*
> *I think the feeling of that distrusting was right there. A person*
> *might be a national guard, or might be the police, or an*
> *ex-soldier, or an ex-guerrilla. So I think it was hard to trust each*
> *other. We communicated for basic things, but there was no sense*
> *of community. We did help each other as much as we could, but*
> *there wasn't really a feeling of community. The strategies of the*
> *governments in Central America has been to divide people, so*
> *there was already something there [in Sanctuary] that we had*
> *been going through. Especially in Guatemala with the civil-*
> *defense patrols and the model villages.*

Adding to this aura of distrust has been the presence of Central American spies who, in at least three cases, posing as refugees, went through the church in an effort to collect information on fugitives for the Salvadoran and Guatemalan governments.

Sanctuary as a Structure of Power

As we saw in chapter 6, North American Sanctuary ideology emphasizes an "inclusive community" based on a shared faith commitment and political orientation. Central Americans, however, often experience Sanctuary as a highly centralized, exclusive organization, dominated by a small, unchanging group of Anglo "officials" who make all the decisions regarding the distribution of social services.[21] Many Central Americans in my interview pool were extremely reluctant to comment on how goods and services are distributed through Sanctuary because, as the recipients of "free" assistance, they feel "guilty" about being critical. Yet many resented the "controls" placed on them regarding requests for aid, in particular having to go through an Anglo to obtain a service. Many perceived this as a subtle form of social control and felt frustrated that there were no independent or alternative channels of access to medical, legal, educational, domicile, or job-related services:

> / *It's a great movement . . . but even in this great movement*
> *there are rotten apples that are destructive. There are many great*

people in it. And may God bless them. They are good people. But there are those who are not aware that they are causing harm. They have broken what they say: "This is for the oppressed of Central America." And this is a great lie . . . because there are people they won't help, that they don't want. And people suffer here . . . because there [in the movement] there are a few people who direct, who have control of the people when they arrive, where they sleep, everything. . . . This is like the way people treat animals.

? In the beginning, there were people that I trusted. We dealt with one Anglo woman who helped us with the social services. Then an Anglo man came along and we liked him so we talked to him. But the first woman didn't like that. And we were punished and afterwards we were not trusted.

/ And if there is a conflict, who in the movement is going to believe us? At times we have differences, but we don't have the option of saying anything.

This perception of centralized command in the movement is accompanied by an awareness of what many Central Americans refer to as "paternalism" among Anglo Sanctuary workers. One Central American noted how important children are for Anglo Sanctuary workers (claiming that refugees with children get greater attention) and implied that in the Anglo mind, a child and a refugee are one and the same thing. Sanctuary literature, for example, frequently features pictures of refugees holding young children, and Sanctuary graphics often include depictions of children or portrayals of the Guatemalan *indígenas* (who are short in stature). In this respect, the paternalism of Sanctuary is also very much a maternalism that has, as Central Americans themselves note, a double-edged quality, since maternalism involves aspects of both self-sacrifice and control.[22] Others see the paternalism/maternalism of Sanctuary as initially necessary but, if it persists, as destructive for the Central American community:

? The paternalistic approach that we see among some of the Sanctuary people . . . helps us with immediate material needs but it makes us dependent on one person. That's one of the bad things. And it also creates division. Because some families think, "Oh, I can't go with this person because she prefers that other person. I call and ask for this person and she doesn't pay any attention to me. On the other hand, I saw her giving all these things to this family and not to me." That increases the sense of division.

This sense of paternalism is often recognized by Central Americans as part of a larger experience of racism and classism in the United States:

> ? *The Anglos sincerely believe that they are superior, a superior race to us, that they know everything, know everybody, and they are able to do everything. And we are like second-class citizens . . . it's a type of racism. We say that the Anglos want to make more money but without doing the hard work. Because they want to make money easily. There is the situation of her [my wife's] boss. Her boss is Anglo and she makes more than we do. And her work is easier. And in my case, the three managers at my work are Anglos. There is a Latino who they said they would train to be a manager but now they are training another manager, an Anglo, and this guy [the Latino] will always have to wait. Where I work, all the good jobs go to the Anglos.*

> ? *I say that the North Americans, the majority of North Americans, do not have frequent contact with other classes. I don't know if it is an educational thing or cultural but there are those who see us as less. There is racism. . . . And there are those who see us as bad. And there are those who are very friendly, very good. . . . But there are some who see us as* mojados, *migrants. That we are lazy. We feel inferior. There is also a lot of indifference because they have no business with us.*

Because so many Central Americans in the Sanctuary community interact with the Anglo community as service employees (as gardeners, house-cleaners, custodians on church properties, caterers, etc.), these differences of class are reinforced and heightened, throwing into relief the vast economic differences that separate the two communities.[23]

Confined to the service sector of the work force, where they often make less than the minimum wage, Central Americans lack the two principal resources (premised on class affiliation) for involvement in the Sanctuary movement: free time and a readily available vehicle. Work schedules are often long and erratic and include the weekends. Moreover, many Central Americans are dependent on an inconvenient public bus system or bicycles for transportation—both of which make attending meetings or religious services difficult. Given the limitations on their mobility, Central Americans are more dependent on household and neighborhood models of support, something that Tucson's Sanctuary churches have moved away from.

As we have seen, North Americans view Sanctuary largely as an experience of "coming together," a moment of convergence and redefinition. In the movement's discourse, Sanctuary has been likened to a "coming home," finding a cultural space that resonates with one's moral values and goals. As my interviews among Guatemalans and Salvadorans indicate, however, Tucson's Sanctuary has not been a moment of "convergence" for some of the refugees involved. Although church asylum can be a kind of haven for Central Americans, it is a temporary, not permanent, respite from the broader structures of power and culture that divide Anglos from Latinos, the lighter skinned from the darker skinned, the First World from the Third World. Sanctuary attempts to confront the forces of inequality that permeate U.S.-Central American relations, but it is pervaded by those very same "structuring" forces. Consequently, even though Sanctuary addresses important human rights issues, it is a limited forum of "empowerment" for Central Americans, primarily because of their linguistic, cultural, economic, and political exclusion from its structure of power—in short, their alienation from its "articulating base."[24]

Chapter 8

Anatomy of an "Underground" Church

There is a new urgency in the life and ministry of the Church; the person in the next pew is no longer a stranger but now a potential co-felon.
                                        —Ignatius Bau, *This Ground is Holy* (1985)

As I have already suggested, the U.S. Sanctuary movement is much more than a social movement focused on a particular "cause." It represents a broader attempt to rearticulate the meaning of "church community" and the role of "faith" in American society. For many Christians, the contours of this new church have involved going "underground," that is, committing civil disobedience and civil initiative, risking prosecution and imprisonment, developing extralegal ways of furthering a specific agenda—all in the name of faith.

By now the reader is familiar with some of the loci within the Sanctuary movement where this resistance has been articulated: Southside Church, the Vigil, and the Desert Pilgrims' worshiping group. One of the most compelling and controversial loci, however, is the movement's "underground."[1]

Tucson's network of safe houses and refugee transporters is not the first such "underground railroad" in the United States, nor the first one to come to Tucson. In the late 1860s, undocumented Chinese laborers established a clandestine underground from Mexico to Arizona in their search for work, and used the many canyons of the Sonoran Desert as hideouts and layover locations. Prior to and during the American Civil War, slaves, freemen, and abolitionists, risking imprisonment under the Fugitive Law Compromise (1850), created underground routes to "freedom" in the north. Tucson's Sanctuary underground, like that of the Civil War, was also established in response to fugitives, but unlike the abolitionist movement, it developed a more explicitly religious character.

Tucson is only one of several hundred underground sites in the United States and is one of three principal locations along the U.S-Mexico border where a Sanctuary underground for Central American fugitives flourished.[2] Underground activities encompass diverse individuals and strategies, but participants tend to think of their Sanctuary work as a "ministry." Although explicit religious discourse and imagery are strikingly absent in the work of Tucson's underground, participants see their activities as the expression of "a faithful community." This chapter explores Tucson's underground as part of the larger Sanctuary church. I attempt to demonstrate that planning runs, transporting undocumented Central Americans, and evading the Border Patrol are as much expressions of "faith" as singing hymns on Sunday, listening to sermons, and attending Bible study classes. These underground activities make a statement about the place of a "conscientious" person in society, primarily because they are viewed as acts of "solidarity with the oppressed" and thus as a way in which privileged, largely white North Americans can become part of a "liberation" church.

The Mexican-American Border

Tucson's underground operates close to the U.S.-Mexico border, a divide that stretches for 1,951 miles between San Diego, California, and Brownsville, Texas. For 1,240 of those miles, the border is the Rio Grande, a river that is only waist deep at many of its bends, thanks to silt bars. At other places, the border becomes a twelve-foot, steel-reinforced fence surveilled by cameras atop poles and patrolled by armed guards. Sometimes, particularly as it winds through the desert, the border dwindles into a few strands of rusty barbed wire, clandestinely monitored in some spots by underground sensors and hidden cameras.

The product of a war (1846-48) that resulted in Mexico's loss of almost half its northern regions, the border has often been a source of tension between the United States and Mexico. Many of the frontier's current tensions are linked to the effects of accelerated population growth and development, both of which have been exacerbated by U.S. businesses in search of cheap labor. In response to dwindling influence in electronics, car manufacturing, and textiles in particular, U.S. businesses began in the 1970s to move out of the union-dominated regions in the Midwest and Northeast and headed south because of cheaper labor. Both Arizona and the Mexican government promised a "business friendly environment" through lower wages, tax concessions, and less regulation of business (Martínez 1988: 128). In Mexico, the new business developments—chiefly large assembly plants or *maquiladoras* (which pay workers around four dollars per day)—have drawn a substantial number of laborers from the south. The factories have produced profits for Ford, Chrysler, General Motors, Zenith, RCA, and other multinationals: as of 1985, these companies, on average, saved $14,520 for each Mexican hired in place of an American employee (ibid.); they have also engendered overpopulation, poverty, and extremely high pollution levels along the border.[3]

Increased traffic in drugs and undocumented labor has made the Mexican-American border a highly volatile region. Border towns have historically been points of entry for thousands of legal Mexican workers who cross daily or seasonally to work in the United States.[4] These towns have also been points of entry for thousands of undocumented Mexicans who usually end up as field hands for U.S. ranchers or growers. Some illegal migrants make their way to Los Angeles, Miami, Houston, New York, or Boston, where they often get work in restaurants, hotels, or construction. Since the 1980s, the stream of undocumented Mexicans has been swelled by thousands of Central Americans fleeing political violence and poverty in El Salvador, Guatemala, Honduras, and Nicaragua.

Along with the Rio Grande, Colorado, and Tijuana rivers, unfriendly stretches of desert, and the international fence, the U.S. Border Patrol forms a blockade against the flow of what the government regards as "undesirable aliens." Organized in 1924, the Border Patrol is the armed, uniformed branch of the Immigration and Naturalization Service (INS), whose job is to "intercept and apprehend" undocumented aliens and those who help them enter.[5] These guards patrol the border on foot, on horseback, in Bronco jeeps, or from airplanes, and have the authority to stop vehicles and pedestrians and request proof of citizenship without a warrant. They can also raid businesses they suspect of hiring illegal aliens. In 1986, the U.S. Congress expanded the Border Patrol's mandate to include drug interdiction. This relatively recent focus on "fighting drugs" has created an even closer alliance among the Border Patrol, the Drug Enforcement Agency (DEA), the U.S. Customs Service, the FBI, the Federal Aviation Administration, the Bureau of Alcohol, Tobacco and Firearms, the National Parks Service, and city, county, and state police (Zanger 1990: 5). Beginning in 1988, the Reagan-Bush administration implemented "Operation Hold the Line," a program designed to quell the wave of undocumented aliens by boosting the U.S. Border Patrol presence, expediting asylum application proceedings, and installing steel plates along the fourteen-mile stretch of fence along the Tijuana-San Diego border.[6]

Border Patrol officers now use infrared goggles and photographic equipment for night vision, air-traffic radar equipment, surveillance planes, photo reconnaissance jets, attack helicopters, and aerostat-radar-surveillance balloons, as well as seismic and magnetic sensors, which are buried along the U.S. side of the fence.[7] Border Patrol officers also carry automatic weapons and recently some have been trained by U.S. Marines in military surveillance and intelligence-gathering techniques. Predictably, this "militarization" of the border has led to greater violence and abuse of undocumented migrants. Attempts to traverse the international line can be extremely dangerous and, increasingly, fatal.[8]

Yet despite the Border Patrol's high-tech equipment, the agency is strangely understaffed. Of approximately four thousand agents in the United States, three thousand are stationed along the U.S.-Mexico border. In the Tucson sector, there are 281 miles of border to monitor and roughly 280 patrol officers who work ten-hour shifts. As one Border Patrol agent related, given sick leave and vacations, it is not uncommon to have one agent per twelve miles of border. In fiscal year 1990, the Tucson sector seized 95,266.70 pounds of marijuana (valued at $66.4 million), 5,505.52 pounds of cocaine (valued at $176.1 million), and 55,000 illegal aliens. Of these "aliens," 90 percent were Mexican; the remaining 10 percent were referred to as OTMs ("Other than Mexican").

Despite improved monitoring devices and techniques at the Mexican-American border, arrests of illegal aliens are expected to reach peak levels during the 1990s. Border Patrol officials in Tucson admit that for every "alien" they apprehend, around twenty make it into the United States.

Illegal Entry

It is estimated that half of all illegal entries into the United States occur at Tijuana–San Ysidro, California. Local "border" industries there have flourished in response to demands to cross the international boundary: "entrepreneurs" dig holes underneath the fence and, for a dollar, one can pass through. Plastic bags with rubber bands are sold to those who wish to wade through the sewage-strewn Tijuana River—again for only a dollar (Langewiesche 1992: 60-61). In the foothills near Tijuana, crowds gather on the Mexican side of the fence waiting for twilight, when they will charge the border in waves. These crowds swarm by the Border Patrol, who position their cars in rows on the U.S. side and try to intercept as many as possible. While prospective undocumented aliens wait for nightfall, vendors sell them drinks and food, and coyotes hawk a good place in line. A few miles away from this daily ritual is another crowd, congregating on one side of Interstate 5. Border crossers hide in the brush and when darkness begins to fall, they attempt to run across the highway—in some places across sixteen lanes of traffic. Drivers in the area average seventy miles per hour on the interstate; since 1987 150 people have been killed by oncoming traffic, prompting the erection of signs warning motorists of these crossings (Mydans 1991).[9]

El Paso and Ciudad Juárez—two border cities separated by the Río Grande—constitute another common point of entry for undocumented aliens. In 1978 (and again in 1988) the United States implemented what it referred to as the "Tortilla Curtain" (steel reinforcement of the international fence as well as the construction of observation towers on the U.S. side of the river). Yet a good pair of wire clippers can dismantle the plates, and on any given day, often in broad daylight, one can see people pay two dollars to a boatman to pull them across the Río Grande in a rubber dinghy or inner tube. Once on the other side, people scramble onto the concrete platforms jutting out beyond the international fence, and from these platforms watch for Border Patrol cars. If none are in sight, they either scramble through holes in the fence and make a dash for a grocery store, a fast-food outlet, or one of the many taxis lurking near the border. The whole process can take less than ten minutes. If Mexicans are caught and deported, it only costs them another two dollars to try again.

Like other ports of entry, Nogales, Arizona, is a town where Mexicans frequently cross legally into the United States (i.e., via Customs). Some have official border-crossing cards, whereas others have to persuade the Customs official that they are only going shopping or to Mass. Illegal crossings, however, are typically done through a hole in the international fence. Nogales's border fence winds down from the hills that encircle the city, and in the center of town (where its height increases), the fence is wedged between two concrete walls. Between the wall and the fence, on the Mexican side, is a kind of gully, filled with garbage and brush. In the early morning and at night, both the darkness and the brush act as effective screens for prospective crossers, who just have to find a hole in the fence, scrunch themselves up into a ball, and slip through undetected by the Border Patrol. Occasionally young boys scale the twelve-to-fifteen-foot fence (in as little as twenty seconds) and sprint toward one of the stores on the other side. Prospective crossers can also traverse the border by climbing up one of Nogales's brush-covered hills and scrambling through the holes that appear, are repaired, and reappear with the regularity of the rising sun.

It is in Nogales, amid the briskly moving traffic of tourists, border shoppers, and undocumented migrants, that Tucson's Sanctuary underground began its operations.

The Tucson Underground: A Brief History

I really felt propelled to get involved [in Sanctuary]. If this were a different time and place, I mean if it were the 1940s in Germany, I'd sure want someone like myself to be helping my children. I didn't stop to think about it. It wasn't like I had a choice. I had no choice. It was just absolutely crystal clear that it was something that I had to do.

—Sanctuary worker

I was impressed by the conflict between Sanctuary and the government. And that seemed sort of neat to me. It seemed very naughty but in a noble sense. Like I can do something naughty but I can be a saint for doing it. . . . I think that there is a tiny bit of that there.

—Sanctuary worker

Tucson's Sanctuary underground has its provenance in an unlikely source of political subversion: a goat-milking cooperative. Convinced that certain breeds of goats, rather than cattle, were better suited to the Sonoran region, a group mostly of Quakers tended and milked one another's goats, and attempted to develop a harmonious, nonexploitative relationship with the desert ecology—in contrast to the impact of Tucson's air conditioners, swimming pools, and golf courses. The group had also spent several years working with seminomadic goatherds in Baja California, and not only had exchanged information on herding, feeding, and medical practices but also had attempted to breed a hardy strain of goat suited to the desert. One of the people in this group was Jim Corbett, a self-described "cowboy, horse-trader, Park Ranger, and teacher of wildland symbiotics," whose Quaker friend, Jim Dudley, had introduced him to the world of Central American refugees via a Salvadoran hitchhiker (see chapter 2). Of this goat-milking group, Corbett recalls:

> During the first stages of sanctuary network formation, the group that was most involved with helping refugees cross through the Arizona-Sonoran borderlands to Tucson was a goat-milking cooperative. We called ourselves "*Los Cabreros Andantes*," which could be translated as "the goatherders errant." We'd just completed a three-year exchange with semi-nomadic goat ranchers in the South Baja Sierras.
>
> The *Cabreros Andantes* weren't a religious organization, but we were "church" in a societal sense. Few groups could have been better prepared, bonded together, and predisposed than the *Cabreros Andantes* to help get refugees through. Errantry shifted from goat herding to refugee aid. (Corbett 1991: 136-37)

Eventually, Corbett and his Quaker cohorts—renaming themselves trsg in the fall of 1981—became heavily involved in assisting Central Americans cross the international fence: they developed a network of crossing points along the U.S.-Mexico border and established strategies for avoiding the Border Patrol, as well as a procedure for determining which Central Americans were "legitimate" refugees. As his participation intensified, Corbett began to travel throughout Mexico, putting in place a network of churches that became an underground refugee route to the United States:

> From late 1981 to July 1984, I traveled throughout Mexico to help with church networking, to counsel refugees, and to accompany those who most urgently needed help. I also spread information about routes and roadblocks, methods and risks, which was more important than accompaniment. If refugees know how to avoid roadblocks and slip through borders, hundreds can get through for each of them who can be personally guided to safety. There's no way to maintain a closed, secure system while helping refugees solely on the basis of need, so I simply shared what I knew about the ways to get through, assuming I'd have to keep updating as immigration officials instituted countermeasures. Surprisingly, the controls and countermeasures remain essentially the same in 1990 as they were during the 1980s. Even the holes in the border fence remain much the same. (Ibid.: 142)

In 1982, the Quaker underground joined forces with the Tucson Ecumenical Council (TEC) task force on Central America. The task force formed its own refugee relay group, directed by Phillip Willis-Conger, a Methodist who had traveled in Central America, spoke Spanish, and had some differences with the Quakers regarding how a refugee determination should occur. (Initially, for example, Willis-Conger was more strict about sticking to UN guidelines for refugee determination.) As a result, the two groups did the same kind of work and used roughly the same pool of people, but remained somewhat separate. Many who were involved in the underground railroad from this early period (between 1981 and 1983) remember it as a rather free-form organization whose participants were often naive about the legal consequences of their work:

> *In those days, and I don't mean to be flippant, it was just a lark. And we certainly had no idea, just none [that it would continue for so many years]. If, in 1981, I had any idea that in 1990 I would be doing this . . . [laughs]. It was just, listen, there's a civil war going on that is just horrible, and these people are fleeing. And it will last for a year or two and then it's all going to go away. . . . So we would just drive right down to Nogales, and then drive right back up the main highway. I didn't resolve the issue of how dangerous it was until Stacey Merkt got picked up. And then when Phil and Katherine got picked up, I started getting anxiety attacks in my sleep. I never had anything like that happen before. But in my sleep I was just scared to death, just*

this deep, deep fear. And I realized that I had been in the same car, on the same road, at the same hour. . . . I had until that time just this really naive notion that God was smiling in us, so that no harm would come to us. And I really believed that—that we were doing the moral or the right thing, and that the powers that be would not allow anything bad to happen to us.

In 1984, however, when Stacey Lynn Merkt and Phillip Willis-Conger were intercepted by the Border Patrol and charged with transporting illegal aliens, the naïveté of the underground began to dissipate and Sanctuary workers began to consider the potentially serious and costly consequences of their actions. Some drifted out of the underground, reluctant to endanger themselves or their families, but, as these excerpted interviews indicate, many decided to remain:

And so I sat myself down, and I said, OK, you've got all these babies. My oldest was six or seven. And my youngest was smuggling when she was two weeks old. She still doesn't know that people don't take picnics on the border and pick up people, that everybody doesn't do that. So I really said, . . . "What is the worst thing that is going to happen to me if I am picked up smuggling?" And I said, "I am a law-abiding citizen, whose family has political ties in Arizona, I have always been extremely active in my church; I have always been doing good works. And I have these babies. They're going to be so embarrassed, they're going to give me probation. And I can live with probation. So I'll keep doing it."

At that time, Southside was holding the first Freedom Seder. And they had a document which said that we believe in such and such, as we will do these things. And then they had you sign your name underneath, and we went out into the parking lot, and they asked us who would drive a Central American from Southside to the temple. I remember holding my baby—this was, I believe, 1983—and trying to decide if I would raise my hand or not. And finally I just handed the baby to my husband. Nobody came with me on the way there, but someone did come on the way back. And I remember being petrified, being so scared. I guess I figured, "Here are these people risking their lives on a regular basis. What excuse do I have?" . . . And then in 1984 I began doing the transporting.[10]

The indictments of the eleven Tucson Sanctuary workers in 1985 and the revelation that government agents had infiltrated the movement increased fears of imprisonment as well as distrust of newcomers among the underground. Following these indictments, a wave of paranoia hit the movement: people were afraid to hold and attend meetings, they were re-luctant to call one another over the phone. Elaborate codes were devel-oped, and members were particularly anxious about admitting newcom-ers into the underground.[11] One participant mused that the whole underground adopted a "cloak-and-dagger" kind of atmosphere:

> I'd get on the phone and there'd be this person on the other end of the phone who'd say, "Hi, can you pack a bag and be ready to go on a little trip overnight by three this afternoon?" I said, "Well, yeah, I suppose I can."
>
> I'd never met this person. I didn't know what was going on. I was just told, "We'll fill you in later." So I went home, packed a bag and came back to the office. I was waiting and this truck pulled up with this woman and they needed someone who spoke Spanish. So I hopped in this truck and we took off and went down to Hermosillo and picked up some refugees. Drove them to the border. At that time there wasn't a split [in the underground] but there were problems. And a lot of it had to do with the wave of paranoia that hit the community around the indictments. Because everything went so underground that there was no accountability within the community. So, like, I got involved not having the slightest idea of what I was doing. I went on this run, and as we were doing it, this woman was explaining to me how they do it. She said, "I want you translate for me, to translate this interview with these refugees for me." So I translated a little bit. And she said, "Well it sounds legitimate, we'll go ahead with it." And it was just sort of a unilateral decision made like that.
>
> And so we loaded them [the refugees] in the truck and left at three in the morning. We got down there at ten o'clock at night and talked to them for an hour. And then as we're driving back in the truck, she says, "I want you to translate a little more." I explained to them if they were detained they had the right to remain silent . . . just sort of doing it like that.
>
> I didn't know that there were meetings. And it was like, "OK, thanks for your help. If we need you again we'll call you." Then I talked to other people and they said, "It's not a good idea to go to the meetings because there could be an informant at them." It made sense to everybody at the time because everybody who was indicted was there because Jesús Cruz [a government agent] had taped them. So it was like, if you just do this freelance, you're OK. But if you go to the meetings, you're likely to be indicted. And people thought—it was this apocalyptic thing—people thought that things were going to grow in terms of the indictments. So I didn't go to a meeting for the first three

runs that I was involved in. I didn't meet anybody except for one or two contact people, who told me when and where there were runs to go on. And I met one or two people every once in a while at the fence, but I never got a chance to talk to them because it was just "Oh, hi. The folks are here. They're safe, you'd better get them across." You know. I met Elizabeth three times at the fence without ever meeting her outside of that. So it was just this whole bizarre thing. My first impression of trsg was of this strange, cloak-and-dagger sort of organization that was real secretive. There was all this fear and paranoia about being indicted.[12]

This "fear and paranoia" lasted throughout the Sanctuary trial, and the convictions of eight Sanctuary workers left several underground members with the strong impression that it was only a matter of time before the government, through another infiltrator, made more arrests. Others saw the increasingly secretive and closed nature of the underground as a negative development, suggesting that the movement was becoming akin to what the government accused it of being: a clandestine alien-smuggling ring. Sanctuary workers consequently struggled to keep the membership "open." As the trial drew to a close, however, the underground faced more than just the effects of distrust. Internal differences over the nature and operating practices of the underground—differences that had simmered in trsg since its inception—intensified in a climate of heightened suspicion and concerns about arrest. These eventually split trsg, and another underground group, calling itself El Puente (the bridge) was formed.

Factionalism within the Underground

In the spring of 1986, a handful of Sanctuary workers in the underground had become frustrated with what they claimed was as an "elite power structure" within trsg. Others felt that certain members of the group were organizing runs without going through the proper channels, thereby endangering the credibility of the whole Sanctuary network. This latter faction felt that the underground had to standardize its procedures while at the same time keeping the group open to new members. The return of some of the indicted (and in some cases, convicted) Sanctuary workers—whom many referred to as the "old underground leadership"—did little to ease tensions. Their conflict-laden reintegration into trsg revealed that, over the course of the trial, the underground had become a different group of people (mostly women) with their own ideas about how an underground should function. Furthermore, the nature

and composition of the underground were being changed by the influx of
newcomers to the movement—young, educated Anglos—who were being supported by various churches and had come to Tucson as church-
sponsored volunteers. Some of the women who had run the underground
during the trial resented the presence of what they perceived as a batch of
young and ignorant "upstarts," as well as the "old" male-dominated underground leadership. As some testimonies of Sanctuary participants attest, the split in this period became bitter and ugly, resulting in what one
described as "irrevocable and unhealable wounds":

> *By April and May 1986, the trial was over, and some of the old
> guard came back and tried to assume command as the Great
> White Fathers. But they had been out of it for so long that they
> didn't really know what was going on. So eventually, because I
> didn't agree with what they were doing, they started really
> lobbying behind my back. And started laying ground that I was
> crazy. Just malicious things that were undermining my credibility.*
>   —El Puente member

> *After 1986, people began to get offended that the underground
> was being run so well by mostly women. These male egos were
> real offended. As far as I am concerned, the whole thing with the
> split was about gender. The problem was that the fathers of the
> Sanctuary movement wanted power and control. And there were
> these dumb women taking over and doing more than they
> thought possible.*
>   —El Puente member

> *The group working during that year of 1984 and 1985—I guess
> we were sort of replacements—that group was almost completely
> female. And we worked in a very different way. What they did
> was they handed around the cards and you put down what you
> were willing to do, or when you were available. And different
> people collected those cards. And then people would call me.
> And I became involved in these actual runs with mostly women.
> So we worked differently than trsg after the trial. Certain things
> were the same. We would have the story, we would talk, and we
> would decide. But it was less structured. And things were
> organized pretty much on the spot. And that went on for quite a
> while. Well, after the trial, other people reentered and the whole
> thing changed. It was completely different. A whole bunch of
> rules started and we had been, well, mostly we trusted each other
> to do the best we could. And I know there was a background to
> why there were all these rules, but that was a privileged circle
> and I wasn't privy to it. After the trial there was an inner circle.
> Whoever presented cases was part of this circle. . . . But by then*

I had been working on the border for a year and I did know
some things. And I wasn't willing to keep quiet.

—El Puente member

Several trsg members, however, argued that the conflict really emerged
in relation to "accountability" at the border and decision-making procedures for refugee cases:

Things got really crazy along the border. Some people just got
out of control. You didn't know who was coming in, who was
bringing them in. And we all had to take responsibility for that.
If one person got in trouble, it meant that the whole group was
in trouble. And there was just all this lying. You couldn't get a
straight answer [from particular people]. There was no
accountability. And we just decided that this couldn't go on.

—trsg member

In addition, those returning from the trial had been profoundly influenced by court arguments and wished to implement procedures that
would underscore the "legality" of Sanctuary work. Among these was
the adoption of the United Nations High Commissioner on Refugees
(UNHCR) guidelines regarding refugee determination. For some trsg
members, the issue of guidelines was becoming particularly important
because runs were being arranged for refugees who, according to some
in the underground, should not have been assisted. The arrest of some
Sanctuary workers in the fall of 1986 was seized upon by one faction
as an example of the incompetence of certain members, and as an indication that decision making, screening, and transporting strategies had
to be clarified. In the rhetoric of the El Puente faction, however, the
bureaucratization of procedures and the implementation of new rules
were a sign that the underground was losing its sense of direction and
purpose:

In the beginning, it was rules about how far can you go to the
fence, can you cross this way. Do this or that. There were those
types of rules around the work. . . . Then it started when we
presented cases. And a pattern began to emerge to me and to
other people, that there was a high degree of caution. I can tell
you some things about people who were turned down by trsg
that really shows that this is true. I called it "trial trauma." It
looked to me that you had to be a perfect case of a refugee to be
passed by trsg. And there were certain people who came up
finally where I said, "I am sorry. I'm not going to have this
person's life on my head. And I am going to help this person."
So I say that due to this trauma of the trial, perhaps, that trsg

*became actually more strict than the U.S. or Canadian
governments.*

—El Puente member

Ideological Differences

Substantive disagreements between trsg and El Puente surfaced
around two issues: one related to affirmative asylum, the other to admitting refugees who already had lived in Mexico for substantial periods of
time.

Affirmative asylum was a concept pushed by Jim Corbett that was designed to reinforce the legal basis of Sanctuary. Under affirmative asylum,
refugees were to apply for political asylum once they were in the United
States. Sanctuary workers could subsequently claim, as a legal defense,
that they were not furthering the illegal presence of aliens in the United
States since they were simply driving refugees to a lawyer's office in order
that they might apply for asylum. Affirmative filing thus built on the case
of Stacey Lynn Merkt, a Sanctuary worker who had been arrested in
1984 for transporting three Salvadorans. A judge reversed Merkt's first
conviction on the basis that persons are legally authorized to bring refugees to INS offices for asylum processing. Some underground members
(including several who decided to remain with trsg), however, were dissat-
isfied with this idea and argued that it placed too much faith in the INS.[13]

The second disagreement revolved around how long a refugee applicant had lived in Mexico. Many Sanctuary workers felt that Central
Americans who had lived in Mexico for a considerable period of time—a
year or more, for example—and who had found "safe haven" there,
should not be crossed via the underground. The trsg Statement Regarding
Refugee Assistance, dated November 19, 1986 (after the split), asserted:

> Trsg currently does not provide direct assistance to those refugees
> who have found safe haven in Mexico and/or who have a
> reasonable alternative to coming to or passing through the
> United States. We do try to direct such refugees to sources of
> other forms of assistance. In spite of the aforementioned dangers,
> many refugees are able to find safe haven in Mexico. In fact,
> there is a very large population of refugees (1 million plus) who
> have found relative safety in Mexico and, although many live in
> the abject poverty endemic to Mexico, are not subject as
> individuals to violence or persecution. Some refugees are able to
> obtain legal status in Mexico as political exiles or as students.
> Some are able to assimilate effectively into Mexican society, get
> jobs, and establish a stable lifestyle. In some cases there is a
> pattern of successfully assimilating into Mexican society by

obtaining legal status and documentation, such as student visas, work visas or political exile status and documentation, or by successfully surviving in Mexico over a number of years, possibly having married a Mexican national or having had children born in Mexico and thus qualifying as Mexican nationals. This pattern would be a strong indicator that in these cases even legitimate refugees may now wish to come to the United States for primarily economic reasons. Conversely, many of these refugees would be unable to find safe haven in the United States or would find themselves much worse off. Because of widespread abuse of refugee rights and deportation of refugees by the United States, many refugees would not be relatively safer here than in Mexico. Furthermore, refugees in the United States face additional problems of cultural and linguistic isolation, as well as exploitation and abuse as a class not under the protection of the law. In the refugee population in the U.S. there is an extremely high unemployment rate (soon to be exacerbated by the new immigration law), high rates of alcoholism, poverty and isolation. Even those few refugees who are sponsored by church groups in the U.S. complain of cultural isolation and difficulties in getting their basic needs met.

Dissenters (as well as many members of the Central American community) regarded this policy as an outrageously unfair way of discriminating against refugees living in Mexico. Many also felt that the dangers facing Central Americans in Mexico were so well documented that they far outweighed any adverse effects a refugee might experience in the United States. Many were particularly concerned about a new cooperation (during the 1980s) between the Mexican and Guatemalan governments. Both Gen. Romero Lucas García, president of Guatemala from July 1978 to March 1982, and Gen. Ríos Montt, president from March 1982 to August 1983, ordered the military to attack refugee camps in Chiapas, Mexico. During these raids, the Guatemalan military arrested people arbitrarily, and many were tortured or disappeared. In 1984, these activities still continued (see Manz 1988: 151). Although the Mexican government did eventually move the refugee camps away from the Guatemalan border, many suspected that some "deal" was reached between the two countries (and with the United States), particularly as deportations of Central Americans from Mexico began to rise steadily from 1981 onward. As a result, some underground members did not agree with the criteria trsg was applying to Central American applicants; they felt that the underground was turning away legitimate refugees.

Conflicts with Consensus

As these substantive issues regarding policy began to emerge, the El Puente faction began to develop reservations about the trsg decision-making paradigm: the consensus model. Influenced by the Quakers who had formed the original underground, and particularly by Jim Corbett, trsg's weekly conference was based on the ideology of a Friends meeting. In trsg's version of the Quaker tradition, decisions were not to be reached by voting, debating, or compromises but by "unity," a condition reached by the group after reflection, silence, discussion, and prayer. Consequently, trsg, like Friends, appointed a "clerk" at the beginning of each meeting who set the agenda in consultation with the group, guided the discussion, and recorded the group's decisions. Theoretically, every member was to assume the responsibility of speaking at a meeting, and, should they object to something, speak up when their conscience dictated it. In the consensus model, no one was to dominate the group, and if unity of the whole group could not be achieved, the discussion was to be set aside until another time.

Although consensus was designed both to establish a unifying set of principles and procedures and to incorporate the opinions of all in the underground, trsg dissenters argued that it was a "smoke screen," a way in which a small handful of people, privy to most of the information regarding refugee issues and the border, imposed their will on the less informed:

I became very uncomfortable with how trsg made its decisions. And very uncomfortable with the leadership. That consensus stuff, and I'll say it straight out, is bullshit. There's an underlying . . . well, let me put it this way. I come out of community organization. And there is one thing that I learned that a core group has to do in order to maintain its integrity, and that is to deal with internal conflicts. The ideological, the personal, the strategic problems. And my reading of trsg is that the one thing they refuse to do is deal with the internal conflict. They smother internal conflicts. And basically, if people do not agree with an underlying philosophy or strategy, or both, my reading was that if you didn't agree with the leadership, you didn't function in that group. It was that simple. And the particular conflict that I saw surfacing [right after the trial in 1986] that they did not want to deal with, and which was very intense—it was between two people in the group. I saw a lot of hidden agendas, a lot of covert material that trsg refused to talk about. And everyone was uncomfortable with the conflict, but no one wanted to push it. . . .

Well, by the summer, I came to the conclusion that trsg was a pretty "sick" group internally. That there were a lot of "yes" people who went along with the leadership. And so several of us said in the summer of 1986, we think that there is room for an alternative group.

—El Puente member

Consensus is a funny thing. It can beget its own form of tyranny. Certain people can dominate others, especially if they are the ones who appear to know everything. And consensus can be reached by people just not giving their input. What started to happen as the new trsg formed, people were brought in that we didn't know—from out of town, who were new, who hadn't gone through our experiences. And who didn't know who we were and the commitment that we had made. And it was a big commitment. And again there was this authority figure. I saw that many people were not willing to say "boo." This person would say certain things and people would just agree. I had done too much at that point to just agree.

—El Puente member

The split, when it did occur, began cordially enough. After much discussion, it was decided that there was room enough on the border for two groups to function. Relations between the two factions, however, deteriorated rapidly and the division became ugly. Both members of trsg and El Puente recall accusations of insanity, demonic possession, and pathological lying, which cluttered efforts to articulate differences. Eventually, underground members began to feel that the divisions were irreconcilable:

It was one of the most painful days of my life. It felt like I was getting a divorce from all these people, whom I loved and respected. The case that I split over was a very interesting case. . . . There was this fellow who, maybe a year before, trsg had decided they would help. We went to get him, and he wasn't where he was supposed to be because he was asthmatic and he could not travel that day. I think there were other people in his group that made it and crossed. He did not. A while later, he came back for an interview and trsg turned him down. And I said, I want to help that person. Here was a thing happening. How long you were in Mexico, that was the big issue. I did not agree with this. But this man was one of the people getting caught in this. . . . And I said I am not rejecting this guy because he could not make it that time. His story is still the same, he is still a refugee. And then trsg said that maybe it would be a good idea to form two groups.

And I was crying, but I knew that I was not going to go through this again.

—El Puente member

So by April or May we had decided to split into two groups. And it was going to be a nice, friendly split. Because some people were very willing to talk about things so we didn't mess up on the border. And it felt good. And it was just a friendly split over some differences we couldn't iron out. Then after this happened, John Fife showed up at a trsg meeting which I wasn't at because I no longer considered myself a member. And he said that we needed to stay together. So I bent to pressure and said OK. But by June, there was a family that was supposed to come up and be part of a caravan to Washington, a family of eleven which had lived in Mexico for a couple of years. Wonderful people. But because they had lived in Mexico for a couple of years, trsg rejected them. And in fact they had tried for asylum but they had been in a flood in Chiapas and they lost all their possessions as well as their documents. So they had nothing to prove themselves. So I said fine. And basically I stood up at this meeting and said, "That's fine, I'm going to help these people. I'm out, bye."

—El Puente member

The splinter group, which started out as four dissenters, eventually became a group of around a dozen people—El Puente—and was active from 1986 on. El Puente forged a relationship with the National Sanctuary Alliance, a network of several hundred Sanctuary churches that were coordinated through the Chicago Religious Task Force. (The connection with Chicago fostered further animosity between the two groups since trsg had disassociated itself from the Chicago-based national network.) Like trsg, this splinter group used the 1980 Refugee Act as the basis of its decisions, but it rejected criteria relating to length of stay in Mexico and willingness to file for political asylum. It also developed its own network of church contacts, though it was never able to establish a permanent representative in Mexico the way trsg had done. El Puente also tended not to do city crossings, preferring instead to move refugees into the United States through the desert.[14]

Despite its status as a dissenting faction, El Puente in fact retained many of the features of trsg; but it defined itself in terms of several differences. Decision making, for example, was not done along a strictly consensual model. Instead, precedence was given to the opinions of those who were "doing the work," that is, doing the run:

The way in which we are different from trsg—those who are doing the work make the decisions, period. If you are not going

*to do the work, then your vote doesn't count a lot. The group
shares the data, processes it, and then just say yes or no. So you
build a lot of trust with eight or nine people that you are
working with. And you don't need to say a lot. If you're not
doing the run, then you don't really say much, unless you feel
warning sirens going in your own gut.*

—El Puente member

*Some things are the same as trsg in our group. People get a call
about a case. But you always know what was said on the phone
and where the cases come from. I never liked that about trsg. We
are a small and close group, and we let each other know
everything. We don't have all these different people come and go
at every meeting. You get a call. You call a meeting. Then we
have people who do an interview. They come back and tell the
story. And people talk about it. It's the same process, basically.
And you say what you feel about it. In our group, if you are not
willing to work on the case, you don't make the decisions. You
may help, but you do not make decisions for others.*

—El Puente member

El Puente did not function as a public or "open" group:

*In the splinter group we do not seek publicity. We are not
comfortable with the way that trsg will have just anybody come
to these meetings. And saying outright things that are really
dangerous to people. So we decided that we would be a closed
group. It's not that we aren't open to new people, but we screen
people before they get involved. If any of us have serious
misgivings, we don't let them in. And we certainly don't invite
them to conspiracy meetings.*

—El Puente member

*Overall numbers have stayed the same. A dozen core people, and
then people on the periphery. Membership usually happens
through a referral of someone in the group and then basically
you just get to know them. A stranger cannot just show up. We
had some real problems with people who aren't familiar with the
area, who aren't familiar with the culture, who aren't familiar
with how things are done, and think they can just come down
here and do this on a lark.*

—El Puente member

Although the underground's split left an ugly blemish on Tucson's
Sanctuary community, El Puente, by defining these differences, engendered a period of critical reflection and clarification among underground participants. The presence of a separate underground in Tucson

prompted trsg to deal with the problems of leadership, power, and authority, and to face the divide between its ideals and what was actually happening in the underground group.[15] Although in 1990 the two groups had very little to do with each other and gossip persisted between them, many of El Puente's concerns continued to be discussed by trsg. The splintering incited the underground as a whole to confront the issues of domination and exclusion that had surfaced despite Sanctuary's commitment to ideals of equality and inclusivity.

The Work of the Underground

Trsg Meetings

The Tucson refugee support group (trsg) is a community of conscience responding to the plight of refugees through civil initiative. The form of our response and our criteria for assistance of refugees evolves as the refugee situation develops. Our group's current experience and understanding have led us to adopt certain criteria regarding who we assist and how we function as a group. Specifically with regard to who we assist in reaching safe haven in the United States, we distinguish, to the best of our ability, between refugees and economic migrants and between refugees who have no other options. We do not distinguish or "screen" refugees based on political beliefs nor on willingness to participate in public sanctuary. With regard to group functioning, we seek to maintain the locus of responsibility and decision-making within the local grass-roots community. We also seek to maintain openness and dialogue with all other groups including the United States government and specifically the Immigration and Naturalization Service (INS). We recognize, additionally, the need to maintain the integrity of the community of conscience for the practice of civil initiative in defense of refugees' rights.

—trsg policy statement, November 19, 1986

Despite its status as an "underground" organization, Tucson's main Sanctuary underground (trsg) uses many of the INS's principles and procedures for screening, evaluating, and determining refugee cases. For the most part, the underground meetings are remarkably businesslike and trsg members stress that correct procedures and principles must be followed (even though frequent "mess-ups" occur). Yet trsg's bureaucratic atmosphere is strangely tempered by the group's dark sense of humor and willingness to laugh or joke about the sordidness of the world in which they function. Overtly religious dimensions to underground work are rarely discussed and the meetings do not open or conclude with a prayer.[16] Yet the activities of the underground are viewed as a core of the

Table 8.1. Underground membership

Member	Age Bracket	Gender	Marital Status	Membership	Attendance at Meetings
James	25–30	M	single	core member	regular
Peter	25–30	M	single	core member	regular
Mike	25–30	M	single	core member	regular
Jason	25–30	M	single	core member	regular
Chris	25–30	M	married	core member	occasional
Robert	25–30	M	single	newcomer	occasional
Kristine	25–30	F	single	newcomer	occasional
Emily	25–30	F	single	newcomer	regular
Anne	25–30	F	single	core member	occasional
Elaine	25–30	F	single	core member	Mexico contact
Adrian	25–30	F	single	newcomer	regular
Sandra	35–45	F	divorced	core member	regular
Rebecca	35–45	F	married	core member	regular
Etty	35–45	F	divorced	newcomer	occasional
Jane	50–65	F	single	core member	regular
Katherine	50–65	F	divorced	newcomer	regular
Beatrice	50–65	F	married	core member	regular
Mary	50–65	F	single	core member	regular
Gwen	50–65	F	divorced	core member	regular
Lois	50–65	F	single	core member	nonattender
Neil	50–65	M	married	core member	occasional

Sanctuary church, and membership in it expresses one of the most fundamental acts of faith that a Sanctuary congregant can make.

The activities of the trsg underground revolve around discussion and evaluation of refugee applications and, if approved, the transportation of the applicants into the United States. Trsg meetings are held once a week in a tiny room (roughly 20′ × 10′) equipped with a telephone. The underground has a core group of fifteen people, and about a dozen peripheral members (see table 8.1), but the meetings are occasionally attended by strangers. Newcomers to trsg meetings are usually brought in by an established member of the underground, and very little effort is made to explain the rubrics of the meeting to neophytes who are left to "sink or swim" as the discussion proceeds.

Trsg meetings last between two and four hours, averaging around 150 minutes. The first half hour or so is normally taken up with socializing—catching up on what happened during the week, reminiscing about runs, distributing photographs of vacations, weddings, and the like, or giving details of refugee reunions. A "clerk" is selected (someone usually volunteers) and asks for agenda items. Various individuals in the group (particularly those who are presenting cases or who have just completed runs) state what they would like to discuss, and the clerk organizes the items in an appropriate order (for example, updates on runs usually come first, budget-related items last). The clerk's responsibility is to make sure that all agenda items are covered and that consensus is clearly reached on any group decisions, as well as the difficult task of keeping the meeting on track. One other person is designated as the note-taker for the meeting, which then officially begins.[17]

If strangers are in attendance, formal introductions take place before any discussion; members of the underground introduce themselves simply by first name, whereas newcomers are expected to give more information about who they are and why they are attending. Most items on the agenda relate to refugee cases (updates of old cases or information on new cases), but other recurrent items involve troubled finances—trsg operated on a thirteen thousand-dollar budget in 1989—and the deteriorating condition of the trsg pool of cars for transporting refugees.

Each application to trsg for assistance is treated, in social-work fashion, as a "case." Refugee cases discussed in the underground originate in a variety of ways. The three most common methods are the following: (1) a Central American already living in Tucson contacts trsg about a family member or a friend; (2) a church from somewhere else in the United States sends a request to trsg to cross a specific refugee and submits a dossier on that person or group; (3) trsg's permanent representative in Mexico City sends information on a case originating through Mexican contacts.

As of 1990, trsg was doing a little work in Guatemala, but mainly depended on refugees to get themselves and their families to Mexico City (or at least to Tapachula) before they could be helped. Some members of trsg had gone to Guatemala and established liaisons there, but the underground railroad had only temporary "depots" in this region. Contacts in Guatemala often were helping refugees cross into Mexico, and then directing them to the trsg person living in Mexico City.

For a newcomer to trsg, listening to the discussion of refugee cases can be like hearing a foreign language. Information is garbled in underground discussions, and presenters of cases often do not give the "full story"; details are left ambiguous, thus ensuring that knowledge is always *segmented* within the underground. Facility with political asylum terms and procedures, as well as Central American and Mexican geography, is usually taken for granted, and participants frequently will not clarify whom they mean when referring to a "she" or a "he" in a case involving three or more people. (Among the most difficult details to absorb are the often serpentine kinship relationships among members in a refugee group, something that many presenters will clarify only if pressed.) Newcomers are discouraged from asking questions about cases and are expected (almost as a rite of initiation) to learn by listening, observing patiently, and figuring out what is going on pretty much by themselves.[18] Initiates are encouraged to take a passive role as far as border work is concerned and any new person eager to do a run is treated with disapproval, and in some cases, suspicion.[19]

Occasionally, trsg holds a separate orientation meeting for new volunteers.[20] In this session, which usually lasts for several hours, one of trsg's core members briefs newcomers on Central American politics, the kinds of refugees coming into Tucson, principles and procedures for helping refugees, the process of consensus, how a run is coordinated, and the legal ramifications of doing border work.[21] The experienced trsg member also explains that border work is legal and that Sanctuary is based on principles established at the Nuremberg Trials—for example, that every person has the responsibility to uphold laws even if the government does not.[22] At the end of the orientation session, new volunteers are handed a packet of information and are asked to pay special attention to a document on the seven principles for joining trsg:

Seven Principles and Procedures that Guide the Sanctuary Practices of the Tucson Ecumenical Council's Task Force on Central America and the Tucson refugee support group (trsg)

1. Only persons who are fleeing persecution or life-threatening conditions of armed violence and who cannot safely remain in Mexico are helped by the Tucson refugee support group to cross the borderlands, but social and legal services are provided for arriving Central Americans by the Tucson Ecumenical Council Task Force, regardless of documentation or refugee status.
2. All refugees who need Sanctuary services are helped, regardless of their political alignment or nationality. None is pressured to go to publicly declared sanctuaries or to speak out. All are informed of available options, provided with legal counsel, and allowed to choose their course.
3. The INS district director is informed by mail whenever trsg helps refugees cross the borderlands. The nationality, age and sex of refugees is provided, but not the name.
4. Trsg will neither buy help from coyotes nor link its Sanctuary services to individuals or organizations that smuggle or hide undocumented refugees for financial or political profit.
5. In the event that trsg volunteers are indicted for helping refugees, they agree to do no plea bargaining and to insist on a jury trial.
6. Volunteers agree to refuse to testify if called before a grand jury. (Refugees need to trust counselors; Mexican coworkers need

anonymity; we would therefore betray our sanctuary ministry by secretly testifying about these matters to the very officials that are violating refugees' rights to safe haven and volunteers' rights to protect refugees. Also, we are open and ready to stand trial to establish the lawfulness of our activities, and our Sanctuary procedures and activities are published and available, so calling Sanctuary volunteers before a grand jury to betray refugees and coworkers would be just a political device to imprison subpoenaed Sanctuary volunteers without trial.)

7. As changing circumstances require new adaptations, the evolution of trsg/TEC sanctuary services is guided by privileges of civil initiative, protecting human rights within rather than outside the law. (If federal officials continue to violate refugees' right to safe haven, the INS must now either validate Sanctuary by failing to challenge our open practice or else put the church on trial until the courts finally rule that, as civil initiative, Sanctuary is lawful. In any case, the Sanctuary church will outlast presidential administrations and partisan judges.)[23]

Any new volunteers who cannot agree to these principles are asked not to attend the trsg meetings (but no formal statement of agreement is solicited).

Deciding a Case

One or two persons in trsg assume responsibility for each refugee case and present preliminary information on the applicant(s) to the group. After trsg has reviewed the case at a weekly meeting, it decides whether the case merits more attention. At this stage, someone is usually assigned to interview the Central American(s). If refugees are still in Central America or in southern Mexico, this is usually done over the phone or through Elaine, the trsg contact in Mexico City. If the Central Americans are in northern Mexico near Tucson, a Spanish-speaking member of the underground goes to interview them. If the information generated through the interview is such that trsg approves the case, the Central Americans (usually located in Guatemala or southern Mexico) are instructed to move to Mexico City and get in touch with Elaine.

Those conducting interviews with prospective refugees are given a printout of "counseling tips." If they are new, they are trained by a veteran trsg member. As counselors/interviewers, they are encouraged to interact with Central Americans according to the following guidelines:

1. Introduce yourself and give background about your religious affiliation to this work.

2. Be politically neutral. Mention of work with solidarity groups, your political beliefs and alignments, etc., will make many refugees feel uncomfortable.
3. If there are children or older people, spend time with them.
4. Don't give the impression of being rushed, even if time is short.
5. Try to work around machismo. Direct questions to women as well as men. Ask for everyone's opinion of their options and of the questions you ask.
6. Always be sensitive to where refugees are coming from—their fear of giving out information, their background, their culture, and educational level.
7. Never make a commitment to help. Explain that a decision must be made first by trsg.
8. Many refugees have survived by not telling much of their stories or experiences. Let them know that everything they say will be respected as confidential by those participating in decisions regarding their case. Let them know that you are aware that there are probably things they don't want to tell about their experiences and that's OK.
9. Try to be introduced by whoever is housing the refugee(s) in order to try to increase your credibility. Building a trust level at the beginning is crucial to the counseling session.

The "tips" document goes on to list the criteria a counselor should use when interviewing refugees. After ascertaining family history, how and why they left their country, what would happen to them if they returned home, and how long they have been living in Mexico, counselors try to establish whether the Central American(s) are refugees under the UN Refugee Protocol or the Geneva Conventions.[24] (Counselors are also instructed to find out what the Central Americans would do if they were picked up by the Border Patrol. If they say that they would sign a voluntary departure form, trsg often takes this as an indication that it is not that dangerous for them to return home.)[25] After explaining the disadvantages of living in the United States (language and cultural differences, the difficulty of finding work, etc.), counselors discuss three options for Central American refugees in the United States:

1. *Affirmative filing.* Trsg interviewers explain that it is unlikely that Guatemalans and Salvadorans will receive political asylum in the United States, but that the process can delay deportation by taking up to three years.
2. *Refugee in transit.* Interviewers suggest that refugees who are afraid to apply for asylum in the United States can begin the process of applying for political asylum in Canada.

3. *Refugees and informed counsel.* Interviewers explain that trsg can put refugees who need to speak to lawyers about their status and options in touch with lawyers in Tucson.[26]

After the interview, the case returns to trsg. Discussion of refugee cases in the underground meetings involves extreme attention to "detail"—which prolongs rather than shortens the meeting—and is frequently dominated by four or five of the same people (usually the presenters of the refugee cases), who have power within the group because of their access to and control of information. Because they "know" more about the case, their opinions are "privileged." Case presenters can often frame an application in a favorable or an unfavorable light, and the rest of the group is expected to extricate the details by looking for inconsistencies in the case, and possibly by playing devil's advocate. Usually trsg splits into two informal "pro" and "con" factions, which argue back and forth until one side concedes. At this point, the clerk may ask if consensus has been reached; if no one objects, it is assumed that it has. The group then moves on to arranging the particulars of a run. Most refugee cases, however, are not decided at one sitting but will span at least two or three meetings. After a case is presented, the group usually will require more information and will instruct the case presenter or the contact in Mexico to conduct further interviews until the group is satisfied with the information it has received. Trsg's decision-making procedures were described as follows in a 1986 orientation packet:

1. Trsg operates by consensus. This means decisions about actions, policies, or other areas relating to the integrity and life of trsg cannot be approved unless everyone attending the meeting agrees to the decision. Consensus must be based on a commitment to trsg as a community and requires openness both in expressing our opinions and in being receptive to the views of others.
2. It is important to speak out in meetings when the question arises as to whether there is a consensus about an issue, especially if you still have doubts or strong feelings of disagreement. A consensus can be blocked by one individual's feelings, and that's OK. You should never feel guilty about blocking consensus, expressing disagreement or doubts.
3. If disagreements are creating a stalemate in decisions, discuss alternatives, compromises, or find a point at which there is agreement and work from there.
4. Persons can step aside from a decision if they are blocking consensus and are willing to step aside so that a consensus can be reached. A person should not step aside from a consensus if they

feel the decision they are blocking will compromise their values, morals, or their ability to participate or function in the group in the future if the decision passes.

In general, trsg accepts personal testimony (in the form of letters or information given in an interview) provided that the story line is consistent and corresponds with its understanding of the history of political violence in Central America. The group does not (as a rule) demand "official documentation" of political repression (such as a newspaper article, a death warrant, or a letter from a human rights group). Personal relations with Central Americans, however, sometimes come into play when making a decision about a particular case, and trsg members find it especially difficult to say no to the relatives of Central Americans already living in Tucson (although in some instances they have done so). For trsg participants, the bottom line in deciding a case is often whether or not they would go to trial on the merits of the case and argue confidently that the individuals involved were legitimate refugees. The following discussion from an underground meeting takes up the case of a Salvadoran man who was waiting on the Mexican side of the U.S.-Mexico border for a commitment of assistance from trsg. The man had previously applied for assistance from trsg but had been turned down because his story did not demonstrate that he was being directly targeted by the Central American police. The excerpt (which condenses the actual discussion) conveys a sense of the issues that surface when trsg members are deciding a case:

JASON: There are two stories to this case. It's a guy named José, a Salvadoran, who's in Agua Prieta now. Some pastor helped him cross. Anyway, the stories he told [to us] were inconsistent. And we're under a bind because trsg has received a lot of calls from many parishes who are sponsoring him. When he first got in touch with us [over a year ago], he told me that he worked for a campesino group and he was fired by the government because he wouldn't do propaganda for them. The first time I talked to him was in April 1989, and he said that the threats to him were psychological. So we [trsg] turned him down. In the second story, and I just talked to him, he says he worked for a union and that he was targeted by the right. He says that because of his family connections, he is being targeted. And I talked to María del Carmen [a member of José's family living in Tucson who has worked with Sanctuary], and she said that he had a strong case. She did say that his family wasn't really in any danger, though. . . .

ANNE: Yes, but he told us that he wasn't picked up [by the police] specifically.

JASON: What happened when trsg denied him the first time?

PAULA: Well, I remember that María del Carmen didn't say anything . . . [but] she wasn't [happy with the decision]. We were caught in a bind. We're still caught in a bind. What are we going to do with this family?

ANNE: I think we need to make a decision on what we have.

JAMES: [José's] relatives aren't in any immediate danger. Now some are in Tucson, and José has just come up to Agua Prieta. He can't really make a claim on their [the family's] claim because he's not immediate family. Are we really in a bind to help? What are the consequences? First, it's against our principles, and second, he would be a bad case to get caught with.

ANNE: I have doubts about helping him because of the stories. I would rather raise money for a bond than have to testify if we were arrested with him. He will apply for asylum anyway in the U.S.

JASON: I'm for giving him the benefit of the doubt. Maybe psychologically he couldn't discuss these things before. Should we confront him about the differences [in the two stories]?

JAMES: Well, I think he's very resourceful.

ANNE: He's going to cross anyway, no matter what we decide.

GWEN: I don't feel that we can penalize him for coming to the border. Lots of refugees do. I am concerned that all these churches and attorneys think that he has a case.

PAULA: And they are going to be upset with us.

GWEN: No, that doesn't enter into it. Everyone in refugee work knows that there are good and bad cases. Every church in the United States wants a nice family case.

JAMES: I don't think I believe his new story. And I wouldn't want to be put on the witness stand.

GWEN: Could we help him, advise him how to cross? Crossing at Agua Prieta is more dangerous than Nogales.

ETTY: Look, he sounds like a pro. Why should we risk our necks?

PAULA: Do we help him at the border?

GWEN: No, we could just help him with transportation to Nogales.

JAMES: Look, if María del Carmen can get herself down to El Salvador so many times, then she can get José across.[27]

ANNE: I feel that this family has the resources.

JASON: Do we give him a reason [for rejecting him]?

GWEN: And someone has to tell María del Carmen. I think Anne should talk to her. (Anne rolls her eyes and sighs.) I think María del Carmen knows the integrity of our group and will respect this decision. We should tell them about the consequences of their actions if they go to get him.

JASON: Do we have consensus? We just advise him?

GWEN: There are all these churches in California really putting pressure on trsg to get him up.

JAMES: We don't owe them an answer.

ETTY: Can't they get someone else?

GWEN: No, they have always called on us. Well, could one of you speak to María del Carmen tomorrow, because she knows that we are meeting tonight?

JASON: OK, it looks like we're not going to help him.

Trsg members make their decisions on a refugee case by "consensus," a long and thorough, but often tedious and aggravating, process. Consensus is most commonly reached when voices objecting to the case become silent, or simply "concede." (Frequently, a case will be tabled if the meeting has gone beyond three hours.) Those presenting the case sometimes try to "push" it through and ask for consensus at strategic moments in the conversation—when the "opposition" seems to have run out of countervailing arguments. The onus in this process is on the objecting voice: a person has to be prepared to defend any reservations against the group's general inclination to approve refugee cases; members often remain quiet rather than enter into argument or prolong a meeting. Although individuals may raise "intuitive" reservations about a case ("I've just got a funny feeling about this one"), objections generally have to be based on "credible" claims (insufficient evidence, contradictory stories, violation of one of trsg principles, etc.). In the discussion below, a frustrated newcomer, Katherine (who became more combative as the meeting progressed) decided to voice her objection to a case by making caustic comments about Central American marriage/family customs. She embarrassed several members of the group and the case was promptly approved, partly to demonstrate that such prejudices were not acceptable critiques:

KRISTINE: (Reads letter from Guatemalan woman.) This is a case about a woman, María. She originally wrote a letter to Southside Church but I talked to her over the phone. I think she has two children—Flori, age ten, and Jorge, age five. She now lives in the United States and she wants to bring them up [here]. She left last February because her house was burned down, and she made it to San Diego in March. She started out as a nurse in Guatemala but lost her job. She worked for the military. But she was intimidated. They suspected her. She had witnessed atrocities, and when she protested they told her to keep quiet. She talked to her coworkers but she was afraid to give the specifics over the phone. She left her kids under the care of a friend named Esther. The military has been harassing her family [and Esther] in Guatemala. The daughter was kidnapped for fifteen days and she had to send a thousand dollars down. María's mother was dragged out of the house in the middle of the night and shot. She thinks that these are ploys to get her back to Guatemala. María is certain that they will kill her if she returns. She hasn't applied for asylum, and she doesn't have a lawyer. She didn't have any problems getting up and now she has a job. She doesn't know how to get ahold of the children.

ANNE: Do we have any doubts about the case? It sounds like a pretty strong case to me. Does everyone think it is? (Silence. Katherine begins to speak but is cut off.) How can we help them?

KRISTINE: María says that her daughter cannot live with the father [who is still in Guatemala].

JAMES: But we need the father's permission. Otherwise it could be kidnapping.

ANNE: If the father has shown no interest and the mother has taken care of them singly, then she is the sole guardian. It seems that Esther doesn't want to take care of the kids anymore.

KATHERINE: I think this is a messy domestic situation. Do we [really want to] get involved?

ANNE: We'll probably need letters signed from the parents if they are going to travel as minors. It would be best if the father could take them to Mexico City.

KRISTINE: Well, it's a little complicated because it seems that the kids have different fathers. And I'm under the impression that she has another one by a different man.

KATHERINE: Oh no, not another one of these [cases]! Did they [the woman and her husband] ever live together? Or do Central Americans just pass a few nights together and produce children? (Silence.)

ANNE (ignoring her): I just don't know how we could get them out. Maybe we should just fly them up. It would cost around a thousand dollars for each.

GWEN: You [Kristine] need to find out if she has filed [for asylum]. And get in touch with her lawyer. Also ask her if the father could take the kids to Mexico.

KRISTINE: OK. I can talk to her tomorrow.

ANNE: Anyway, we do have consensus on this, right? (Said quickly.) OK. Next case.

As this exchange suggests, tensions frequently erupt when a case is discussed. The consensus model, however, abhors personal conflict, and the clerk usually tries to cut conversation off before the tension becomes too serious. In the following excerpt, Ellen and Peter (both veterans of the underground) took opposing positions on a case, and Peter began to "needle" Ellen about why she was objecting to it. Mike, the clerk, terminated the discussion by tabling the case to another date:

JASON: All right, this is that case about Oscar's [common-law] wife. He's in the States and she's still in El Salvador. He wants to bring her up. We talked about it last week. Do you want me to review the case? (Reads letter from Oscar.)

KATHERINE: Does he really miss her? Does she really need to be here?

JASON: Yes. He's really worried about her.

MIKE (the clerk): Have we had contact with this Oscar guy before? Do we really know him?

JASON: No.

PETER: How did he contact us?

JASON: He was a university professor. And he left because he heard the military was looking for him because of some papers he wrote. He came to the United States with a six-month travel visa, but the wife couldn't get one. So she's been down there for a year, alone with a son. Four people connected to the office where the wife works have been captured. Oscar thinks that she is in potential danger.

PETER: Could he send us his I-589 [form for requesting asylum] for more information?

PAULA: Because she's not [officially] married to him, we need to look at her as a separate case.

ELLEN: What do we have that is new in this case? Last week he thought it was dangerous. This week he thinks it is dangerous. What's new? (Jason was supposed to have interviewed Oscar for more details but did not.)

JASON: (Ignores question.) Well, we could get her to Chihuahua [Central Mexico].

ELLEN: But we don't have any overt action on her part to contact us. It seems that she should have contacted us. This concerns me.

PETER: There are two grounds to help her. First, on the grounds that he has a legitimate case and that she is his wife, even if the government doesn't [think so]. And second, we simply recognize the merit of her case.

JASON: Do we have to wait until she gets kidnapped and tortured before we can help her?

PAULA: I lean strongly on the pieces of information from her own case. We know that the disappearances are real.

MIKE: OK. Before deciding, let's make sure everyone agrees.

ELLEN: Wait a sec, guys. I am really uncomfortable with this woman. This lady has an office job, she's at home, she's happy.

PETER: Well she's contacting . . .

JASON: No one is going to force her to leave. I don't see what the problem is.

ELLEN (growing irritated): The problem is soliciting people to leave El Salvador and becoming a travel agency.

PETER (also irritated): What's the problem, is it because she's [a] common-law [wife].

ELLEN: Come on! You know I don't care about things like that!

MIKE: Wait. What's your issue, Ellen?

ELLEN: Well, are other people making decisions for her?

MIKE: That's a good question.

JASON: Well, what do we want? A letter from her?

MIKE: Can we fax? Can we get a personal statement? I don't know.
I'm just asking if that is the next step.

PETER: But the implication in Oscar's letter is that she's tried to leave.

ADRIAN: Well, I think it's hard to tell from the letter. I can't distinguish
who is who.

MIKE: Well, he is her husband. They do have a child. . . . I don't think
that we are close to consensus on this one. What we need to do
is get the letter as an in-between step.

PETER: I hate to drag this meeting on, but I'm not clear on what the
issue is.

PAULA: I'm willing to listen to concern. Maybe we haven't dealt with
this for a while. A lot of cases have gone by and I feel we are
getting too abrupt. I don't feel as strongly as you [Ellen] do.

ETTY: Is it going to take another week? Maybe she's at risk.

JASON: Oscar said that she is planning to leave in a month.

ELLEN: There is something about saying to a woman who has never
contacted us . . . (Peter cuts her off and is told by the clerk
[Mike] to let Ellen finish.) I am just uncomfortable that this
compañera has not said, "I want to get out." I don't think a
personal statement is necessary, but I do think that if we get
caught it would be nice to talk to her first.

MIKE: Well, this would not be the first time that we have reunited
families that did not want to be reunited.

JASON: Yeah, but it says in the letter that his wife is "getting nervous."

GWEN: How did Oscar get in touch with Tucson? (No one answers.)

JASON: (Rereads part of the letter.) Look, I don't want to rip this letter
apart like biblical criticism.

PETER: And I don't think people have to write us with "Dear Tucson
Support Group. . . ."

MIKE: Yeah, and it has to be in a hundred words or less. (Laughter.)
OK. Let's drop this for a minute and go back to the last case.
We can come back to this one later.

If approved, the next step is to decide on how to get the refugee(s) up
to the U.S.-Mexico border. Usually, Central Americans are required to get
themselves to Mexico City (trsg will give them advice about how to do
this and, in the case of small children and high-risk cases, will send someone down to collect them). The trsg representative in Mexico City then

puts them on a bus for a northern city, not more than twelve hours from Tucson. The finances for these trips are paid out of trsg's budget (consisting mainly of donations made through various churches) or by a church group that has offered to sponsor the refugee case.

Doing "Runs"

The most important tip about refugee accompaniment is never to act like prey. In Mexico, it's helpful at times to seem to have official connections. Carry a list of government notables, with their phone numbers. Never threaten, never show contempt for a corrupt functionary; avoid all gringo arrogance. Just move with the confidence of one who belongs. The appearance and manner of clergy is often a good model. Instead of pretending to be invisible when you meet those who are hunting you, be sociable and seek positive interaction. When they might be of help, ask.

—Jim Corbett (1991: 144)

Trsg refers to the transfer of Central Americans from Mexico to the United States as "refugee accompaniment," or a "run." Under the influence of the Sanctuary trial, runs were split into two parts involving two separate teams (thereby distributing the potential felonies among a larger group).[28] Runs are coordinated by one or two people who are not directly involved in the operation but supervise the whole procedure. A coordinator is a person who finds an adequate number of people for the run (usually two teams of two persons), one of which will do the Mexican side, the other the American side; locates *reliable* vehicles for the run (a U.S., a Mexican, and possibly a "lead" car);[29] ensures that the "debt coordinator" (the treasurer) gives the runners enough money for the trip (including money for car insurance, visas, and to bribe a Mexican official if they are stopped); makes sure that a legal appointment has been set up for the refugees; has a letter mailed (regular post) to the INS informing it that trsg is picking up refugees (see figure 8.1); has a letter ready to be signed by the refugees indicating that they are going to a legal appointment (see figure 8.2); ensures that the driving teams have adequate equipment (food, water, first aid, maps, baby seats, etc.); arranges housing for the refugees. In a prerun meeting (held separately from trsg meetings), the coordinator and the driving teams discuss how the run is to occur. Usually, the Mexican team drives down to a city in northern Mexico, picks up the Central Americans, and drives them to a safe house on the Mexican side of the border. The runners discuss routes, potential immigration checks, and how people should be seated in the car. The Mexico drive is the most arduous and dangerous part of a run. Drives often take ten or

Tucson refugee support group
c/o Name of Signator
c/o Pima Friends Meeting House
Tucson, AZ 85719

Date

INS Official
District Director
Federal Building
230 N. 1st Ave.
Phoenix, AZ 85025

Dear District Director,

The Tucson refugee support group is helping the following refugee(s) reach legal counsel in order to determine the best way for them to establish and document their legal status in the United States.

These refugees meet the requirements of the 1980 Refugee Act and the UN Refugee Protocol for entry into the United States without visas or prior inspection. They are at risk in Mexico as well as in their home country.

Under advice of counsel that they have a reasonable prospect of establishing their legal status only with the assistance of a qualifying attorney, we defer to them and their legal counsel the determination of the best way for them to establish and document their legal status.

Because of the frequent need for confidentiality and the risk of prejudicing an application if a refugee should use a false name, we also continue to defer to their legal counsel verification of refugees' names.

Sincerely,

Name of signatory
for Tucson refugee support group

Figure 8.1. Sample letter to the Immigration and Naturalization Service.

A quien corresponda:

La oficina de la Directora del Distrito de Arizona del Servicio de Inmigración ha
sido notificada de mi presencia en los Estados Unidos. Estoy en ruta a recibir el
consejo de un abogado para determinar la mejor manera de establecer mi
estatus legal en los Estados Unidos. Tengo una cita con mi abogado el
día _____ de _____ a las _____ . Tal vez el Servicio
de Inmigración puede usar la siguiente información biográfica:

Nombre:

País de origen:

De mi propia voluntad, no daré más información, ni oral ni escrito, antes hablar
con mi abogado. No firmaré nada más sin el consejo de mi abogado. Por eso,
cualquier firma o información adicional que yo dé sin la presencia de mi abogado,
está extraída por coerción y es con estas palabras renunciada.

To whom it may concern:

The office of the INS District Director for Arizona has been notified of my presence
in the United States. I am on my way to receive legal counsel in order to determine
the best way to establish my legal status in the United States. I have an appointment
with my lawyer _____ at _____ .

My name, birth date, and nationality are given above.

I will not voluntarily give any additional information either orally or in writing until I
am in the presence of my attorney. In addition, I will not voluntarily sign anything
until I consult with my attorney. Consequently, anything I may sign, or any
additional information I may give, in the absence of my attorney, is extracted
through coercion and is hereby renounced.

_____   _____
(firma)   (fecha)

Figure 8.2. A reproduction of the original text of a letter that refugees sign and carry once
they arrive in the United States. Transporters for the U.S. side of a run have each of the
refugees sign two copies of this letter before they get into a car; one is retained by the refugees, the other by trsg. This letter and the letter sent to the INS whenever trsg assists refugees constitute trsg's effort to give transporting a legal basis. In 1985, a Fifth Circuit Court
reversed Stacey Merkt's conviction for transporting, arguing that a person intending to help
an alien to obtain legal status is not acting in "furtherance of the alien's illegal presence in
this country."

192 Anatomy of an "Underground" Church

more hours each way, and drivers frequently have to take back roads and navigate washes to avoid *la migra*. Arrest by the Mexican police can result in lengthy imprisonment in one of Mexico's unsavory jails.[30]

Once the Mexican side of the run is coordinated, participants decide on what type of crossing should occur. Trsg uses two types: a city crossing and a canyon crossing. In a city crossing, Central Americans are taken to a border town by the Mexican team and instructed on where there are holes in the fence. Runners frequently advise them on how to dress and suggest various disguises, as well as the time of day for slipping through the fence. The Central Americans are told to go to a designated location on the other side of the international fence where they will be picked up by the American team and driven to Tucson. (Originally, Sanctuary used a church that held a daily Spanish Mass as a rendezvous point. Mexicans frequently cross the border in order to attend masses and, when carrying a Bible or a religious candle, often are not bothered by the Border Patrol, even if their entry is illegal.)[31]

In a canyon crossing, Central Americans are taken to a remote place near the U.S.-Mexico border, and have to hike (usually for two to three hours) to a designated meeting point.[32] (These hikes can be dangerous, since they take runners into isolated parts of the desert. Consequently, trsg members have developed a careful system of landmarking and timing, and they update each other continuously on changes in the desert landscape.) Once there, the Central Americans cross the international fence by themselves (they either climb over it or shimmy underneath it) and are met by the American team. (Refugees cross borders by themselves because it saves trsg members a felony.)

During the coordinator's meeting, run participants also discuss how the drive back to Tucson should proceed, and, in particular, how to avoid detection by the Border Patrol. One of the most important features of the U.S. part of the run is the "profile" of the car—that is, what the left-hand side of the car will appear like to a Border Patrol car stationed in the middle of the highway on the lookout for suspicious vehicles. Runners carefully design the profile of a car; ideally, it should look as if the passengers are on a picnic, going shopping, or innocently taking a Sunday drive. Trsg often follows these guidelines in creating a profile:

> The trick is to work out a profile that lets you slip through. Use a local car (economy models are best) with clear windows. Move no more than three refugees at a time, always during daylight, accompanied by several passengers who are readily recognized as Anglos. Blonde is better than brunette; female is better than male; old is better than young. (Corbett 1991: 150)[33]

In the final stage of the meeting, the coordinator instructs drivers where to drop off the Central Americans and ensures that transporters empty their pockets of all important or incriminating information and gives the drivers a number where he or she can be reached for the duration of the run.[34]

The Role of Storytelling

Runs are frequently hair-raising experiences with unexpected twists, but for the most part they are successful.[35] Sanctuary workers like to recount particular runs, incorporating humorous elements into their stories and emphasizing the role that "luck" often plays in a successful run. The run stories, which perhaps are the underground's most overtly "religious" feature, not only act as an introduction to the culture of the underground but also serve as parables that convey a moral message. One of the most common themes in these "run parables" is a focus on the interaction of Anglos and Latinos, and on the courage and poise of Central Americans, which they exude even in their most desperate moments. In the first run parable below, the speaker conveyed the lesson of humility she was taught on a run:

> The Martínez family was huge. A father, a mother, a
> grandmother, four teenage boys, a teenage daughter, and a
> younger son, like nine or ten maybe. This was one of the earlier
> runs. And I got preoccupied with all the things you have to do.
> And this was going to be a huge family. And we got a pickup
> truck to take us into this canyon. We used to always tear out all
> the labels of their clothes so they couldn't be identified as Central
> Americans. We had to tell them all the regulations and rules. It
> was kinda like instant culturalization, you know, all on this one
> little ride from the time you got them.
>   So I was at the point where I was hooking up with the truck
> that had gone to get them. And I jumped in the back of the
> pickup, not really used to riding in the back of a pickup with so
> many people. And it was through this canyon with all these
> bumps. And I had just light pants on, so every bump seemed like
> just murder to me. But these people seemed to be so stoic sitting
> there as if they had done this all their lives. And I kept looking
> at them. And every time it would bump, I would wince. And
> they kept handing me their clothes. And it got to be kind of
> funny, and I would say "gracias." And so we were almost
> halfway there and I thought I'd better start the instructions.
>   By the way, this woman had led a walkout at her factory. She
> was a member of a labor union. (The mother, not the

grandmother.) *She used to work in an undergarment factory, it was a* maquiladora, *and she led a walkout. And then after that, several of her family members were killed. Her seven-year-old nephew's arm had been torn off. Many things had happened. So I started talking to them. And I say, "See these tags. We need to get all these tags torn off because they might identify you."*

And the grandmother, who was like seventy-eight, I think, says to me: "No tags."

So I said: "Oh. You took all the tags out. Great."

Then I said: "Let's check our shoes. Here's a bag of shoes I brought. Different sizes."

And they go: "Nikes!" They already had tennis shoes. "We sold all our blankets for shoes. U.S.-made."

Oh. OK. What's the next thing I should tell them?

Then all of a sudden a voice goes: "Timex watch. From the U.S. Timex. We eat lunch at 12 o'clock."

I said: "Who taught you that?"

He said: "I read it in a book. We eat dinner, five or six."

I said: "How about breakfast?"

"Seven A.M.*"*

Then I said: "We can't take any extra luggage. Everybody take one plastic bag"—'Cause I'm looking around to see where's their luggage and I didn't see any. Grandma was always outsmarting me, and she had one plastic bag with her and one dress.

"Anybody else got luggage?"

"No."

I said: "What's all those? Out they go." OK, out they went.

"Two oranges," I said, "in your plastic bag, everybody, in case you get hungry." Grandma already had some fruit in her bag. She must have been thinking, "Who is this nitwit? What does she think I came along on the trip for?" So we get to this stupid gate. And I looked at it and Joe [the driver] says, "This is a new gate." So I jumped off and I couldn't get the damn gate open. This kid gets off who is ten and just whips this thing open.

"I get on the truck, you close the gate," I said.

We had to do that three times. So we got to the point where we were abandoning the truck and I'm moving on with this family. So we get there, and I'm looking at this seventy-eight-year-old lady and I said: "You know, we really have a long hike here. What we are going to do is all hike, and I will be in the front so that all of you stay behind me. And if I think we need to take a break, or if you do before I do, we'll sit down under a tree and you can have your first piece of fruit or orange. And I have two bottles of water here. And you can take a sip of water.

*And you will have a break for five minutes and then you can
follow me. And I won't have to speak to you again."*

*OK. They go. So we did this like three times. We took our
five-minute break. And grandma comes up to me, she taps me on
the shoulder, and she says: "Mira. Enough of this* descanso," *she
says. "Enough of this resting," she says. "We're not going to sit
down again until we are on the other side. When you tell me
that we're in the United States of America, and we're in those
cars and we get to where we're going, then we'll have a* gran
celebración."

And I said: "But you're going to get very tired."

*"No. No more. I'm telling you we're just going to keep
going."*

*So I said: "OK." And I was huffing and huffing, 'cause it's
miles you go in these mountains. And I'd turn around saying:
"You OK?" She just goes like this [waves her hand].*

*We got to the fence. I had told them already that we were
going to do it in threes. I had another person meeting us, and
she was going to take the first three, then the next three five
minutes later. And grandma wanted to go first, but I had her last
on the list. And I said [to the group]: "Now, mira, it's [the fence]
six feet here. And the Border Patrol can see you from the tower.
You gotta get under this fence and then you gotta wookie like a
rabbit." And then I said: "I'm gonna say it one more time so
everybody understands. I have this piece of plastic sheeting here,
and you can sit down on it, scoot it under, scoot your body
under this fence, and then run like a bat out of hell."*

*And I'm trying to explain this and I look down and here is
grandma underneath the fence and she's gone. She just flies
across. And once she's across, she turns around and goes like this
[wiggles her behind like a rabbit] to me. (Laughs.) And then she
was in the bush before I could say anything! (Laughs.) And I
thought to myself, here is this woman, after all she's been
through. This woman is wonderful! What a sense of humor!
Wiggling her fanny like that.*

*And my friend Marlene was at the other end. And we had this
signal with a handkerchief. Marlene was a friend from back East
and she'd never done this before. She said, "I'm out there
looking around and I couldn't see anything. And all of a sudden
this figure comes out of the bushes and goes [wiggles her
behind]." . . . And she told me that grandma rushed like a
cottontail right into the car. And they got three in, and the next
three. And Marlene told me that they got in front of Lettie's
house and grandma said: "Is this the place now? Is this the safe
place? Where's that other woman who told me that she would*

*meet me here?" Marlene kept trying to explain that I had to go
all the way through Mexico and come out through the border; so
I would be quite delayed. And the whole time grandma kept
checking her watch, worried about us. And they weren't going to
have dinner until we came. And they had all this food waiting.
But she said: "Uh-uh, you don't do that. We sit here and pray
for them now."*

*And when I finally walked in the door she said, "¡Qué viva la
revolución!" And she said: "Now we're going to have a
celebration."*

These people are really incredible sometimes.

A second, common type of run parable celebrates inter-Anglo relationships and emphasizes that actions of solidarity on behalf of the poor (a
liberationist theme) lead to special, enduring friendships—that is, that
the attempt to do what is just, especially when it involves self-sacrifice
and risk, always unites, rather than divides people:

*There's one story I like to tell. Most of my runs have gone really
smoothly. In fact I've never had a bad run. Gracias a Dios. I
don't think I've ever aborted a run. A few times I've had things
go wrong where somebody was delayed or something. I've never
been stopped by the Border Patrol. I've been stopped on the
Mexican side a few times, but I've talked my way out. So one
that I remember very fondly was Andrew's first run. And it was
pretty funny. It was a woman from El Salvador and her three
children. There was a little girl. The cutest little girl. She was
maybe . . . she was walking but not talking, so she must have
been twenty or twenty-two—no, less than that—probably 16
months. Really cute. There were two men also from El Salvador
who were lay catechists from this base community. And we
decided that we were going to move all of them, all six of them
at one time.*

*And it was right around the time that everything had broken
loose in Agua Prieta and also Matamoros with the satanic cults.
You know, seven people were found murdered, who had been
dropped into a well outside of Agua Prieta. It was really gross
and all drug-related. Northern Mexico went berserk. There was
military everywhere. They moved in six hundred troops into
Nogales and close to 350 in Agua Prieta. And they were doing
house-to-house searches. Just gone berserk. And it lasted for
months. And they had roadblocks, military roadblocks in
northern Mexico. [It was] really hard to move anybody.*

*So there's this place, it's a canyon where we decided we were
going to do this crossing. And the way we normally do a*

crossing is, first of all, we do all the counseling with them beforehand, and tell them all of what they have to know about the crossing, that they have a legal appointment, and what their options are, and all that kind of stuff. And I had done all of that. So we agreed that Andrew and I would go down and do the Mexico side. And I can't remember who was on the U.S. side. Anyway, a couple of the older women were going to do the U.S. side. But when we do these, one group goes to one side and the other stays on their side, and then [they] walk in toward the fence at a prearranged time, and then only the refugees cross the fence. And then we on the Mexico side go back out and come back [to the United States] in the same car. So Andrew and I borrowed Lettie's truck, this little gray pickup with a camper on the back. And we drove down in this beat-up old pickup truck and we arrived at the church, and we were really worried that they hadn't been eating right. They had been at the church for a week and they had no money. So we thought, "Before we take them on this long hike—it was a two-and-a-half-hour hike total—we really ought to give them something to eat." So we fed them fruit, I think it included bananas. And some bread and some peanut butter. And some juices. And we were really early because Andrew was so nervous. It was his first run. So we left really early, and when we got down there, we were early. Everything was going—we were at least forty-five minutes early. So we hung around and wasted time, and ate a lot of food and everything. Finally, we put them all in the back of the truck.

It was about a forty-five-mile drive out to this canyon. And Andrew—we had all of them in the back camper and he and I were in the cab. We pulled in. It was right off the highway. And we were just going to pull off in this little area. And so we pull off in this little area. And I was going to jump out and take them and drop right down over the hill and on to the trail that I knew and try and get right out of sight. And Andrew was going to go on in the truck and then come back and pick me up later on. So I would do the hike with them alone. Well, we're starting to pull off the road, and as we pull off, another car pulls up, coming the other direction, and it pulls in. And Andrew says, "Oh, shit! Now what do we do?" And I said, "We can't do anything. We've already stopped. It would be really stupid if we leave and then come back."

So we jumped out and opened the back door and we're shepherding all these people out and I had said hello to these two guys who had pulled off the road. And they said, "Oh, hi. Whatcha doin'?" And I said, "Oh, just hangin' out, havin' a picnic." And they said, "Oh, that's great. We're doin' that too."

And we got these folks out [of the camper] and the middle boy, who was maybe nine years old, got out of the car and just started to throw up. All over the place. And the poor kid, I felt so bad—he was heaving all over the place and I kept saying, "I'm sorry, I'm sorry, but we've got to go." And I'm like making to go over the hill. And the two guys are going, "Oh, just a picnic, huh?" And I go, "Yep. Just a picnic." And the poor kid is literally throwing up while I'm making him walk. He was so sick. But we finally got him over the hill and we could sit down and rest. And he did his business. And then everybody was fine. And we did the hike. And we hiked about forty-five minutes and then I left them under a tree when we got close to the fence so that they couldn't be seen. And I walked up to the fence and got there at the same moment as Tom. Tom met me within three minutes of me getting there. And we shook hands. And I went back and got them and sent them around the corner on their own. And they finished the trip with no trouble.

So I went back out, and this is the part I like the best. Andrew pulled in at just the right moment. And he got out of the car and when he heard that they were gone and everything was OK, he just let out this scream. And he gave me this great bear hug and we just stood there and hugged each other. And I remember it really well. It was just a really cool moment. I don't think I'll ever forget it.

Like biblical parables, these run tales function as a kind of "wisdom tradition" in which certain social values (of humility, humor, trust, courage in the face of adversity, etc.) become part of the historical memory of the underground and a moral legacy to future runners. Usually told at the beginning of trsg meetings by "veterans," these tales establish seniority, give practical information to other underground members, and convey a moral message—of the wisdom and tenacity of Central Americans, the bonds of friendship engendered through adversity, and the uniting of laughter and faith through Sanctuary work.

The Underground as "Church"

Do something really revolutionary. Practice your faith.
                                        —Sanctuary bumper sticker

Tucson's underground is a group that, like church sanctuaries themselves, reflects "liminal" or "betwixt-and-between" characteristics. Trsg often walks an ambiguous line between the legal and the criminal, the public and the clandestine. The underground claims that it is an "open" group—yet one must be invited to its meetings, and information about cases is garbled and always discussed judiciously. Trsg stresses that it operates with the full knowledge of the INS, even to the extent that immigration is notified of runs by letter before they occur. Yet the group often disguises fugitives, takes circuitous and dangerous routes around immigration checkpoints, and counsels border crossers on how to evade the Border Patrol.

The U.S. government attempted to portray trsg as an "alien-smuggling ring" and convicted eight of its participants as felons. In contrast, Sanctuary supporters advocated the underground as a "church" activity, and celebrated the figurative martyrdom of eleven of its members. Within the underground, the line between God and Caesar is oftentimes unclear, lending ambiguity to efforts to label Sanctuary as either a religious or a civil activity. Perhaps one of the most striking features of the underground, which supports Sanctuary's claim that it is indeed a "religious institution," is the presence of young church volunteers who are financially supported by congregations across the United States. These churches view "border work"—activities that are regarded by the government as illegal—as part of the mission of their churches; these missioners have become a standard feature of the Sanctuary underground, and in many respects they form the backbone of the group.

For those without "official" missioner status, however, the underground is an extension of a larger religiosity, and the transporting of undocumented Central Americans, like going to church, is a way of practicing one's faith. Most of trsg's participants risk prosecution and imprisonment, and endure long, tedious, and often frustrating meetings, not because they are thrill seekers (even though the draw of adventure is a factor for some individuals), but because of deeply held religious convictions. Consequently, Sanctuary's border work is viewed as an "act of faith," the underground is seen as a "community of believers," and the principles and procedures that bind the group are regarded as a "sacred covenant." This underground is very much a part of Sanctuary's attempt to redefine "church."

- Go through checklist every time—entire runs have been canceled when experienced people forgot little details.

1. PREPARATION

KNOW: GENERALLY
- refugees' story—you may have to defend in court why you were helping these people
- a lawyer
- what to do if stopped ["why did you stop me?"—remain silent, reassure refugees (nonverbally, if necessary), call contact person—don't call lawyer yourself]

KNOW: SPECIFICS
- routes, timing, waiting time, backup plan
- lead-car procedure, what to look for

DO:
- clean out purses, cars, etc., of names, phone numbers, flyers, bumper stickers, etc.
- check vehicle:

• registration	• brake lights
• proof of insurance	• turn signals
• registration stickers	• lights
• oil	• radiator

- gas
- automatic trans. fluid, power steering, brake fluid
- extra water for radiator
- key to door—keys to ignition—keys to gas tank
- if vehicle has 2 tanks (trucks), know how to operate them

Note on vehicle check:
- every vehicle should meet legal specifications
- don't give the police reason to stop you or to spend time with you if they do stop you

HAVE FOR TRIP:
- PHONE NUMBER of contact person
- HOUSING: address, directions, and phone number
- DRIVER'S LICENSE
- LETTERS for refugees based on category (2 Spanish and 1 English for each refugee that will be in your car)
- WATER: 1 quart for yourself and each refugee/hr. of hike, plus a gallon or so at car for end of hike
- FOOD: for yourself and REFUGEES; snacks for hike, and a small meal (fruit, sandwiches, etc.) for end of hike or during the trip. (The refugees will probably have eaten before beginning their long trip and hike.)
- MONEY: for phone, emergencies, and any planned expenses

2. HAVE FOR TRIP
Equipment

• first aid	• rain gear
• blankets	• sunscreen/hat
• baby pack	• flashlight

- Baby seat (Arizona Law requires a baby seat for any child under 4 yrs. old or under 45 lbs.)
- small backpack—for food, water, first-aid kit on hike
- Spanish-English dictionary
- sturdy shoes for hiking and appropriate (not brightly colored) clothing

IF YOU ARE CAMPING:
- extra food and water
- sleeping bag
- insect repellant
- matches—but you will probably not be able to have a fire
- tent
- flashlight
- pocket knife

HAVE FOR PROFILE:
- equipment—e.g., for birdwatching: binoculars, guidebook
- extra "Americanizing" clothing, i.e., a "U of A" [University of Arizona] sweatshirt can make a refugee look much more American

3. KNOW FOR DURING A TRIP
Meeting [with refugees]
- be quiet, sounds carry
- someone wait with vehicles
- let refugees cross themselves, stay back
- confirm to refugees they have arrived in the U.S.
- introductions and review rights (say nothing, sign nothing, right to speak with lawyers)
- have refugees sign letters
- give refugees phone number of lawyer
- make sure bathroom stops are made before departure

On Road
- obey speed limits, traffic signs, etc.
- offer food to refugees
- call contact when you arrive safely at destination

Afterward
- evaluation
- return all equipment, maps, etc.

4. MEXICO TRANSPORTERS
- notify safe house of expected arrival
- bring: shoes for refugees to hike in
          backpacks for refugee luggage
          money for *mordida* [bribe] ($20+ per refugee minimum)
- papers: proof of citizenship (passport, birth certificate, voter registration)
          driver's license
          vehicle registration
          notarized letter authorizing vehicle use
          before leaving, review refugees' dress for profile/hike

Figure 8.3. Transporter's checklist (from trsg information packet, 1986).

Chapter 9

Reconstructing Religious Identity and Practice: Churches, States, and the "Global Order"

The problem is to understand the embattled efforts to establish order on a globe that has become one, yet is also becoming more self-consciously diverse. . . . At [the] core of [world history] is no longer the evolution and devolution of world systems, but the tense, ongoing interaction of forces promoting global integration and forces recreating local autonomy. This is not a struggle for or against global integration itself, but rather **a struggle over the terms of that integration**.
—Bright and Geyer (1987: 69; emphasis mine)

Narratives of Tucson's Sanctuary movement are firmly located in the world of individual experiences—of homemakers driving Central American fugitives to safe locations, of pastors confronting intransigent INS officials, of retired ranchers plotting Border Patrol evasion techniques. Yet Sanctuary is also a story deeply embedded in a larger social reality, one that encompasses the shifting contours of both U.S. religiopolitical culture and the larger global economy. Throughout this book, I have argued that Sanctuary is not just an example of personal religious practice or simply an expression of social protest: it is also an attempt to define the articulating presence of faith and religion in American society. Yet, at a level that transcends national boundaries and issues of domestic church-state relations, Sanctuary also reflects a response to a particular hegemonic vision of global integration—it is itself a response to the specific ways in which the state, under Ronald Reagan and George Bush, attempted to define the terms integrating Central and North American communities within a world economy.

By integration, I am not referring to a simple, functional interconnection among different parts. Rather, I am suggesting that globalization is a set of structured relationships—historical, political-economic, cultural, and moral—that represent a network of linkages among different human communities. These linkages entail not only the flow of commodities and cultural symbols but also specific values—ideologies of intersection, so to speak—which, like market forces, impose particular patterns of interconnection among different groups. In this sense, global economies can also be viewed as *moral* economies and Sanctuary is one instance in which

202

church and state representatives engaged in a struggle over who and what interests define the undergirding moral terms of Central American-North American integration.[1]

In the summer of 1993, I returned to Arizona to find Tucson's Sanctuary community in a moment of profound transition. Refugee flows had dwindled considerably and the underground had become dormant. Sanctuary participants were seeking new directions for the movement and were reflecting deeply on the meaning of their experiences over the past thirteen years. It is perhaps fitting, then, that this final chapter explores Sanctuary as a social movement that involved several interrelated levels of experience: (1) a *personal* level defined by the moral imperative to respond to the "stranger in need"; (2) a *national* level that focused on re-articulating U.S. models of religiopolitical practice; and (3) a *global* level involving both a critique of the United States as a world power and an effort to develop new transnational models of Christian identity and practice.

Articulating a Social-Justice Church

The substantive issue that drew Sanctuary into conflict with the state was Central America—a region that, under Ronald Reagan, became a battle-ground between the polarized orientations of U.S. churches. As I have already indicated, left-leaning churches became aware of Central America largely through the assassination of Salvadoran Archbishop Oscar Romero and the rape-murder of four American churchwomen in 1980. Outraged and shocked by these events, these churches began to question the government's material and ideological support for what many began to see as oppressive Central American regimes. Much of this questioning was informed by frequent visits to Central America, where church groups collected their own information on what was occurring, and from eye-witness accounts of U.S. missionaries in the region. One result of this in-dependent data gathering was a phenomenon referred to as "reverse mission" whereby church groups began to disseminate information on political conditions in Central America and mobilize opposition to Reagan's foreign policy:

> On average, 1,000 Catholic missioners return to the United
> States each year, for leave or reassignment. They form the core of
> a new type of work known as "reverse mission" that developed
> in the early 1980s. Although traditional missionary appeals for
> prayers and money continued, the emphasis shifted from good
> works to reforming public opinion about the U.S. role in the
> Third World. Reverse mission was a way to get Americans to

hear what the poor were saying, particularly in Central America. It was also a way to stimulate Americans to ask tough questions about what it meant to be Christian in one of the world's wealthiest, most powerful nations. The missionaries spoke of their experiences to churches, schools, civic groups—to anyone who would listen. With firsthand information, with photographs and documents, reverse missionaries put many countries on the amorphous map of Christian consciences, rousing in Catholic parishes an unprecedented interest in Third World affairs. . . . One result of reverse mission was that thousands of Americans who had never considered themselves "activists" joined organizations, staffed picket lines, and circulated petitions to protest U.S. policies in El Salvador. (Lernoux 1989: 179-80)[2]

The Christian left's understanding of Central American politics was profoundly different from that of the Reagan administration and right-wing churches. While conservative, anticommunist factions saw Central America as the embodiment of *East-West* conflict, left-wing church groups, and particularly the Catholic bishops, began to perceive it as the product of *North-South* domination. Such a perspective reflected a radically different view of the global economy and the ideological principles articulating integration between rich and poor nations. Reaganism and its right-wing supporters utilized cold war ideology to define the political, economic, and moral ties linking human populations around the globe, and argued that Central America was deeply embedded in a communist versus a democratic struggle. The left-wing churches, however, saw these same strands in terms of economic disparity and as the historical product of the First World's exploitation of the Third World: Central America's violence was thus in part the historical legacy of U.S. imperialism.

Consequently, left-leaning sectors within the churches, and movements such as Sanctuary, articulated an alternative vision of the role of the church in the international community: its proper function, one Maryknoll priest remarked, was not only "to feed the hungry," but also (and more important) "to question the causes of hunger." Such questions reflected the viewpoint that the role of the churches was not only to influence government policies but also to evaluate the broad moral ramifications of foreign policy and its concomitant implications for globalization. Sanctuary, then, despite all its diverse manifestations, underscored the global nature of human morality and located human belief and action ultimately in a global context.

Yet, despite this global focus, the starting point for the articulation of a Sanctuary church was confrontation with the government. Sanctuary practices, therefore, can be said to grow out of a rearticulation of domestic church-state relations, and Sanctuary activism adopted two distinct ways for reconstituting this relationship. In one stream of activism, Sanctuary workers practiced their moral vision through underground activities (either in the sense of civil disobedience or civil initiative), and indeed this form of activism dominated Sanctuary throughout the 1980s. In another stream, participants attempted to use the existing legal apparatus to propel their political agenda, namely, by taking the U.S. government to court.

Sanctuary Vindicated

One effective example of this second strategy occurred in May 1985 when a group of churches filed suit against the U.S. government for illegal application of domestic asylum laws. (Those named in the suit were the U.S. Attorney General, the Commissioner of the INS, and the Secretary of State.) The civil suit, *American Baptist Churches et al. (ABC) v. Thornburg*, involved more than eighty religious and refugee organizations and charged that the Reagan administration's policy of routinely denying Salvadoran and Guatemalan requests for asylum was in violation of the U.S. Refugee Act of 1980. At the time of the suit, the U.S. government was granting asylum to 3 percent of Salvadoran applicants and fewer than 1 percent of Guatemalan applicants. The plaintiffs argued that the government was improperly using foreign-policy considerations in determining political asylum.

In July 1990, the government realized that the court was probably going to rule in favor of the plaintiffs, and offered to settle out of court. Potentially affecting five hundred thousand Salvadorans and Guatemalans, the suit resulted in the following revisions in INS asylum proceedings:

1. All Salvadorans and Guatemalans in the United States who had been denied asylum since the Refugee Act was passed in 1980 became eligible to receive a de novo asylum adjudication by a newly trained corps of asylum officers.[3] Salvadoran or Guatemalans in the country who had not previously applied for asylum also became entitled to the de novo adjudication. In addition, applicants became entitled to employment authorization throughout the period of the de novo adjudication.
2. Foreign-policy and border enforcement considerations, the government's opinion of the political and ideological beliefs of the applicant, and the fact that the individual was from a country that the United States supported politically were excluded in determining eligibility for asylum.

3. The INS was prohibited from forwarding an application to the State Department without a specific preliminary assessment by the INS of whether the applicant was entitled to asylum. (This provision prevented the INS from bowing to the State Department's recommendation.)

4. A new corps of asylum adjudicators was trained by the INS; these individuals were educated about the political and economic conditions of the countries from which they received cases.[4]

Sanctuary workers seized upon the settlement as a vindication of the movement, but more importantly, as an indication that progressive religious groups could effect positive change in the political realm.[5] The *ABC* decision asserted that churches had a legitimate right (as well as a responsibility) to influence government policies, and encouraged churches to take governments to task (even to the point of a court suit) for violating moral/religious values.

As I have intimated, however, for Sanctuary groups, confrontation with the U.S. government was but an intermediate level of activism located in a broader religious ideology that extended well beyond the boundaries of national accountability. Like their right-wing counterparts, Sanctuary communities tended to view state as a moral entity that produced policies with moral implications, but ethical discipline of the state in and of itself was not the ultimate objective of the movement. Because Sanctuary theologies gave the individual a transnational identity, they emphasized a *global* church whose values and programs of action surpassed the boundaries of nationalism. (This differed considerably from the right-wing churches, which have tended to articulate their position vis-à-vis the state in a *complementary* fashion; that is, they saw the state as a vehicle of public morality that enacted and enforced religious values.)[6] Hence, the transnational dimension of religious identity in movements such as Sanctuary (and, for example, in the peace, ecology, and feminist movements) reflected a distinct conceptualization of what a church, in both a local and a global sense, is or should be.

Theological and Organizational Influences

The theological and activist traditions that are the principal historical wellsprings of Sanctuary and many other U.S.-based progressive and transnational church movements are Latin American liberation theology and the U.S. Nonviolent Direct Action (NVDA) coalitions. Both traditions emphasize the local-global continuum of religious identity and both have profoundly shaped the ideological and organizational directions of Sanctuary.

U.S. Nonviolent Direct Action coalitions, which grew out of the civil rights movement and coalesced around opposition to nuclear militarization in the 1970s, have been most influential in terms of organizational and strategic initiatives. Basing their activism on a morally charged vision of the world and adhering to ideologies of nonviolence, these groups have promulgated a number of principles for the practice of religious belief. By building on these NVDA principles, Sanctuary communities were able both to define religious belief in terms of the empowerment of the local community and to situate moral activism in a larger context of church-state struggle. Many Sanctuary communities, for example, used the NVDA affinity group (a small support group) as their basic unit of organization and tended to identify themselves in terms of community clusters rather than sets of distinct individuals. Decision making within these affinity groups generally followed a consensus model, and the ideological focus has been on inclusivity and community building rather than on drawing clearly marked boundaries around "correct" political behavior. In keeping with NVDA principles, Sanctuary groups also stayed focused on a particular issue (refugees/U.S. foreign policy in Central America) and used mass civil disobedience/civil initiative as a way to articulate their political opinions and mobilize public support (see Epstein 1991: 4-5).

The base communities in the Latin American liberation tradition reflect some of these organizational and strategic principles, and also situate the expression of religious belief in the context of struggle. Critical, however, in a liberationist framework is first, recognition of the tremendous disjuncture between the rich and poor nations of the globe, and second, a focus on the unique responsibility of dominant northern cultures in the creation and maintenance of poverty. For northern churches such as Sanctuary, then, the appropriation of "liberationist" themes has meant not only a focus on the affinity group, consensus, and community building, but also a rejection of dominant cultural values. As William Tabb has noted, this countercultural dimension of groups such as Sanctuary is a distinct feature of northern, social-justice churches:

> The rejection [within these churches] of possessive individualism, of national chauvinism, and of the implicit racism that characterizes the American notion of patriotism is both a return to the ethical beliefs of an earlier Christianity and a challenge to the secular religion of America, which celebrates getting rich and being important as reflections of God's favor. For the theologies of liberation, the central message of the Bible is to know God is

to do justice, and that women, men, and nations are to be judged by how they treat the most vulnerable members of the human family, rather than by rituals they observe or their private experiences of conversion, which leave the individual's social role unchanged. . . .The inspiration that the more affluent churches of North America have received from their sisters and brothers to the south has profoundly shaken the comfortable and challenged them to a new understanding of faith. (Tabb 1986: xv, xix)

Central to the liberationist agenda has been moral and practical engagement with situations of social inequality, and Sanctuary, emerging out of a point of intersection between First and Third Worlds, has played a key role in articulating a U.S. version of a "liberative" church. Continuing to evolve in the present day, this liberative church encapsulates not only a local dimension in which small support groups seek community empowerment, but also a global dimension in which a solidarity-with-the-poor morality transcends national identities and obligations. The underlying transnational morality of Sanctuary is distinct from the nation-based cold war and national-security ideologies that have undergirded conservative groups and, specifically, their interpretation of U.S. relations with Central America. It is in this sense that one can begin to see the U.S. Sanctuary movement as the articulation of a distinct church identity based in a local-global continuum. A church-state confrontation that entailed a struggle over the terms of U.S.-Central American relations, Sanctuary was ultimately a manifestation of conflicting moral economies about global integration.

Conclusion

This ethnography has explored how a particular group of people used religious beliefs and practices both to respond to state authority and to interpret the moral implications of a particular globalizing vision. It has analyzed how, in doing so, they attempted to reconstitute their cultural world—from their place in the family and church to their identity within the nation and the global community.

This study began with a consideration of some important social-scientific questions about religion and its role in the modern world, and endeavored to emphasize the importance of looking at religion as a dynamic social force, creatively contextualized in a political economy, a culture, and a history. I have suggested that it is also critical for social scientists to include studies of religious groups in the current burgeoning interest in processes of globalization. The integral presence of religious groups in shaping both national and global relationships challenges traditional social-scientific understandings of globalization—many of which have been dominated by neo-Marxist scholarship and its emphasis on economic forces. This study suggests that global processes are not just political and economic; that intricately shaping global networks are not only markets, systems of production, and the division of labor but also symbols, cultural representations, and social values. As such, global orders also represent *moral economies*. Clearly, we need to understand more about the shaping role that religious groups and movements are playing in the generation of these cultural, political, economic, and moral webs of significance.

It is my hope that this ethnography has raised more than just "academic" issues for the reader, as fieldwork among Sanctuary participants did for me.

Refugees compel both the ethnographer and the homemaker, the university professor and the preacher, to view power structures and processes of globalization in a particular light. In many respects, refugees are the human flotsam and jetsam of the contemporary world order, and Central Americans are the victims of a particularly heinous process of globalization. Refugees are most commonly the products of floods, drought, starvation, environmental devastation, civil wars, repressive governments, and flagging economies that, more recently, have been worsened both by International Monetary Fund- and World Bank-sponsored austerity programs that concentrate rather than expand wealth. Refugees are often people who have been moved off their land for cash crops, hydroelectric projects, or road construction. The 1980s witnessed a tremendous increase in human displacement: Southeast Asian "boat people" desperately taking to the sea, Ethiopians evading famine, Afghans escaping war, Cambodians flooding into Thailand, Salvadorans, Guatemalans, Kurds, Tamils, and Bosnian Muslims fleeing political repression, as well as the thousands of Haitians intercepted by the U.S. Coast Guard and repatriated without proper asylum proceedings. The number of refugees grew from 2.5 million in 1970 to 4.6 million in 1980 and to more than 14 million by 1989. According to the United Nations High Commissioner for Refugees, there are now some 19.7 million refugees worldwide, and more than 24 million internally displaced refugees—most of whom are from the Third World. This increase has occurred despite the return of 2.4 million refugees to their countries of origin during 1992.

The increased presence of displaced people in our world, at a time when many nations are closing their borders to refugees, raises important questions about who the winners and losers are in the evolving global economy. Although we are indeed experiencing a unique kind of global integration and unprecedented world *creolization*, globalization has engendered the displacement of millions of individuals. Do we accept such massive displacement as a permanent feature of the world order, or are there important political and economic as well as moral questions to be pondered?

The presence of Central Americans in the United States challenged a group of North Americans to reflect on who and what defines the political-economic and moral power relations that link the peoples of the world together. They were also challenged to evaluate the human consequences of the U.S. government's vision of a "world order." Sanctuary became a response to this challenge, a different vision, developed within a Christian and humanitarian context. Yet the presence of Central American political fugitives and the growing number of refugees, on a broader level, also compel each person, Christian or not, to engage in a critical reassessment of global relationships, of national policies, of the relation of morality to politics. When so many seem to be resorting to a xenophobic stance, one can also, like the Sanctuary workers, formulate an "alternative vision." This vision is perhaps discovered by seeking out those liminal spaces—those moments of betwixt and between that have been discussed throughout this work—in which the conflicting discourses of our social world are drawn together. In my experience, the most compelling of these liminal spaces are those that point to the social inequities dividing the First and Third Worlds, the privileged from the oppressed. It is here that the affluent North is most cogently challenged to discern its responsibilities in the face of overwhelming poverty and suffering. The stark encounter with victims of poverty and cruel repression raises, for each of us, issues of conscience versus issues of cultural and political practice. We are challenged to do what we sense to be "right and just," despite the cultural, political, and ideological currents that tell us otherwise, that whisper words of compromise and indifference. Perhaps we, too, need to ponder and ultimately heed the words John Fife so often has said to his Sanctuary congregation: "These are the choices we have to make."

Notes

Introduction. On the Steps of Sanctuary: Religion and Politics in the United States

1. Prior to the development of the U.S. movement, a sanctuary tradition for political refugees had evolved in Western Europe during the 1970s. In the Netherlands, for example, several congregations offered sanctuary to migrant workers and refugees threatened with deportation, and in Britain, Bishop Colin Winter set up an International Peace Center for South Africans fleeing apartheid, Chilean exiles, and Filipino and Bengali migrant workers. Sanctuary gained momentum in Britain, West Berlin, Belgium, the Netherlands, and Switzerland after the 1985-86 trial of the U.S. Sanctuary workers, but adopted a much more interfaith quality, involving Christian, Jewish, Islamic, and Hindu congregations. In September 1986, an international conference, "Sanctuary: The Congregation as a Place of Refuge," was held in Driebergen, the Netherlands, and brought together Sanctuary workers from the United States and Western Europe (Weller 1987).

2. Although Reaganism created a broader role for Christianity in politics, there were some important differences between the way in which conservative and progressive churches viewed the state. For example, although both factions viewed the state as a moral entity, right-wing churches tended to articulate their position vis-à-vis the government in a "complementary" fashion; that is, they saw the state as a vehicle of public morality and focused their efforts on legislating religious values. Left-leaning churches also viewed the U.S. state as a moral body, but they tended to underscore an "ascendant church" whose values and programs of action transcended the power of the nation-state. As a result, the leftist churches adopted a distinctively adversarial position in relation to the government, even though they shared with their right-wing opponents some important paradigmatic points on the necessary linkage between religion and politics.

3. NVDA movements generally involve a radical wing of activists who "believe in nonviolence, engage in political action through affinity groups, practice decision-making by consensus, and employ the tactic of mass civil disobedience" (Epstein 1991: 1).

4. I also conducted several interviews with INS and Border Patrol officials from the Tucson sector.

5. In addition, through his own publishing career, my husband had made the acquaintance of Gary MacEoin, one of the principal organizers of the movement in Tucson, and a distinguished Catholic writer and lecturer. A few weeks before we left New Haven, Connecticut, for research in Tucson, Gary MacEoin had dinner with us and offered to contact a friend in Tucson. He telephoned his associate that night and immediately gained us an invitation to stay with her in Tucson. This woman ended up being our introductory link to Tucson's principal Catholic Sanctuary group, a community of Sanctuary refugees, and a political protest held every week in response to U.S. foreign policy in Central America.

6. For contrasting approaches and studies, see Susan Biber Coutin (1993), who focuses on Sanctuary as a language of protest that transformed the seemingly nonpolitical realms of daily life, and R. Ovyrn Rivera (1987), who examines Sanctuary in terms of resource mobilization and value frameworks.

1. Sanctuary and Theoretical Frameworks: Anthropology, Religion, and Power

1. Five topics or types were of special interest to anthropologists during this period: (1) *nativistic or revitalization movements*—these movements were characterized by the strong reaction of a minority group to a ruthless, dominating culture, and the desire among the minority for a revival of their own culture; (2) *cargo cults*—the cargo cults of the South Pacific, in which various groups coalesced around a prophetic leader who promised the resurrection of the dead, the destruction of the colonial population, and the arrival of a miraculous cargo of trade goods, became an area of intense anthropological scrutiny; (3) *messianic and millenarian movements*—in these movements a divine emissary was expected to intervene on behalf of the oppressed population and to transform the earth into a paradise for both the living and the dead; (4) *syncretic churches*—the "syncretic" churches in Southern and Central Africa were prophetic, messianic churches that blended traditional African beliefs with the Christian missionary message; (5) *"ecstatic" religions*—these groups, in response to political oppression, developed cults around spirit possession and became a way for the powerless to advance their interests.

2. Although the subjects of these postwar studies—millenarian movements, cargo cults, and religious revolutions—have long been, and continue to be, significant themes of human history, it is worth noting that they have not received the kind of social-scientific attention they warrant. Lincoln (1985a) suggests that this is a broad trend in both the social sciences and the humanities and illustrates his point by demonstrating that among scholars who have studied the great revolutions—the French Revolution (1789-99) and the Russian Revolutions (1905 and 1917)—there is an implicit acceptance of a classical Marxist theory of religion. Religion in these classics is treated as an established church aligned with the state, and is regarded as simply sanctioning the established political order.

3. Several anthropologists (e.g., Eric Wolf) have noted that serving in World War II frequently stimulated a greater interest among social scientists in issues of power, domination, and resistance.

4. These ethnographies that explore religious culture as "processes" span a great number of topics and ethnographic areas. They encompass both processes of "resistance" and "domination" in their treatments of religious culture. Several authors, for example, have analyzed how traditional religious culture articulates processes of "resistance," "rebellion," and "revolution" (e.g., Lincoln 1985a; Scott 1985; Apter 1984; Lan 1985; Ranger 1982). Several ethnographies in the "domination" genre have focused on how hegemonic groups (such as the state) successfully appropriate and reconstitute traditional religious cultures to further their own control (e.g., Brow 1988; Bossy 1970; Goody 1983), while others delin-

eate how states fail to manipulate local religious traditions (Weller 1985), and hence experience diminished social power. An interesting debate within the resistance-domination literature on religion has involved disputes over whether Christian missions are essentially a vehicle for indigenous sentiments and interests or a Western import that functions solely in the direction of imperial control (Glazier 1980). Although scholars have explored topics as diverse as Pentecostalism, Protestant fundamentalism, and liberation theology, and have lined up on both sides (e.g., Higgins [1990], Berryman [1984], and Garma Navarro [1984] representing the former position, and Manz [1988] and Annis [1987] the latter), there is a growing consensus that missionary efforts and effects must be treated dialectically (see Lancaster 1988; Gill 1990; Comaroff and Comaroff 1991; Stoll 1990).

5. Attempting to compensate, perhaps, for the theoretical tendency to treat religion simply as a form of social glue, many anthropologists have been particularly interested in how religion is implicated in struggles over power. Talal Asad, for example, claims that it is not appropriate to approach religion with questions about "the social meaning of doctrines and practices" and the "psychological effects of symbols and rituals" (1983: 252). He argues, rather, that one should begin with questions about the historical conditions (the "movements, classes, institutions, ideologies") that gave rise to religious culture so that one can understand the "different ways in which it [religion] created and worked through institutions, the different selves which it shaped and shaped it and the different categories of knowledge which it authorized and made available" (1983: 238). Eric Wolf's edited collection, *Religion, Power and Protest in Local Communities: The Northern Shore of the Mediterranean* (1984), furthers this perspective. Wolf suggests that anthropologists should look at how symbolic processes construct individual identities and how they "anchor" them within a symbolically constituted world. Wolf argues that anthropologists should analyze how dominant groups attempt to control these symbolic processes in order to further their own political and economic interests. Wolf's collection explores, among other topics, how religious ideologies construct gender identities, how states penetrate and control kin groups through ecclesiastical intervention, and how some of these processes are linked to a global economy in which Christianity allied itself with the centralization of European state power during the modern era. (In a more recent edited collection [1991], Wolf delves more deeply into the nature of religion and power by focusing on religion and state-making processes.)

6. Other important examples included Jean and John Comaroff's work (1991) and a collection on popular religion in Middle America edited by Stephen and Dow (1990).

2. Local History, Part 1: Declaring Sanctuary for Central Americans (July 1980 to December 1982)

1. During the 1980s and early 1990s, Southern Arizona's top ten employers were Fort Huachuca, the University of Arizona, the state of Arizona, Davis-Monthan Air Force Base, Tucson's Unified School District, Pima County, Hughes Aircraft Co., the city of Tucson, Magma Copper Co., and IBM.

2. Since the U.S. Drug Enforcement Agency's crackdown on Miami in the early 1980s, Tucson has also become one of the main gateways to the United States for heroin, crack, and cocaine.

3. Coyotes are smugglers of human cargo who, for a specified sum of money, will get clients into another country illegally. The price varies: two coyotes in Guatemala City told me (in June 1991) that the average price from Guatemala City to Los Angeles was between $2,000 and $2,500 per person. (Another name for these smugglers is *polleros*, chicken rustlers.) The term coyote implies someone who is wily enough to get around the police, but who scavenges on other people's misfortune by charging too much money (see Conover

1987). Most coyotes, depending on the route, use bus and train transportation, bribing immigration officials along the way until they reach the Mexico/U.S. border, where clients hike (or, near the Rio Grande, float on rubber tubes) across the international border. I was told by Central Americans and church workers in Tucson that, without a coyote, it usually takes three or four attempts before entering the United States successfully.

4. A detailed reconstruction of these events is provided by Miriam Davidson in *Convictions of the Heart: Jim Corbett and the Sanctuary Movement* (1988).

5. Sanctuary participants warned me not to think of Sanctuary as only a story involving Anglo, North American churches. They pointed to the Mexican tradition of ecclesial sanctuary developed in response to the wave of Central Americans flooding into southern Mexico during the mid-1970s, when Mexican churches created special ministries for Central American fugitives and established a network of "safe" churches or an "underground railroad" up to the U.S border. For several years before the declaration of Sanctuary in the United States, an informal, quiet, yet widespread network of Sanctuary churches in Mexico was facilitating the movement of Central Americans toward the U.S.-Mexico border.

6. Several churches in Tucson had also been involved in resettlement of Southeast Asian refugees.

7. Between 1980 and 1982, Salvadorans were by far the main Central American population making their way to Tucson. By the fall of 1982, Guatemalans also began to arrive, and their numbers grew dramatically from 1983 to 1986. The original profile of both groups was urban professionals, students, human rights and union activists, catechists, and their families. The second wave of Central Americans (late 1982 on) included increasing numbers of campesinos and Guatemalan Amerindians from the highlands.

8. The Vigil was inspired by a series of public protests that Father Ricardo had organized around a 1977 incident in which a Tucson police officer was acquitted of involuntary manslaughter for shooting and killing of a young Hispanic man (José H. Sinohui Jr.). In a civil case protesting the acquittal, the judge awarded the Sinohui family damages, and the police officer lost his house in payment of the judgment. Father Ricardo's protests had successfully alerted the Tucson community to discrimination and abuse in the local police force, and, importantly, had brought together a coalition of people intent on appealing the original acquittal. The eventual conviction of the officer convinced Father Ricardo of the effectiveness of public protests. The Vigil, which continues as of this writing, is considered the longest-running demonstration of its kind in the United States.

9. The Vigil is where Jim Corbett met John Fife. (Father Ricardo and John Fife had known each other principally from their work among farmworkers.)

10. The church's membership steadily became Anglo after Fife's arrival. In 1990, it had 163 active members, of whom 66.9 percent were Anglo.

11. One of the younger men, for example, had a close friend who did not show up for his second tour of duty with the Salvadoran National Guard. Shortly afterward, ORDEN (a civilian paramilitary group organized in the 1960s) came to his house and abducted him. The following day his body was discovered in a dump. His teeth were broken off and his lips had been sewn together. After he had been tortured, his abductors had apparently run a truck slowly over his body to kill him (Davidson 1988: 8). During the first five months of 1980, the Archdiocese of San Salvador estimated that 2,000 to 2,500 people had been killed by political violence.

12. See Manz 1988: 15-16; Diskin and Sharpe 1986: 53-54. Some of these organizations were linked to armed groups (e.g., FECCAS with the FPL [Popular Liberation Forces] and CUC with the EGP [Guerrilla Army of the Poor]).

13. Until Vatican II, Catholic doctrine held that there was no grace—no salvation—outside of the Catholic church (*extra ecclesiam nulla salus*), and that the principal task of

the church was to get people into it and keep them there. Theologically, Vatican II acknowl-edged that God's grace was everywhere, *saving humans on its own* (Berryman 1984: 26). As a result of this doctrinal shift, new questions about the proper role of the church were raised, and many Catholics began to question traditional models of ministry that privileged the sacraments (baptism, communion, marriage, etc.) over education, literacy, and lay-related programs.

14. See Coste (1985), McGovern (1989), and Aman (1984) on Marxism and liberation theology.

15. Liberation theology does not underscore the separation between spiritual and tem-poral planes, and prefers instead to see a single history of humankind in which God is "in-carnated." This notion, which suggests that the kingdom of God can be realized in the hu-man world, contradicted traditional Catholic theology in which the kingdom of God is realized only in the afterlife. The liberationist perspective also rejected the traditional sepa-ration of the church from politics, and argued that conflict, even class conflict, was an im-portant part of realizing "God's kingdom."

16. Leonardo Boff was a Franciscan priest whose principal offense was authorship of *Church: Charism & Power*. The Vatican organization that "silenced" him, the Congrega-tion for the Doctrine of the Faith, is the modern successor to the Catholic Inquisition. Boff eventually decided to resign from the priesthood (see *Catholic New Times*, July 19, 1992).

17. The program adopted by El Salvador and Guatemala was primarily influenced by Israeli and U.S. counterinsurgency theory. This form of counterinsurgency argued that in-surgents must be confronted not only militarily, but also politically, economically, and ideo-logically: a central target of counterinsurgency is not just guerrillas but the populations that sustain them. Counterinsurgency must therefore bring "the environment in which the people live under the spatial, social and economic control of the government in order to diminish or cut off the possibility that they may support the guerrillas" (Aguilera Peralta 1988: 154). In Guatemala, this required army control of the countryside and was accom-plished along three lines. First, the Guatemalan military instituted civil patrols, or PACS (Patrullas de Auto-defensiva Civil), whereby local inhabitants protected their villages from guerrillas through rotating, twenty-four-hour patrols. These patrols often entailed forced labor and became a means by which the military controlled the indigenous population. Sec-ond, the army created "model villages" (reminiscent of the "strategic hamlets" of the Viet-nam War era), which forcibly concentrated indigenous populations in army-monitored compounds. Third, a structure called the National Interinstitutional Coordinator (CIN) was established in each department or province and was presided over by a military com-mander. The CIN regulated civilian government and permitted only army-approved civil groups to emerge. (See Trudeau and Schoultz 1986: 40-42.)

18. Among the first priests to be killed was Rutilio Grande, a fifty-five-year-old Jesuit who was machine-gunned on March 12, 1977.

19. Ximena Bunster-Burotto has documented the sexual dimension of repression di-rected especially at Latin American women in "Surviving Fear: Women and Torture in Latin America," in *Women and Change in Latin America*, ed. June Nash and Helen Safa (1985).

20. Lernoux notes that opinion polls showed a two-thirds opposition to Reagan's policy in Central America at the beginning of his first term (1989: 183-84).

21. The G-28 form legally retracts anything an alien might have signed (including a vol-untary departure form) and guarantees him or her a hearing before an immigration judge.

22. These letters and various other documents written by Jim Corbett are collected in a two-volume xeroxed packet entitled *Borders and Crossings*. The packet comes with the fol-lowing words written across the front : "WARNING: The U.S. Attorney General may con-sider the acquisition of these papers to constitute participation in a criminal conspiracy."

23. Quakers refer to themselves and each other as "Friends," in reference to John 15:12-14: "This is my commandment, that you love one another as I have loved you. Greater love has no man than this, that a man lay down his life for his friends. You are my friends, if you do whatsoever I command you."

24. Historically, Mexico has maintained a tradition of informally providing safe haven for diplomats, ousted politicians, and political refugees. It is not, however, a signatory to the United Nations 1967 Protocol Relating to the Status of Refugees. The Mexican government usually allows political refugees to remain in the country on a temporary basis (for thirty days) while they are applying for asylum in other countries. In the late 1980s, however, under pressure from the U.S. government, Mexico began to deport Central Americans aggressively. (In general, poor Third World countries are more generous in offering asylum than are Western First World nations [*New Internationalist*, September 1991: 19].)

25. Another factor prompting the beginning of an underground was the dwindling supply of money among the Sanctuary churches (bond for detainees was $1,000 to $3,000 per person).

26. The movement also spawned what was termed an "overground" railroad. In this system "high-risk" refugees were bonded mainly out of south Texas and became wards of a Quaker group working with the Canadian government. In the overground, Central Americans were processed for asylum in Canada, even though they had been arrested in the United States. Under this program, the Canadian government frequently paid transportation costs. The system was termed "overground" since it involved no illegal activities.

27. By the fall of 1981, the group had made a commitment to bail out five to ten people per week. This work continued until May 1982.

28. There is some discrepancy in the record as to exactly what government source transferred this information. Several participants in the movement claimed that the warning came as a message from Border Patrol Intelligence.

29. Fife had read the letter distributed by the Lutheran Social Services in October 1981, which recounted the incident of a Central American arrested in a church and presented the idea of sanctuary for Central Americans as a possible way to halt the deportations. Fife's idea for sanctuary was sparked by this letter.

30. Apparently these lawyers felt that if the churches rejected "the system," they would be left on their own with an overwhelming number of cases to be processed. Margo Cowan and Lupe Castillo of Manzo saw sanctuary as "primarily a tactic to educate middle- and upper-class American churchgoers on the Central American refugee issue. In their view, most refugees didn't need gringos helping them across the border. . . . They needed more help in the tedious and unglamorous work of fighting their cases through the courts" (Crittenden 1988: 78). Following the sanctuary declaration, Manzo began to remove itself from TEC. The Manzo Area Council was eventually incorporated into TEC and renamed Tucson Ecumenical Council Legal Aid (TECLA).

31. Archbishop Oscar Arnulfo Romero, who had appealed to Salvadoran soldiers not to obey the murderous commands of their superiors, and who had called for an end to U.S. support of the Salvadoran military junta, was assassinated by a death squad on March 24, 1980, while he was celebrating mass at the Convent of the Good Shepherd in San Salvador. Evidence shows that the death squad received its orders from Roberto D'Aubuisson, a military officer who became the head of the right-wing ARENA party until his death in 1991 (Lernoux 1989: 157).

32. On March 19, 1982, reporter Randall Udall—who had recently accompanied Jim Corbett as he brought "Alfredo" and some other Salvadorans into the United States from Mexico—published a front-page article in the *Tucson Citizen* on the upcoming sanctuary event. The article reported that, next week, Fife "will publicly defy the U.S. government to

arrest him as a felon in violation of immigration laws." Sanctuary organizers were worried that the prepublicity would enable the government to act quickly and arrest them before declaring sanctuary. As it turned out, the precoverage alerted several other newspapers and television stations to the event. As a result, media coverage was greater than expected.

3. Local History, Part 2: The U.S. Sanctuary Movement on Trial (January 1983 to July 1986)

1. Presumably named after agent Thatcher's reference in his memorandum to *Sojourners* magazine, a left-leaning Protestant monthly that had taken a strong stance against U.S. foreign policy in Central America.

2. News reports indicate that, throughout the 1980s, the FBI spied on U.S. secular and religious groups that were critical of the Reagan administration's foreign policy in Central America (see Kahn 1992; McCarthy 1985). In July 1984, Jesús Cruz secretly taped an ecumenical service held for a Salvadoran man in the Camelback Presbyterian Church north of Phoenix, Arizona. Sarah Bard, a member of the congregation and a lawyer, found out about the taping and organized a group of ministers, churches, and denominations (including Southside Presbyterian in Tucson) to file a suit (in 1986) against the U.S. government, the U.S. Department of Justice, the INS, and the agents involved. In *Presbyterian Church et al. v. The United States of America et al.*, the churches claimed that the government had violated their First Amendment right to the free exercise of religion. On December 10, 1990, a district court judge in Phoenix ruled that "the government in conducting criminal investigations does not have 'unfettered discretion' to infiltrate religious services" (Morrell 1990; see also Leslie 1990).

3. The INS also hired Gina Sánchez as an undercover agent. Her one appearance was terminated after she appeared at Quiñones's Santuario de Guadalupe wearing bright lipstick and dark eye shadow, an open blouse, and tight-fitting shorts. Quiñones sent her back to Tucson, telling her that she could not visit a Mexican jail dressed in such a way. After this incident, Rayburn decided to drop her from the case (Crittenden 1988: 166 n).

4. The characterization of these camps as Tucson and Chicago is problematic since the divisions—although geographic—extended throughout the movement and encompassed Sanctuary communities in the Midwest, the East Coast, California, and Tucson itself. (See also Bau 1985: 29–30.)

5. All financial sources of the CRTF came from "individual contributions, denominational grants, speakers fees, membership fees, literature sales and fund-raising events" (*Basta!* January 1985: 6).

6. Although several Central Americans approved of this concept (and indeed requested a public forum), for many others it was problematic. Many Central Americans found the idea of "speaking out" on political matters contradictory to their own interests: it was something that could get them killed. (Some North American organizers referred to this reluctance to speak publicly as "campesino reticence," but it was something that was politically and culturally much more complex.) According to the Tucson Ecumenical Council task force, only one in twenty Central Americans wanted to go into public Sanctuary—most, they argued, just wanted to find a home and a job, and blend quietly into U.S. society.

7. In the beginning, churches were coordinated so that they could declare sanctuary on either March 24 or December 2—the anniversaries of Archbishop Romero's assassination and the murder of the four American churchwomen, respectively. As the number of churches wanting to become sanctuaries burgeoned, it became impossible to hold all declarations on these dates.

8. The Geneva Convention of 1948 and the United Nations 1967 Protocol Relating to the Status of Refugees, for example, forbid signatories to forcibly deport persons back to "war zones." The fact that these persons may or may not qualify for refugee status by domestic laws, or may have entered the country illegally, has no bearing on this rule. The United States is a signatory to both.

9. The legal implications of this concept were far-reaching for the Sanctuary participants, since, in effect, it turned the tables and put the government on trial. Under civil initiative, the government would have to defend *its* actions. Civil initiative thereby had the potential to subvert the culture of the courtroom, which was based on the assumption that the state was (1) always a law-abiding institution and (2) an impartial arbiter of the law.

10. One of the most contentious cases between the CRTF and TECTF occurred in February 1986 while the Sanctuary trial was going on. Five Sanctuary transporters were arrested while driving a group of Salvadorans to Tucson. As it turned out, several men in one family were members of ORDEN—an extralegal police organization that was responsible for some of the worst human rights atrocities in El Salvador. When they learned of this incident, the CRTF was furious. As Darlene Nicgorski noted, several of those already in Sanctuary had family members who had been murdered by ORDEN and were fleeing El Salvador because of ORDEN persecution (Davidson 1988: 129-36). The case also divided the Tucson underground, with some arguing that Sanctuary could not discriminate against anyone on the basis of political affiliation and others refusing to have anything to do with the case.

11. Sanctuary workers from Tucson explain these differences between the CRTF and TECTF as the result of their different positions vis-à-vis undocumented Central Americans. Situated closer to the border, Tucson participants had to deal with hundreds of refugees and their needs on a day-to-day basis. In the Chicago "hinterland," without a face or name to deal with, Tucson participants contended, the CRTF could reject or select refugees on the basis of their ideological orientation.

12. The one concession Tucson made to the centralizing trend was the formation of the National Sanctuary Defense Fund, a fund-raising group for legal expenses. Tucson acknowledged that as a fund-raising body it needed a central body and a cohesive set of policies. The tensions between segmented versus centralized organization within U.S. leftist activisim are succinctly documented in Barbara Epstein's work on nonviolent direct-action groups (1991). (See also Laclau and Mouffe 1985; Wittner 1984; Davis and Sprinker 1988; and Boggs 1986.)

13. The reversal was significant since the court ruled that Merkt was legally authorized to bring applicants (who qualified as refugees under the U.S. 1980 Refugee Act) to an INS office for processing. Merkt had claimed that she was not furthering the Salvadorans' illegal presence in the United States because she was driving them to an INS office so they could apply for political asylum. This ruling profoundly influenced underground procedures for transporting Central Americans in the United States. As soon as Central Americans got into cars on the U.S. side of the border, they were instructed to sign a statement indicating that they were going to a lawyer's appointment in order to apply for political asylum. This was done in order to give some legal basis for challenging any potential arrests of Sanctuary workers (while transporting aliens).

14. After the sentencing, Amnesty International adopted Merkt as a prisoner of conscience. Merkt was three months pregnant when she began serving her term (a point that sympathetic reporters emphasized). She was released after seventy-eight days in prison and put under house arrest for the remaining part of her sentence. In April 1984, Jack Elder, the director of Casa Romero and Merkt's supervisor, was arrested and served 150 days' community service in 1985. Also in 1985, Lorry Thomas, the succeeding director at Casa

Romero, was charged with transporting an undocumented Nicaraguan in her car. Thomas pleaded guilty and was sentenced to two years in prison, of which she served one and a half years.

15. Conger managed to eat a few very incriminating documents along with some business cards before the knapsack was confiscated.

16. Father Quiñones and Doña María, as Mexican nationals, were not legally required to attend the trial (without extradition), but both agreed to appear voluntarily. Nena Mac-Donald, a Quaker, had come to Tucson for two months in the summer of 1984, and had driven undocumented Central Americans around Tucson as well as offered them a place to sleep in her residence. Because she was a quiet woman with two young children back in Texas, prosecuting attorney Don Reno wanted to drop charges against her. He felt she would stir up too much sympathy in the jury, but was advised by U.S. attorney Stephen M. McNamee that she should stand trial.

17. The unindicted coconspirators were subpoenaed to testify against the defendants under a grant of immunity, whereby they had no right to refuse to testify or to invoke the constitutional protections of the Fifth Amendment.

18. U.S. criminal law recognizes two types of criminal offenses, *malum in se* and *malum prohibitum*. The former, which are crimes in themselves, are linked to community morality; these are actions that are wrong because they transgress social morals. In the latter, actions are wrong because they are prohibited; they are not considered social evils but simply violations of regulatory laws. Usually in a criminal trial there is one defendant and one crime, where the crime is *malum in se*. The Sanctuary defendants were tried for crimes *malum prohibitum*. Thus the legal issues posed were whether they did or did not instruct an alien on how to cross the international border, or did or did not harbor an alien on their property. As a result, the moral and social issues undergirding the legality/illegality of the defendants' actions technically were not part of the trial (Matas 1989: 76).

19. Polls by local media indicated that 71 percent of those residing in the Phoenix area did not believe that giving sanctuary to refugees was a legitimate excuse for violating laws (McCarthy 1985).

20. As a result, many journalists were the first chroniclers of underground activities, and their articles are rich sources on early underground transporting and crossing techniques. One of the most vivid of these was a series of articles by Michael Williamson in the *Sacramento Bee*, published between August 26 and 30. Williamson accompanied Jim Corbett on a "run" that began in southern Mexico and lasted several days.

21. Judge Carroll also ruled out any testimony or evidence referring to the State Department, the Central Intelligence Agency, or departments affiliated with them.

22. A person who claims that religious belief motivated his or her actions has the burden of documenting these motivations. If successful, the burden is discharged and shifts to the state, which must justify why it is placing limitations on religious conduct (Matas 1989: 51-52).

23. Duarte's eldest daughter had been kidnapped by guerrillas in September 1985, and his family had received death threats. In October, after his daughter was released, he had members of his family sent to the United States. Judge Carroll ruled on this motion that "[there are] powers . . . reserved to the political branch [of government]" that cannot be exercised by others (Crittenden 1988: 243-44).

24. This ruling is largely responsible for the dismissal of all charges against Jim Corbett. Cruz had had very little contact with Corbett, and the one Central American whose testimony could convict Corbett—a woman named Juana—had evaded the INS. Corbett, along with some journalists and a photographer from the *Arizona Star*, had helped cross Juana into the United States from Mexico. Judge Carroll ruled that the newspaper photographs

showing Jim Corbett helping Juana climb over a wire fence were not conclusive evidence of his guilt. Reno tried to get the Justice Department to issue him subpoenas for the *Star* photographer and reporters, but the department refused, citing a reluctance to start a First Amendment conflict with the press.

25. From 1980 to 1983, Cruz had taken undocumented Mexican laborers to a gun shop in Phoenix where he bought arms for them, and then helped cross them (along with the guns) back into Mexico. Judge Carroll ruled that this evidence was inadmissible since the government had no knowledge of Cruz's actions at the time it hired him for Operation Sojourner. This information could have impeached Cruz as a witness and ended in the dismissal of charges—but the jury never heard about his misconduct.

26. One of the Central American witnesses, José Argueta, testified that he had told Father Quiñones that he was going to the United States only for economic reasons. He also stated that his hometown of San Miguel, El Salvador, was very peaceful, and that he would not mind being deported there. This testimony was damaging to the defendants. The defense lawyers suspected that Argueta had been told by the INS that the U.S. government would look "favorably" on his application for residency if he cooperated during the Sanctuary trial. Argueta was the only one of the Central American witnesses who did not have to post bond and was released on his own recognizance (Crittenden 1988: 279).

27. A twenty-nine-year-old Salvadoran woman, Elba Teresa López, also refused to testify on the grounds that she was afraid that her testimony might adversely affect family members in El Salvador. Carroll had the courtroom cleared of the press, but López stated that her main fear was testifying before the government, believing that the INS and the Salvadoran police cooperated with one another. Carroll also held her in contempt, and she was placed under house arrest. As a result, Reno was permitted to introduce a tape recording on which López was speaking.

28. As a national body, the Presbyterian church was quite supportive of Sanctuary. Its support was very different from that of the Catholic church, which did not endorse Sanctuary. The Catholic bishops as a group never publicly endorsed the Sanctuary movement, though individual bishops such as Archbishop Weakland of Milwaukee, did. During a visit to Texas in September 1987, Pope John Paul II praised those Catholics who were assisting refugees from Latin America, but he did not cite any specific organizations (see Suro 1987, September 14, *New York Times*). Although several Catholic nuns declared sanctuary, the only Catholic male clerical orders to do so were the western Redemptorists and the Maryknollers.

29. The Sanctuary trial cost the government just under $3 million and the Sanctuary defendants approximately $2 million.

30. Amnesty International had indicated that if the defendants were sentenced to jail, it would adopt them as political prisoners. In June 1991, the Supreme Court rejected, without comment, an appeal by the eight convicted Sanctuary workers to overturn their convictions.

31. For churches that did not declare sanctuary, see *National Catholic Reporter*, March 15, 1985.

4. Sanctuary and the Judeo-Christian Tradition

1. Turner's notion of liminality (1964) built upon the ideas of anthropologist Arnold Van Gennep, who had argued that all rites of transition (rituals, for example, in which boys become men and girls become women) involve three stages: *separation* from the social group; *margin* or *limen* (the in-between stage); and *aggregation* or reunification with the social group. Turner was struck by the notion of interstructural or "liminal phases" in which ritual subjects become "declassified" (suspended in a kind of limbo) and then are reclassified by religious specialists before they can reenter the community.

2. The Romans and Greeks also practiced their own versions of sanctuary. The Greeks had created an extensive network of sanctuaries or sacred places that were originally intended to be places of refuge for slaves, debtors, and criminals but eventually became "resorts of murderous slaves, insolvent debtors and notorious criminals" (Siebold 1934: 535). Under the Romans, Greek sanctuary was restricted and regulated: when the privilege was invoked, the fugitive had to "undergo a formal inquisition and submit what amounted to a full legal defense before being admitted to sanctuary" (Bau 1985: 130). Sanctuaries, however, never officially became part of the blood-feud system in Roman culture since vengeance for murder was handled directly through Roman civil law (Siebold 1934: 535). Since slaves were the only ones who had no legal rights under Roman law, the Romans adapted sanctuary from the Greek tradition, and permitted it largely for the benefit of slaves. It is important to note that sanctuary under Roman rule was granted to an individual slave not as an alternative to civil law but as a special privilege allowed to those who had no rights within Roman law.

3. Joshua established three more sanctuary cities in the west region: Kedish, Shechem, and Hebron (Josh. 20:7).

4. The practice of altar sanctuary also made its way into Christianity via some of the Germanic cultures. In the Germanic tradition, religious temples were places of supreme peace and purity; any desecration of this peace was punishable by death. Hence, in this tradition, religious shrines were never places of asylum for criminals who had been tainted by vice or misfortune, for fear that they would sully the shrine (Siebold 1934: 535).

5. Such a dualistic understanding of power would make no sense in the Islamic tradition, in which the "state" is not a sister to "religion." In Islam, the "state is nothing at all by itself . . . the state is not an 'extension' of religion; it is an instrument of Islam, a transparent instrument which vanishes when one tries to regard it per se" (Rahman 1986: 154).

6. As it evolved, the Republica Christiana took shape around a tripartite structure of government consisting of the Sacerdotium (the ecclesial body), Imperium (the imperial or civil body), and Studium (the intellectual body that provided Christendom with a "reasoned" understanding of the Bible). Although different roles and powers were accorded each branch, and although theoretically power was "dialogic" or shared within the tripartite structure, the structure was perceived (particularly by the church) as a single unit presided over by the pope.

7. In the Germanic tradition, *fryth* or the church's peace was different both from the king's general peace *mund* (which every free man enjoyed) and *gryth* (special protection granted by the king). *Fryth* was a protection based in "the power of the church and rested in any sacred place" (Bau 1985: 135).

8. To some extent, Charlemagne's plan to entrench church authority established, ironically, the structural conditions for its demise. Charlemagne made bishops powerful, but their authority was issued largely on the authority of kings. As the Carolingian dynasty declined and Europe fragmented in to separate monarchies, church leaders attempted to assert a power independent of the secular king, but failed to achieve autonomous authority. This occurred owing in part to the fact that church power had become contingent upon, rather than coexistent with, the power of the king.

9. The institution of "proprietary churches" (*Eigenkirchen*) especially jeopardized church authority. Germanic law specified that property owners who built churches on their own land retained control of the church; the landowners could appoint and remove the clergy and collect revenue from the "proprietary church." By the ninth century, the *Eigenkirchen* churches greatly outnumbered episcopal churches (those under a bishop's authority). For the next 150 years, much to Rome's dismay, the landed nobility exercised increasing influence in church affairs thanks to their control of these proprietary churches, abbeys,

and monasteries (Lynch 1988: 17). The threat of these independent proprietary churches to church control was exacerbated by a kind of tenurial system that engulfed the clergy. The church's cash-flow crisis in the medieval period did not always permit a salaried clergy, paid by and loyal to a bishop. Instead, like feudal lords who had to maintain their dependents through land granting (fiefs), bishops from the sixth century on were compelled to grant lands (called *beneficia* or *precaria*) to the clergy, who, though allowed to manage the income from the property, were not permitted to transfer it. Frequently, the distinction between ecclesial and lay property became confused: revenues and taxes were often diverted to laypersons, and many married clergy, ignoring Roman episcopal authority, left their benefices to offspring.

10. Secular asylums also existed in England during this period. They were purely civil jurisdictions where the king's "writ" could not immediately penetrate (Bau 1985: 140). Protection within these jurisdictions, which were often a lord's courtyard or central churches on his property, were limited in time and space (civil sanctuary usually lasted not longer than six weeks and three days) and functioned much in the same intercessory way (between feuding parties) as did ecclesial sanctuaries (Siebold 1934: 536). As the English monarchy consolidated its power, this form of secular immunity from the king, like ecclesial immunity, was also increasingly restricted and regulated.

11. The records for St. Cuthbert's in Durham (1464-1524) show that 332 persons sought sanctuary for 243 different crimes, 195 of which were homicide. At St. John's in Beverly, between 1478 and 1539, 469 persons sought sanctuary: 173 of the cases were for homicides (52 of which involved tailors as the murderers), and 200 were related to debt (31 debtors were butchers). The largest number of asylum seekers, however, were peasants. The records show that very few women sought church sanctuary. Most of the crimes committed involved the use of knives and daggers (Bellamy 1973: 110).

12. In one famous case, Robert Haulay, an esquire, broke out of the Tower of London in 1378 and sought refuge in the abbey church at Westminster. Haulay, along with a sacristan, was slain in the church while high mass was being celebrated at the high altar. The event created a public stir and made the government unpopular. Haulay's assailants were eventually excommunicated and had to pay a fine to the church (Bellamy 1973: 109). This event is similar to the assassination of Archbishop Oscar Romero, who was gunned down while saying Mass in San Salvador in 1980. Substantial evidence suggests that Romero's assailants were members of the Salvadoran military—none of whom were ever arrested or prosecuted for the murder. The event sparked widespread international criticism of the Salvadoran government's abuse of human rights. As we saw in chapter 2, the first church sanctuary established for Central Americans in the United States was declared on the second anniversary of Romero's death.

13. Henry II, for example, attempted a bold recasting of the church-state paradigm by having Thomas à Becket, archbishop of Canterbury, murdered in 1170 (while he was saying vespers at the cathedral) for being an insolent prelate who was confounding his plans to fuse church and state in the office of the king. This was yet another historic violation of church sanctuary.

14. In English law, this meant taking an oath and swearing to leave the country and never return.

15. Under Henry VIII, a fugitive could not request sanctuary unless he or she confessed to committing a felony.

16. In 1530-31, under Henry VIII, abjuring the realm was ended for sanctuary seekers because many of the fugitives were mariners, archers, and soldiers who carried valuable military information with them as they left the realm. For these individuals, ecclesial asylum became permanent exile or life imprisonment within a sanctuary church.

17. The eventual demise of ecclesial sanctuary, it seems, was also linked to causes other than royal consolidation of power, one of which was abuse of sanctuary within an "increasingly commercial society" (Bau 1985: 150). Debtors, for example, who could not (or would not) pay their creditors often signed over their properties to family members, and then fled to sanctuary where they would wait until the creditor agreed to settle for a much-reduced payment or simply gave up on collecting the debt. Westminster Cathedral and St. Martin-le-Grand in London were both such "debtor's resorts." In 1377 and 1378, both the canon and civil laws outlawed debtors from using ecclesial sanctuary, but the abuses persisted and provided ample fuel to those who wished to abolish the privilege. Criticism of sanctuary emerged particularly in relation to St. Martin-le-Grand, where, according to local complaints, a den of thieves was using the church as a safe house and headquarters for further escapades (Mazzinghi 1887: 45; Bellamy 1973: 110). Some historians argue that perhaps deeper economic interests underlay these complaints: many of the fugitives were craftspersons or foreign artisans who could not or did not wish to pay guild taxes. At one point, St. Martin's developed an alternative market in which those who could not join the guilds or pay its fees were able to sell their wares at competitive prices. As "new bearers" of capitalism, in a time when the economy was still organized around guilds and commodity controls, the sanctuary asylees were perhaps threats to the medieval system of production (see Bau 1985: 151).

18. Historians note that, though abolished by statute, the practice of church sanctuary continued for several years after 1624. In France, sanctuary continued until the French Revolution.

5. Separation and Covenant: Church Sanctuary in the U.S. Tradition

1. Probably the first recorded case of sanctuary in the United States involved two regicides who fled to the colony of New Haven in the early 1660s. Col. Edward Whalley and his son-in-law, Col. William Goffe, were officers of the Cromwellian army and members of the High Court of Justice that had convicted Charles I of treason. The sentence, faithfully executed, was death by beheading. When the Stuarts were restored to the throne in 1660, Charles II sent out officers to find the regicides and bring them to trial in England. The New Haven Puritans, however, were sympathetic to Whalley and Goffe, and hid them in a cave at the top of West Rock, a craggy, fingerlike ridge stretching across the northwestern tip of New Haven. Once in New Haven, the pursuing officers appealed to the governor to arrest the fugitives; they were told that nothing could be done until after the Sabbath. Fuming with impatience, the royal officers attended Sunday services only to hear a sermon on Isa. 16:3: "Give counsel, grant justice; make your shade like night at the height of noon; hide the outcasts, betray not the fugitive." Eventually it became clear to all at the service, including the king's officers, that the regicides were not going to be returned to England. Neither man ever again left North America; both lived in New Haven for three years and then moved to Massachusetts, where Whalley died in 1674 and Goffe in 1680 (Osterweis 1953: 55–57). The same nonexplicit use of sanctuary is found in the abolition movement and the network of safe houses that formed an Underground Railroad for slaves seeking freedom in the north.

2. The First Amendment applies only to the federal government. The state conventions called to ratify the Constitution advocated a stronger guarantee of local state regulation of religious freedom, and many states ratified the document on the assumption that more amendments protecting local state autonomy would follow (Wilson 1990: 83). The states, however, eventually followed suit by adopting provisions similar to those of the First

Amendment in their own constitutions—some did so "freely," others as a prerequisite to joining the Union. By the beginning of the nineteenth century few vestiges of religious establishment remained in local state constitutions—the exception being the religious test for office.

3. Leo Pfeffer writes that this distinguishes European models of church-state separation from that of the United States. In European countries, freedom of religious practice "is conceived as belonging to minority sects or religious groups, often with the qualification that they be officially recognized by the State; it is, in other words, a corporate rather than a personal freedom. In the United States, from the very beginning, freedom was deemed to belong to the individual rather than to any group to which he might or might not belong" (Pfeffer 1974: 13).

4. Following this constitutional model, "church" and "state" are *structurally* separate governments—each constitutes a separate organization with independent clerical and civil offices, different personnel staff these offices, each division has a separate system of law, and each owns property independently (Weber 1989: 26).

5. Church-state conflicts within the Court are usually framed in terms of the "establishment" and "free exercise of religion" clauses of the U.S. Constitution. In the former, the Court must evaluate whether a government's involvement with a religious group is preferential; if it is, then it is deemed unconstitutional because it suggests the establishment (through government) of one favored religion. In the latter, the Court must not only protect an individual's right to practice religion freely, but also determine the limitations of religious practice.

6. The Supreme Court has consistently ruled, for example, that prayers in public schools are unconstitutional and violate both the establishment and free exercise clauses of the Constitution (Sheldon 1990: 239) (see *West Virginia Board of Education v. Barnette*, 319 U.S. 624 [1943]; *Engel v. Vitale*, 370 U.S. 421 [1962]).

7. One of the first cases in which the Court limited the First Amendment provisions on freedom of religious practice involved the Mormon sect and the practice of polygamy. Although polygamy was never widespread among the Mormons (involving not more than 5 percent of Mormon men), it engendered strong public opposition. In 1862, Congress passed the Anti-Polygamy Act, which made polygamy a crime in any U.S. territory. In the one polygamy case that reached the Supreme Court (*Reynolds v. United States*, 98 U.S. 145 [1879]), the right of Congress to make a law prohibiting a specific religious practice was contested on the grounds of freedom of religion. The court unanimously upheld the criminal conviction of polygamy. Significantly, the ruling underscored the impartial nature of the state as supreme judge but indicated that it was bound to intervene in local affairs when basic values, the "laws of the land," were threatened. The justices argued that the First Amendment left the court "free to reach actions which were in violation of social duties or subservient of good order." The ruling explicitly limited the free exercise clause of the First Amendment, but, more important, made clear that the clause did not exempt a person from the general reach of the law.

8. Although the Court recognizes a legal basis for conscientious objection, it has "repeatedly affirmed the supreme defense of State against a foreign enemy as taking precedence over constitutional guarantees of civil liberties and individual rights" (Woods 1969: 375). During World War I, Congress enacted a draft law with exemptions from combat duty for conscientious objectors that was upheld by the Supreme Court (*Aver v. United States*, 245 U.S. 366 [1918]). The Court, however, has never acknowledged conscientious objection as a constitutional right under the Amendments (see *U.S. v. Mackintosh* [1931]).

9. Influenced by Durkheimian "integrationist" themes, Bellah stressed that this nationalistic cult pulled Americans *together*. It could be argued, however, that nationalistic

religion has played a very divisive role in American politics: Protestant nativism at the turn of the century, anti-Semitism in the 1930s, and the election of a Catholic president in the 1960s are examples.

10. A significant religious development of the period was the pursuit among liberal Christian churches of a new interdenominational (and later interfaith) dialogue under the rubric of "ecumenism," a movement whose parent organization was the World Council of Churches (founded in 1948) and which sought unity among the Christian churches around themes of mission, doctrine, and social action. For American Catholics, the 1960s were also powerfully framed by Vatican II (1962-65), a council called by Pope John XXIII, which became one of the most widely discussed and media-covered religious events of the twentieth century. Vatican II was an opportunity for the Catholic church to articulate a role for Catholics in the "modern" world, and to develop new strategies and goals for the future. "Progressive" Catholics were deeply influenced by this council and were inspired by its message to respond, in conscience and in action, to crises in the current global order. The council produced sixteen documents (ranging in content from the nature of the church to Catholic perspectives on the press, the cold war, and motion pictures). It also radically changed the Roman Catholic liturgy, mandating that masses be conducted in the vernacular rather than in Latin.

11. Philip Gleason notes that because the nationalism that dominated post-World War II America was based on social values, it became inevitable that cracks within national unity developed primarily along "ideological rather than ethnic faultlines" (1981: 517). The point is interesting in light of the split between conservative and liberal churches that emerged around this time. The split had begun to appear during the civil rights movement over the issue of appropriate church activism (the most controversial form of which was civil disobedience), but by the 1960s the divide had become explicitly ideological, separating supporters from critics of the Vietnam War.

12. The conviction rate for draft resistance peaked in 1966 and 1967: in 1966, 72 percent of those arrested were convicted; in 1967, the percentage was 75.1; and in 1975, it dropped to a low of 16.6 percent (Kohn 1986: 90). (For histories of resistance to the draft in the United States, see Keim and Stoltzfus [1988] and Kohn [1986].)

13. Sermon cited in Denis Willigan, "Sanctuary: A Communitarian Form of Counter-Culture," *Union Seminary Quarterly Review* 25 (1970: 519-20); also quoted in Bau 1985: 161.

14. Several universities also declared themselves sanctuaries for draft resisters (e.g., Harvard, Brandeis, City University of New York, Columbia, Massachusetts Institute of Technology, Boston University School of Theology, and the University of Hawaii), but the student movements undergirding these sanctuaries often disassociated themselves from any religious affiliation.

15. These convictions were overturned on appeal in 1969.

16. One reason why the dissenting anti-Vietnam War churches became so controversial was that they were among the first religious groups to challenge state hegemony over U.S. foreign policy in the postwar period. Although the structure of state power in the United States is dispersed and offers different interest groups considerable access to central decision-making processes (Skocpol 1985: 12), some "arenas of power" are insulated from public opinion. These arenas, notes political scientist Stephen Krasner, are those controlled by the White House and the State Department and involve foreign policy and war-making capabilities (Krasner 1979: 86). In the post-World War II period, access to these arenas of power increasingly contracted under the influence of national-security ideology, a doctrine of beliefs popularized by the School of Munich during the rise of Nazism and one that exalted state military objectives (see Comblin 1979).

17. Interestingly, during the Vietnam War period, Supreme Court rulings consistently underscored a separation of church and state, reaffirmed that the conscience was a distinct sphere of religious identity independent of government, and even amplified the legal basis for claiming exemption from military service on the basis of religious conviction. See *United States v. Seager* (1965) and *Welsh v. United States* (1970) in Miller and Flowers 1987: 104-42.

18. Polls from the early to mid-1980s show that the U.S. population was fairly evenly divided between these two camps. Of those polled, 43 percent considered themselves liberal (19 percent very liberal); 41 percent identified themselves as conservative (18 percent very conservative); and only 16 percent claimed that they did not fit either category (Wuthnow 1988: 133).

19. Some of these groups (such as the Presbyterian Church U.S.A., the Lutheran Church in America, and the American Baptist Convention) also took a "liberal" position on women's issues, including reproductive rights (Burke 1987: 256).

20. More recent additions to this agenda are a burgeoning interest in the ecological crisis, structural adjustment and development issues in the Third World, the General Agreement on Trade and Tariffs (GATT), and the North American Free Trade Agreement (NAFTA).

21. The liberal model of separation of church and state still survives, however, and many religious leaders are critical of this new fusion of religion and politics. In the early 1990s, for example, the National Council of Churches sent a letter (signed by twenty-three church leaders) to President George Bush and the Republican party, stating that "any partisan use of God's name tends to breed intolerance and to divide" and that it is a "blasphemy . . . to invoke the infinite and holy God to assert moral authority of one people over another or one political party over another." Other such letters were issued by the Baptist Joint Committee on Public Affairs and the People for the American Way (*New York Times*, August 30, 1992).

22. This was not the case for all sanctuaries emerging at this time. Quaker theologies in Tucson, for example, never saw sanctuary principally as a place, but rather as a protective community of people.

6. Creating "Social Space": Sanctuary and the Reconstitution of "Church"

1. At the time of my research in Tucson there was only one synagogue involved in the Sanctuary network.

2. Saguaro Friends are more of an "open" community in that they, like Southside, have a regular meeting place and welcome visitors to their Sunday services. Because Saguaro Friends and Southside hold worship services at roughly the same time on Sundays, I was unable to gain sufficient data on the Quaker community, and therefore have confined my analysis to Desert Pilgrims (Catholic) and Southside Church (Presbyterian).

3. In addition, women in the movement have used a Sanctuary-based identity to survive painful divorce scenarios in which separation from their husbands deprived them of any socially acceptable corporate identity. (Christian cultures often shun the divorced or separated woman.)

4. The first base communities appeared in Northeast Brazil and in the San Miguelito slums of Panama. By 1978, there were 80,000 such communities in Brazil and 150,000 to 200,000 in all of Latin America. The proliferation of base communities was in part spurred by a severe shortage of priests in Latin America during the 1960s.

5. The term "liberation" emerged from Latin American theology of the 1960s as part of an effort to understand what role the church had to play in socioeconomic "development." At this time, many Latin American theologians were writing on a "theology of development." Peruvian theologian Gustavo Gutiérrez first used the term "liberation theology" in 1968 during a lecture in Chimbote, Peru. Gutiérrez's classic, *A Theology of Liberation*, was published in 1971 (1973 in English translation).

6. Fundamentalist groups in Latin America also make use of the BCC model. Fundamentalist and evangelical sects emphasize community relations and a personalized atmosphere, and highlight the importance of popular religiosity. In many cases, fundamentalist groups are most successful in the areas where Catholic BCCs already exist (see Lernoux 1988; Stoll 1990).

7. One sanctuary participant had some insightful comments about this phenomenon. Quoting Leonardo Boff, he suggested that the Latino BCCs in the countryside are more successful because community (based on proximity) "naturally" exists in a rural context. In urban areas, however, this powerful residential basis to community breaks down. A similar process occurred in the United States in the post-World War II period with massive immigration to cities: the country chapel gave way to the large and more alienated urban church. According to this participant, U.S. Sanctuary churches attempted to transpose into the urban environment the tradition of a town meeting, whereby people who might not have much daily contact come together out of interest in a political issue. In some respects, Sanctuary churches are like town meetings, in that current political issues are always discussed at the worship services, and people are drawn to these churches precisely because of this.

8. To some extent, this cell reflects the shift in the composition of the Sanctuary network in the posttrial period. Sanctuary was originally staffed primarily by local women who were housewives and/or employed outside the home, or retired. As Sanctuary became a national issue, churches across the country began to fund volunteers (mostly young, college-educated Anglos), who became the modestly paid staff of the Sanctuary network. There has been some tension between the senior, locally based participant and the newer "professional" Sanctuary worker regarding how meetings are to be conducted, how work is to be divided, and whose authority is ultimately respected.

9. In 1993, Southside Presbyterian moved into new buildings, constructed on the same site. In the new church, they have retained a circular seating pattern as well as the same basic structure of service.

10. Both communities, and particularly Desert Pilgrims, also try to use nonsexist language in their services. The Desert Pilgrims, for example, never refer to God as a male, and infrequently use the term "Lord." Ironically, many of the Protestant hymns sung during Southside's service contradict the community's inclusive ideology, containing militaristic images of Christianity and the idea that there is no salvation outside of the church. Other hymns stand in stark contrast to Southside's theme of political empowerment—hymns that imply that poverty is a holy state, and that God is satisfied with the plight of the poor (traditional Christian messages that have been soundly rejected by liberation theology).

The most traditional of all the services that I attended in the Sanctuary network was the refugee Mass. The seating arrangement followed that of the typical Catholic church: the congregants were meant to face forward toward the priest, focused on the altar. Significantly, this seating arrangement had been deliberately selected by the priest (since the chairs were all movable and could have been arranged otherwise). The priest who ran the refugee Mass was himself heavily involved in alternative, nonpriest-centered liturgies, and when I asked him why the refugee Mass was so traditional, he responded that most Central Americans preferred it that way. Several of the Central Americans who were attending the Mass in 1990 and 1991 confirmed this.

11. The Phoenician is a luxury hotel, a project masterminded by Charles Keating Jr., one of the handful of Arizona entrepreneurs who was convicted of criminal misconduct during the savings and loan scandal of 1990-91.

12. In Southside, ethnic divisions within the community became particularly acute in 1991 over the issue of ordaining homosexuals. This issue split the congregation along racial and ethnic lines (with blacks, Hispanics, and Native Americans overwhelmingly against ordination), and tensions became so severe that some members threatened to leave the community.

13. The term "People of God," popularized by Vatican II, built upon the notion of the Israelites as Yahweh's "chosen people." The phrase reflects a sense of a corporate, not individual, identity in relation to God.

14. Sanctuary members tend to be critical of conservative politics regarding U.S. imperialism and capitalism. Many, however, are conservative themselves on issues of abortion, homosexuality, and capital punishment.

15. As in Latin American liberation theology, "causes" of poverty tend not to be seen by Sanctuary participants as individual shortcomings or sins, but as part of larger social and economic patterns, referred to by some theologians as "social sins." These larger causes of oppression demand individual responses if they are to change, but cannot be redeemed as long as poverty and injustice exist. In this respect, "individual" salvation, traditionally celebrated in Christianity, is transformed into "covenant" salvation.

16. The theologies of these two Sanctuary communities share several core features with Latin American liberation theology. First, both emphasize that the interpretation of the Christian Scriptures should be "contextual," that is, dictated by what is going on around people in the everyday world (see Boff 1987: 22). (Father Ricardo is particularly strong on this point and frequently uses newspaper clippings as the basis of his theological reflections.) Second, theological reflection is not restricted to "spiritual matters" but encompasses political, economic, and cultural issues. Third, class analysis and questions of how poverty is generated in relation to wealth become central. In the sermons of John Fife and Father Ricardo, for example, class privileges and wealth, and the culture that celebrates them, are the most common targets of theological criticism. Fourth, like liberation theologians, Fife and Father Ricardo characterize God as a "God of the poor" who always takes the side of the poor against the rich (see Boff 1987: 50-51; Gutiérrez 1983: 7-8). God and Jesus Christ are viewed as "liberators" of the poor.

17. In Latin American liberation theology, this notion of a God of the poor who exists *in* the world is joined to a concept termed "the unity of history." Latin American liberation theologians tend to dismiss dualistic understandings of history that distinguish between sacred and profane history. They argue that there is only one history and that the evolution of God's kingdom occurs as part of the evolution of the human world (see Gutiérrez 1973: 72; Bandera 1975: 297-303; Bonino 1975: 137-38).

7. Sanctuary and the Central American Odyssey

1. Fugitives on the Pacific Coast cross the border from the southern bank of the Suchiate River. The river forms sixty miles of the Mexico-Guatemala border and is usually crossed in an inner tube or rafts pulled by boatmen for a small fee. Fugitives then enter Mexico through a hole in the fence. (Undocumented Mexicans sometimes refer to Central Americans as *mojados doblados* [double wetbacks] because they often cross rivers twice [the Suchiate and the Rio Grande] to get into the United States.)

2. Those who have money often fly directly into a Mexican airport and bribe immigration officials there with twenty-dollar bills (which their travel agents have advised them

to bring along). Other Central Americans who have money, and manage to hold onto it, can make it from the Mexico-Guatemala border to the United States by bus in a week. (Most Central Americans I spoke to in Tucson said it took them fourteen to twenty-five days to get through Mexico. Women with small children, of course, have greater difficulty.) For men, another common method is simply to cross into Chiapas and then get a job as a fieldhand in the banana, cacao, and coffee plantations until they earn enough to move on to another town.

3. See Amnesty International 1990: 14-16. John Crewdson wrote a five-part series for the *New York Times* (January 13-17, 1980) documenting Border Patrol and INS abuses at the border. Some of these abuses included bribe taking, narcotics trafficking, sexual abuse, and beatings.

4. There are roughly two pools of refugees in Tucson's Sanctuary movement: those brought into the United States through the underground and those who have crossed into the country on their own and made their way to Southside Church.

5. There is some resentment directed at this family by other members of the Central American community. The father is referred to as a "paid refugee" by some of the other Central Americans because he was "adopted" and supported financially by Southside.

6. Some Central Americans find their role in this process frustrating because of the nature of these North American audiences, which are usually quite unknowledgeable about Central America. Some expressed dissatisfaction that they never get beyond telling people about the horrors they endured as targets of political oppression, something that stigmatizes them as "educational tools." Moreover, in certain cases North Americans will reject refugee speakers who are prone to give "too much political analysis" in favor of those who will "just tell a good story" about the violence.

7. Refugees sometimes feel that "bad behavior" or "dissent" will result in being cut off from these services; others have left the movement because they have found these resources too limited. Some refugees have attempted to restructure this culture of dependency into a culture of obligation whereby North Americans are expected to atone for the sins of their government by helping out Central American refugees.

8. Most Central Americans in the church sanctuary are single men. Women and families with children tend to be moved into house sanctuaries and often spend several weeks with a particular family. In these cases, certain Anglo families have developed strong ties with Central American families independent of the activities organized through Southside.

9. Central Americans living outside of the church also report to this office. It is quite possible that the history of infiltration in the Sanctuary movement is responsible for why this office acts as a kind of semisurveillance center. Evangelical churches have also tried to recruit Central Americans into their churches and, although the social workers do not prohibit evangelicals from entering Southside, they like to know when they are coming and to whom they are speaking. These two factors, combined with the presence of U.S. Border Patrol cars lurking outside, give Southside Church, and this office in particular, a "watchful" and "wakeful" quality during the week.

10. The inclusion of Spanish in Southside's service strikes one often as "tokenism." The Gospel, after being read in English, is read in Spanish. Southside also usually includes a Spanish hymn in its services, but, as one Sanctuary participant observed, it is most often a traditional WASP hymn translated into Spanish and sung valiantly but timidly by the congregation.

11. For others, retaining linguistic identity is linked to maintaining a semblance of unity within the displaced Central American community. To some extent, this objective clashes with the North American Sanctuary ideology, which underscores intercultural (and, by extension, interlinguistic) contact between Latin Americans and Anglos.

12. In northern Mexico, I heard some Mexicans refer derogatively to a group of black and Hispanic Americans as "gringos." They later explained that the term "gringo" can designate an English-speaker, which for them means an American. Thus, for these Mexicans (as may be the case for the Central American community in Tucson), being an English-speaker has certain political implications. The same is the case, incidentally, in Quebec where French-speakers (francophones) often refer to the rest of Canada as anglophone, or English-speaking. In Québécois nationalist politics, anglophone is frequently a derogatory term, designating the "imperialist enemy."

13. Protestant cultures typically minimize the devotional dimensions of Christianity and emphasize simplicity in church decorations. They frown upon the worship of "idols" in the form of saints or devotional pictures. One statue of a Guatemalan woman, donated to Southside for fund-raising purposes, was transformed by Central American refugees into a Virgin figure, and one frequently sees Guatemalans and Salvadorans praying to her.

14. Gudeman (1988) argues that it is through the cult of the *manda*—in which an individual asks for a favor of a saint in return for the performance of holy acts—that individuals can influence their own salvation. Because the saints are not strictly organized in a hierarchical fashion, a person can "play" the saints—that is, find one who seems sympathetic to one's request and establish a *manda* with that saint.

15. Until the late 1970s, Latin America was almost uniformly Catholic. According to studies conducted by the Catholic church, four hundred Latin Americans convert to Protestant fundamentalist sects each hour; by the year 2000, half the population will have converted (Lernoux 1988: 51).

16. In one village of twenty-five families that I visited in Guatemala (1991), there were seven different fundamentalist sects, which had torn apart the community. Two of the sects were struggling for control of the civil patrols and, by extension, the favor of the military. Fundamentalist sects also use a BCC model of organizing and usually offer members some kind of economic benefits. In Guatemala, they move into remote villages with public-address systems—microphones and speakers—and sponsor daily rallies for prayer and singing. These rallies are so loud that virtually everyone in the village is affected by them. This, in particular, has a uniquely coercive effect. Several scholars see fundamentalism as a way in which the government has divided (and thereby conquered) the Central American population, primarily by taking away Catholicism as common ground for political action. Fundamentalism has indeed splintered kin groups, and it is not unusual for families to be divided along religious lines.

17. Ríos Montt is a member of the California-based Gospel Outreach Church. Most of the evangelical Protestant churches in Latin America are offshoots of U.S. churches.

18. Because many *indígenas* were affiliated with the Catholic church (and in some cases, with armed groups), they became a principal target of the Ríos Montt repression. The association between Catholicism and Guatemala's indigenous population is, in some respects, historically ironic. In the late 1940s and early 1950s, the Catholic church instituted "Acción Católica," a program aimed at purging the Latin American church of syncretic "heathen cults." What started out as purgation, however, developed some progressive elements as priests and nuns encouraged literacy campaigns, local political parties featuring Indian concerns, and native-owned cooperatives (see Warren 1978; Falla 1978; Burgos-Debray 1984).

19. This has been particularly the case with members of the Salvadoran left in Tucson. Certain FMLN factions attempted to organize Tucson's Central American community in the mid-1980s, but failed partly as a result of bitter internal polemics.

20. GAM is the Mutual Support Group, a human rights association in Guatemala consisting of relatives of the disappeared. GAM's objectives are to locate the bodies of the disappeared and bring those who killed them to justice (Manz 1988: 27).

21. Some Anglo Sanctuary workers also have experienced Sanctuary as an "exclusive" organization. I explore this in chapter 8.

22. Interestingly, some Central American women use Sanctuary's maternalism (as a woman-dominated form of power) to criticize their own often marginalized gender roles within the Latin American cult of machismo. Models for critiquing male domination are particularly important for Central American women in the United States who, as refugees, are usually making an asylum claim through their husbands' applications. This dependency makes Central American women acutely subject to their husbands' authority and many remain in abusive relationships partly out of fear that they will not obtain political asylum otherwise. (Central American women, for example, benefit directly from Sanctuary's intolerance of domestic violence.)

23. In 1986, the U.S. Immigration Reform and Control Act (IRCA) implemented employer sanctions in order to quell the hiring of undocumented aliens. Under IRCA, employers are required to keep I-9 forms on all employees hired after November 6, 1986; the form confirms that the employee is legally eligible to work. Failure to file this form can lead to a ten thousand-dollar fine or a jail term. Agencies such as the Center for Immigrants Rights (CIR) in New York, the Central American Refugee Center (CARECEN) in Washington, and the American Friends Service Committee have documented extensive discrimination against people of color (documented and undocumented) as a result of this law. IRCA also offers amnesty to any migrants who can prove that they had been living in the United States since 1982 and to others working in the agricultural sector. One unforeseen consequence of IRCA has been the growth of a massive black market for fake documents; in Los Angeles, for example, green cards, birth certificates, and Social Security cards sell for thirty to fifty dollars.

24. In contrast to the Tucson experience, some Central Americans in New York and San Francisco formed their own Sanctuary committees and played central and influential roles in the structure of these communities.

8. Anatomy of an "Underground" Church

1. Central Americans in Tucson have developed their own underground railroad, but it operates independently from that of Sanctuary's Anglo-only underground group. Several Central Americans I met had moved members of their families into Tucson without the assistance of trsg. In cases involving young children, however, Central Americans seemed more inclined to go to the Sanctuary underground for help.

2. In this chapter I focus on the Sanctuary underground that extended from Mexico to the U.S. border and into Tucson. The larger underground, of course, extended across the United States and into Canada.

3. Pollution, one of the border's most severe problems, has been exacerbated by industrial emissions, agricultural dust, pesticide residues, and the dumping of raw sewage, all of which have contaminated water supplies and resulted in alarming rates of hepatitis, typhoid encephalitis, and various birth defects.

4. The United States has often used Mexico as a source of cheap labor during prosperous times. In 1948, it instituted the notorious Bracero Program by which thousands of Mexicans were allowed to cross into the United States to work in the agricultural sector for cheap wages. (Thousands of illegal crossings were also made into the United States at the same time.) Mexico tried to negotiate some labor protection for its citizens, but the United

States unilaterally decided to open the border up to some seven thousand Mexicans, who were promptly arrested and then "paroled" out to growers. During the the Great Depression, half a million Mexicans were forcibly returned to Mexico, and in 1954 the United States implemented "Operation Wetback," by which it repatriated more than one million Mexicans.

5. Created in 1891, the INS was transferred from the Labor to the Justice Department in 1940. Unauthorized entry into the United States became a misdemeanor in 1929.

6. The program also included putting pressure on the INS's Mexican counterpart (Servicios Migratorios) to apprehend undocumented aliens from Central America and deport them. As a result, the United States set up an intelligence network among the Mexican and Guatemalan governments with the express purpose of halting the flow of Central American migrants. The number of Central Americans apprehended and deported in Mexico went from 14,000 in 1988 to 80,000 in the first six months of 1990 (Hughes 1990: 2). (See also U.S Committee for Refugees [1991: 2-4, 20].)

7. Tucson, in particular, uses the air as a way to intercept drug and alien smugglers. The radar planes are Lockheed P-3s (a four-engine turboprop), the interceptors are Cessna Citation jets (which can land on short runways), and the "attack" helicopters are $16 million Sikorsky Blackhawks (see Langewiesche 1992). The sensors, which detect human presence by weight, movement, and metal content, were used by the United States during the Vietnam War. When activated, the sensor's number lights up on a board in a communications room and Border Patrol agents are dispatched to its location. One of the biggest factors contributing to the ineffectiveness of this system are roving cattle, which frequently trigger the sensors.

8. Civil rights groups have found these developments to be particularly unsavory, fearing that they will lead to a military body with domestic police powers—something that is forbidden by the Comitatus Act of 1878 (Zanger 1990: 4). See Alfaro Clark 1991: 94-105 on frontier violence.

9. The signs feature a silhouetted picture of a running man and a woman holding the hand of a little girl. People crossing the freeway in this manner often hold hands in long chains, which slows them down considerably. In some sections of the highway, the median has become a kind of neutral zone where people camp out, rest, or wait for rides. Journalist William Langewiesche observed people dancing and playing cards on these medians (1992).

10. The Freedom Seder was a liturgical publicity event intended to stress the public transportation of Central American refugees. Underground members felt that Tucson had to emphasize the public nature of what they were doing in order to counter government accusations that they were really a clandestine smuggling ring. The event started at Southside Church, where refugees were picked up and then driven to temple Emanu-El, a Reform synagogue in Tucson. The first Freedom Seder was held just after Jack Elder's arrest in April 1984. Elder was charged with three counts of transporting illegal aliens and faced a maximum of five years in prison on each count. This arrest stimulated serious reflection regarding participation in the Seder. As it turned out, around seventy Guatemalans and Salvadorans attended the Seder, and the car caravan was two miles long.

11. By this time the Sanctuary underground had a person stationed in Mexico who was interviewing prospective refugees from Central America. The code for discussing refugee cases seems to have originated from the Mexican contacts. Unfortunately, underground members in Tucson did not remember much of the code or were unwilling to discuss it; many claimed that it was so elaborate that no one ever managed to use it properly.

12. One Sanctuary participant recalled: "Sometimes we went to the [Sanctuary] trial to set up a run. I mean, you'd go to this trial and everybody was there who would be willing to do things. So it worked real well."

13. Trsg requests that Central Americans sign a slip of paper indicating that they had an appointment with a lawyer. As mentioned earlier, this is part of their legal defense, since transporters can claim they are furthering the legal presence of aliens by taking them to an appointment with a lawyer.

14. Although the National Sanctuary Alliance did not fund El Puente, it assured the group's members that if they were arrested it would provide funds for legal services. El Puente also accepted money from the Central American families they were helping.

15. For Central American families in Tucson, El Puente became a kind of alternative underground: those who had their claims rejected by trsg often turned to the splinter group for assistance.

16. When discussing a particularly high-risk case, someone frequently asks, "Should we say a prayer about this one?" The reference comes from the experience of the Sanctuary trial, and is intended to protect the confidentiality of the case in the event the meeting is being clandestinely tape-recorded. Praying establishes that the group is an explicitly religious one, and government infiltrators are expressly forbidden from taping during religious activities.

17. Although there is considerable concern that the cases discussed be kept confidential, someone usually takes notes as a way of keeping track of the case and recording the details of the case in the event of arrest and trial.

18. In this way, trsg trains new people to submit themselves and their needs (e.g., the need for clarification) to the authority of the group. One speaks in the underground on the basis of knowledge and experience, and newcomers are expected to bow to the seniority of others unless their consciences dictate otherwise.

19. As noted earlier, one of the most suspicious features of the INS agents during the undercover investigation of Sanctuary was their availability to do runs around the clock.

20. Most people in the underground, however, had not gone through an orientation meeting. Mine, for example, occurred four weeks after my first meeting, at which time I was enlightened about the legal ramifications of attending the meetings—a potential of five years in prison for each person one conspires to bring into the United States.

21. In the orientation meeting, it is explained that it is a felony to (1) attend the meeting (conspiracy), (2) counsel someone in Mexico on how to cross the border, (3) drive someone to the Mexico-United States border for the purpose of crossing it without documentation, and (4) facilitate the entrance of an undocumented person into the United States. Trsg argues that driving someone to a lawyer's appointment in the United States is not illegal because it is furthering the legal presence of an alien.

22. Sanctuary work is thus distinguished from civil disobedience ("the attempt to change bad laws") and is characterized as "civil initiative" ("the attempt to get the government to uphold good laws already in existence").

23. This document is also reproduced in Corbett 1991: 171-72. An eighth point, which failed to achieve consensus, was to have Sanctuary volunteers agree that all donations to Sanctuary for legal aid would go to the refugees rather than North Americans (ibid.: 172-73).

24. The UN Refugee Protocol defines a refugee as a person who is outside his or her country of origin and who cannot return "because of well-founded fear of being persecuted for reasons of race, religion, nationality, membership in a particular social group or political opinion." The Geneva Conventions applies to persons residing in areas of armed conflict. The convention aims to protect civilians from the effects of war (including direct military attacks on civilian populations or acts/threats of violence aimed at terrorizing civilian populations). Under this convention, refugees are people who are not protected by any govern-

ment and cannot be returned to their country of origin while the hostilities and armed conflict persist.

25. The "counseling tips" document, however, acknowledges that sometimes refugees would "voluntarily depart rather than create risks for family back home that could result from their exposure during the asylum process."

26. Trsg also does "family reunification" with refugees. Under these guidelines, all dependents under twenty-one, spouses, and dependent parents are eligible for refugee status under the original applicant's claim for political asylum, which is contingent upon the applicant's gaining political asylum. (If the applicant has not received official refugee status and the family is in immediate danger, trsg treats them as a separate case.) The U.S. government does not recognize common-law marriages, and the immigration courts will not even look at a spouse's case (it is usually the wife) if she or he is not legally married to the primary applicant. (Consequently, in some cases trsg has had spouses get married just before crossing the border.) Children have to be the biological or legally adopted offspring of the refugee claimant in order to qualify for family reunification.

27. Although it is dangerous, many Central Americans in Tucson, even those with political asylum, travel back to Central America.

28. The idea here is to avoid having one person commit several felonies. An entire run can involve seven or more felonies per Central American; by using teams, the underground distributes these among several persons.

29. In addition to the surveillance of the Mexican *migra* and the U.S. Border Patrol, transporters face many dangers in the course of a run, including those posed by the vehicles that trsg has to use. Because the INS confiscates the vehicles of any person caught with an undocumented alien, underground members are reluctant to use their own cars for runs. Consequently, over the years, trsg has collected a number of cars that serve as transporting vehicles; often, these are donations made to a church that are on their last legs. Drives through the desert and on Mexico's back roads wreak havoc on the cars' suspension, steering, and overall reliability. ("Lead" cars are discussed in note 34.)

30. No Sanctuary worker has ever been imprisoned by the Mexican police, although some have been stopped by them. The usual procedure is to pay the officer twenty dollars per person in the vehicle. The technique used is to feign confusion, appear to think that some traffic violation has occurred, and suggest that a fine might be paid.

31. Trsg developed other ingenious ways of "interfacing" with local Mexican customs. For example, in Mexico families often name a child after a saint and celebrate the saint's feast day by dressing up their daughter or son in a *habitos* and attending Mass on that date. Many Mexican families in Nogales just slip through the fence with their child and walk up the hill (on the American side) toward the church, unmolested by the Border Patrol. Trsg sometimes had Central American mothers dress their children up in this fashion and cross the border as if they were going to Mass on a saint's feast day.

32. In the early days of the underground, Jim Corbett sometimes took high-risk refugees on two-to-three-day hikes through the desert.

33. Trsg members do not always follow the advice about clear windows but, when possible, use cars with tinted rear windows. (Cars that are completely tinted draw the immediate attention of the Border Patrol, but, because of the intense sunlight, it is not unusual to see tinted rear windows in Arizona.) In earlier days, trsg also used "lead" cars. A third vehicle would leave Nogales first and check if the immigration checkpoint on the highway was in operation. If it were operating, the lead car would go through it, take the next exit and then park the car on the opposite side of the highway several miles in front of the last exit before the checkpoint. The lead car would then create some kind of signal (an elevated hood, for example, meant that the checkpoint was open and to get off the road at the next

exit; a shut hood meant that it was closed and proceed as planned.) During my fieldwork in 1990-91, lead cars were no longer being used because fewer drivers were available.

34. The U.S. side of a run can take as little as three hours, but the Mexico side usually involves two or more days. The coordinator is expected to be available (by phone) at all times in the event of a "hitch." Often the Mexican and American sides of the runs are done on separate days and different coordinators are designated for each part.

35. Trsg transporters have been arrested on three occasions since the eleven indictments in 1985 (on February 2, 1986; June 15, 1987; October 4, 1988) but no charges have been laid.

9. Reconstructing Religious Identity and Practice: Churches, States, and the "Global Order"

1. For discussion of the role of religion in processes of globalization, see Robertson and Chirico 1985; Swatos 1989; Beckford and Luckmann 1989; Beyer 1990; Shupe 1990; Sahliyeh 1990; and Robertson and Garret 1991.

2. In contrast, the fundamentalist churches tended to use the electronic media (radio and television broadcasting) to mobilize support for their agendas.

3. The settlement affected all Guatemalans in the United States as of October 1, 1990, and all Salvadorans in the United States as of September 19, 1990, except for those who were not eligible for asylum because they were aggravated felons under the Immigration and Nationality Act. Prior to the *ABC* agreement, George Bush had also signed (in November 1990) an immigration reform bill that granted refugee status for eighteen months to Salvadorans; the program was called Temporary Protected Status (TPS). Salvadorans became eligible for both TPS and asylum adjudication under *ABC*. The settlement prohibited the asylum officer conducting the de novo adjudication from taking into consideration that the prior decision was a denial, or that the previous recommendation by the State Department's Bureau of Human Rights and Humanitarian Affairs (BHRHA) was not positive.

4. In September 1993, the new system was dealing with a backlog of 300,000 refugee applications, of which 145,000 were from Guatemala and El Salvador (see Conover 1993: 75-76).

5. A group of Sanctuary churches also filed a suit in 1986 against the government for spying on church activities. On December 12, 1990, Judge Roger Strand ruled that the government is constitutionally prohibited from "unbridled and inappropriate covert activity" (see Martínez 1988).

6. See Worsley 1990 on the contrast between liberal and conservative reactions to globalization among religious groups (pp. 387-88).

Bibliography

General Bibliography

Abrams, Philip. 1982. *Historical Sociology.* Ithaca, N.Y.: Cornell University Press.

Abrams, Ray. 1969. *Preachers Present Arms: The Role of the American Churches and Clergy in World Wars I and II, with Some Observations on the War in Vietnam.* Scottsdale, Pa.: Herald Press.

Aguilera Peralta, Gabriel. 1988. "The Hidden War: Guatemala's Counterinsurgency Campaign." In *Crisis in Central America: Regional Dynamics and U.S. Policy in the 1980s,* ed. Nora Hamilton, Jeffrey A. Frieden, Linda Fuller, and Manuel Pastor Jr. Boulder, Colo.: Westview Press.

Ahlstrom, Sidney. 1978. "The Radical Turn of Theology and Ethics: Why It Occurred in the 1960s." In *Religion and American History: Interpretive Essays,* ed. John M. Mulder and John F. Wilson. Englewood Cliffs, N.J.: Prentice Hall.

——. 1972. *A Religious History of the American People.* New Haven: Yale University Press.

Alfaro Clark, Victor. 1991. "La violencia fronteriza." In *Audencia informativa sobre derechos humanos de los trabajadores migratorios mexicanos.* Tijuana: Senado de la República.

Aman, Kenneth. 1984. "Marxism(s) in Liberation Theology." *Cross Currents* 34 (winter): 427-38.

American Friends Service Report. 1990. *Human Rights at the Border.* Philadelphia: American Friends Service Committee.

Amnesty International. 1990. *Reasonable Fear: Human Rights and United States Refugee Policy.* New York: Amnesty International USA.

Annis, Sheldon. 1987. *God and Production in a Guatemalan Town.* Austin: University of Texas Press.

Apter, David. 1984. *Against the State: Politics and Social Protest in Japan.* Cambridge, Mass.: Harvard University Press.

Aronoff, Myron J., ed. 1984. *Religion and Politics.* New Brunswick, N.J.: Transaction Books.

Asad, Talal. 1987. "Ritual and Discipline in Medieval Christian Monasticism." *Economy and Society* 16: 159-203.

———. 1983. "Anthropological Conceptions of Religion: Reflections on Geertz." *Man* 18: 237-59.

Bandera, Armando. 1975. *La iglesia ante el proceso de liberación*. Madrid: La Editorial Católica.

Barbe, Dominique. 1987. *Grace and Power: Base Communities and Nonviolence in Brazil*. Maryknoll, N.Y.: Orbis Books.

Barreiro, Alvaro. 1982. *Basic Ecclesial Communities: The Evangelization of the Poor*. Maryknoll, N.Y.: Orbis Books.

Bax, Mart. 1991. "Religious Regimes and State Formation: Toward a Research Perspective." In *Religious Regimes and State Formation*, ed. Eric Wolf. Albany: State University of New York Press.

Beckford, James A. 1987. "The Restoration of 'Power' to the Sociology of Religion." In *Church-State Relations: Tensions and Transitions*, ed. Thomas Robbins and Roland Robertson. New Brunswick, N.J.: Transaction Books.

Beckford, James A., and T. Luckmann, eds. 1989. *The Changing Face of Religion*. London: Sage.

Bellah, Robert. 1970. *Beyond Belief*. New York: Harper & Row.

———. 1967. "Civil Religion in America." In *Religion in America*, ed. W. G. McLoughlin and R. N. Bellah. Boston: Beacon Press.

Berger, Peter. 1968. *The Sacred Canopy*. New York: Doubleday.

Berryman, Phillip. 1985. *Inside Central America*. New York: Pantheon Books.

———. 1984. *The Religious Roots of Rebellion: Christians in Central American Revolutions*. Maryknoll, N.Y.: Orbis Books.

Beyer, Peter F. 1990. "Privatization and the Public Influence of Religion in Global Society." In *Global Culture: Nationalism, Globalization and Modernity*, ed. Mike Featherstone. London: SAGE Publications.

Bloch, Ruth M. 1990. "Religion and Ideological Change in the American Revolution." In *Religion and American Politics: From the Colonial Period to the 1980s*, ed. Mark A. Noll. New York: Oxford University Press.

Boff, Leonardo. 1987. *Introducing Liberation Theology*. Maryknoll, N.Y.: Orbis Books.

Boggs, Carl. 1986. *Social Movements and Political Power: Emerging Forms of Radicalism in the West*. Philadelphia: Temple University Press.

Bonino, José. 1975. *Doing Theology in a Revolutionary Situation*. Maryknoll, N.Y.: Orbis Books.

Bossy, John. 1970. "The Counter-Reformation and the People of Catholic Europe." *Past and Present* 47: 51-70.

Bourdieu, P. 1977. *Outline of a Theory of Practice*. New York: Cambridge University Press.

Bright, Charles, and Michael Geyer. 1987. "For a Unified History of the World in the Twentieth Century." *Radical History Review* 39: 69-91.

Brow, James. 1988. "Representations of Authority and Justice." *American Ethnologist* 15: 311-27.

Burgos-Debray, E. 1984. *I, Rigoberta Menchú: An Indian Woman in Guatemala*. London: Verso.

Burke, Patrick. 1987. "Religion and Politics in the United States." In *Movement and Issues in World Religions: A Sourcebook of Developments since 1945*, ed. Charles Wei-hsun Fu and Gerhard E. Spiegler. New York: Greenwood Press.

Burridge, K. 1985. "Millennialism and the Recreation of History." In *Religion, Rebellion, Revolution*, ed. Bruce Lincoln. London: Macmillan.

_____. 1969. *New Heaven, New Earth: A Study of Millenarian Activities.* New York: Schocken Books.

Cano, Luis Carlos. 1991. "Veteranos de Vietnam entrenan a policías fronterizos de E.U." *El Universal*, May 13.

Carmack, R. M., ed. 1988. *Harvest of Violence: The Maya Indians and the Guatemalan Crisis.* Norman: University of Oklahoma Press.

Chidester, David. 1988. *Patterns of Power: Religion and Politics in American Culture.* Englewood Cliffs, N.J.: Prentice Hall.

Chopp, Rebecca S. 1986. *The Praxis of Suffering: An Interpretation of Liberation and Political Theologies.* Maryknoll, N.Y.: Orbis Books.

Cohen, N. 1957. *In Pursuit of the Millennium.* London: Secker and Warburg.

Colson, E. 1962. *The Plateau Tonga of Northern Rhodesia: Social and Religious Studies.* Manchester: Manchester University Press.

Comaroff, Jean, and John Comaroff. 1991. *Of Revelation and Revolution: Christianity and Consciousness in South Africa*, vol 1. Chicago: University of Chicago Press.

_____. 1986. "Christianity and Colonialism in South Africa." *American Ethnologist* 13: 1-22.

Comblin, José. 1979. *The Church and the National Security State.* Maryknoll, N.Y.: Orbis Books.

Conover, Ted. 1993. "The United States of Asylum." *New York Times Magazine*, September 19, 1993.

_____. 1987. *Coyotes: A Journey through the Secret World of America's Illegal Aliens.* New York: Vintage Books.

Cook, Guillermo. 1985. *The Expectation of the Poor: Latin American Basic Ecclesial Communities in Protestant Perspective.* Maryknoll, N.Y.: Orbis Books.

Coste, René. 1985. *Marxist Analysis and Christian Faith.* Maryknoll, N.Y.: Orbis Books.

Crahan, Margaret. 1988. "A Multitude of Voices: Religion and the Central American Crisis." In *Crisis in Central America: Regional Dynamics and U.S. Policy in the 1980s*, ed. Nora Hamilton, Jeffrey A. Frieden, Linda Fuller, and Manuel Pastor Jr. Boulder, Colo.: Westview Press.

Davidson, Miriam. 1990. "The Mexican Border War." *Nation*, November 12.

Davis, John, ed. 1982. *Religious Organization and Religious Experience.* ASA Monograph 21. London and New York: Academic Press.

Davis, Mike, and Michael Sprinker. 1988. *Reshaping the U.S. Left: Popular Struggles in the 1980s.* London: Verso.

Davis, S., and J. Hodson. 1982. *Witness to Political Violence in Guatemala.* Boston: Oxfam America Impact Audit no. 2.

DeHainaut, Raymond K. 1988. "The FBI's Political Intimidation." *Christian Century*, April 27: 420-21.

Diskin, Martin, and Kenneth Sharpe. 1986. "El Salvador." In *Confronting Revolution: Security through Diplomacy in Central America*, ed. Morris Blachman, William M. LeoGrande, and Kenneth E. Sharpe. New York: Pantheon Books.

Douglas, Mary. 1982. "The Effects of Modernization on Religious Change." *Daedalus* (winter): 1-19.

_____. 1966. *Purity and Danger: An Analysis of Concepts of Pollution and Taboo.* New York: Praeger

Edel, Wilbur. 1987. *Defenders of the Faith: Religion and Politics from the Pilgrim Fathers to Ronald Reagan.* New York: Praeger.

Epstein, Barbara. 1991. *Political Protest and Cultural Revolution: Nonviolent Direct Action in the 1970s and 1980s.* Berkeley: University of California Press.

Evans-Pritchard, E. E. 1965. *Theories of Primitive Religion.* Oxford: Oxford University Press (Clarendon).

Fabian, Johannes. 1979. "The Anthropology of Religious Movements: From Explanation to Interpretation." *Social Research* 46: 4-35.

Fagan, Patricia Weiss. 1988. "Central American Refugees and U.S. Policy." In *Crisis in Central America: Regional Dynamics and U.S. Policy in the 1980s*, ed. Nora Hamilton, Jeffrey A. Frieden, Linda Fuller, and Manuel Pastor Jr. Boulder, Colo.: Westview Press.

Falla, R. 1978. *Quiché Rebelde: Estudio de un movimiento de conversión religiosa, rebelde a las creencias tradicionales, en San Antonio Ilótenango, Quiché (1948-1970).* Guatemala City: Editorial Universitaria.

Fernandez, James. 1979. "On the Notion of Religious Movements." *Social Research* 46: 36-62.

Firth, Raymond. 1981. "Spiritual Aroma: Religion and Politics." *American Anthropologist* 83: 582-601.

_____. 1972. "The Skeptical Anthropologist? Social Anthropology and Marxist Views on Society." *Proceedings of the British Academy* 58: 3-39.

_____. 1964. *Elements of Social Organization.* Boston: Beacon Press.

Frederick, Howard. 1988. "Media Strategies Stifle Democracy in Central America." *Media Development* 2: 32-38.

Freire, Paulo. 1972. *Pedagogy of the Oppressed.* New York: Herder and Herder.

Garma Navarro, Carlos. 1984. "Liderazgo protestante en una lucha campesina en México." *América Indígena* 44: 127-41.

Geertz, C. 1965. "Religion as a Cultural System." In *Anthropological Approaches to the Study of Religion*, ed. Michael Banton. London: Tavistock Publications.

_____. 1964. " 'Internal Conversion' in Contemporary Bali." Reprinted in *Reader in Comparative Religion*, ed. W. A. Lessa and E. Z. Vogt. 4th ed. (1979). New York: Harper & Row.

Giddens, Anthony. 1984. *The Constitution of Society: Introduction to the Theory of Structuration.* Berkeley: University of California Press.

Gill, Leslie. 1990. "Like a Veil to Cover Them: Women and the Pentecostal Movement in La Paz." *American Ethnologist* 17: 708-21.

Gillet, Richard W. 1986. "The Church Acts for Economic Justice." In *Churches in Struggle: Liberation Theologies and Social Change in North America*, ed. William K. Tabb. New York: Monthly Review Press.

_____. 1984. "Jailing Grand-Jury Resisters: Implications for Church Activists." *Christian Century*, September 26: 872-75.

Glazier, Stephen, ed. 1980. *Perspectives on Pentecostalism: Case Studies from the Caribbean and Latin America.* Washington, D.C.: University Press of America.

Gleason, Philip. 1981. "Americans All: World War II and the Shaping of Modern Identity." *Review of Politics* (October): 483-518.

Gluckman, Max. 1963. "Rituals of Rebellion in South East Africa." In *Order and Rebellion in Tribal Africa.* New York: Free Press of Glencoe.

Gomez, Leonel. 1984. "Feet People." In *Central America: Anatomy of Conflict*, ed. Robert S. Leiken. New York: Pergamon Press.

Goody, Jack. 1983. *The Development of the Family and Marriage in Europe.* London: Cambridge University Press.

Gorostiaga, Xabier, and Peter Marchetti. 1988. "The Central American Economy: Conflict and Crisis." In *Crisis in Central America: Regional Dynamics and U.S. Policy in the 1980s*, ed. Nora Hamilton, Jeffrey A. Frieden, Linda Fuller, and Manuel Pastor Jr. Boulder, Colo.: Westview Press.

Gudeman, Stephen. 1988. "The *Manda* and the Mass." *Journal of Latin American Lore* 14: 17-32.

Guth, James L., Ted G. Jelen, Lyman A. Kellstedt, Corwin E. Smidt, and Kenneth P. Wald. 1988. "The Politics of Religion in America: Issues for Investigation." *American Politics Quarterly* 16 (3): 357-97.

Gutiérrez, Gustavo. 1983. *The Power of the Poor in History*. Maryknoll, N.Y.: Orbis Books.

————. 1973. *A Theology of Liberation*. Maryknoll, N.Y.: Orbis Books.

Hamilton, Nora, and Manuel Pastor Jr. 1988. "Introduction." In *Crisis in Central America: Regional Dynamics and U.S. Policy in the 1980s*, ed. Nora Hamilton, Jeffrey A. Frieden, Linda Fuller, and Manuel Pastor Jr. Boulder, Colo.: Westview Press.

Hammond, Philip. 1974. "Religious Pluralism and Durkheim's Integration Thesis." In *Changing Perspectives in the Scientific Study of Religion*, ed. Allan Eister. New York: John Wiley & Sons.

Handy, Jim. 1984. *Gift of the Devil: A History of Guatemala*. Boston: South End Press.

Harding, Susan. 1987. "Convicted by the Holy Spirit: The Rhetoric of Fundamental Baptist Conversion." *American Ethnologist* 14: 167-81.

Harrison, Beverly W. 1986. "Agendas for a New Theological Ethic." In *Churches in Struggle: Liberation Theologies and Social Change in North America*, ed. William K. Tabb. New York: Monthly Review Press.

Hebdige, Dick. 1979. *Subculture: The Meaning of Style*. London and New York: Methuen.

Herberg, W. 1956. *Protestant, Catholic, Jew: An Essay in American Religious Sociology*. New York: Anchor Books.

Higgins, Michael James. 1990. "Martyrs and Virgins: Popular Religion in Mexico and Nicaragua." In *Class, Politics, and Popular Religion in Mexico and Central America*. Washington, D.C.: Society for Latin American Anthropology Publication Series, vol. 10.

Hobsbawm, E. J. 1959. *Primitive Rebels: Studies in Archaic Forms of Social Movement in the 19th and 20th Centuries*. Manchester: Manchester University Press.

Hughes, Candice. 1990. "Deportation Crackdown Produces U.S. Delight, Local Fear." *Arizona Daily Star*, September 30.

Hughey, Michael W. 1983. *Civil Religion and Moral Order: Theoretical and Historical Dimensions*. Westport, Conn.: Greenwood Press.

Johnston, David. 1992. "Rise in Crossings Spurs New Actions to Seal U.S. Border." *New York Times*, February 9.

Kahn, Robert. 1992. "New Documents Detail FBI Spying on Refugee Advocates." *National Catholic Reporter*, March 13.

————. 1990. "Use U.S. Foreign Policy as Your Guide, INS Video Tells Workers." *National Catholic Reporter*, June 1.

Keim, Albert N., and Grant M. Stoltzfus. 1988. *The Politics of Conscience: The Historical Peace Churches and America at War, 1917-1955*. Scottsdale, Pa.: Herald Press.

Kelly, Dean M., ed. 1986. *Government Intervention in Religious Affairs*. New York: Pilgrim Press.

Kohn, Stephen M. 1986. *Jailed for Peace: The History of American Draft Law Violators, 1658-1985*. Westport, Conn.: Greenwood Press.

Krasner, Stephen. 1979. *Defending the National Interests: Raw Materials Investments and U.S. Foreign Policy*. Princeton, N.J.: Princeton University Press.

Laclau, Ernesto, and Chantal Mouffe. 1985. *Hegemony and Socialist Strategy: Toward a Radical Democratic Politics*. London: Verso.

Lan, David. 1985. *Guns and Rain: Guerrillas and Spirit Mediums in Zimbabwe*. London, Berkeley, Calif.: John Currey; University of California Press.

Lancaster, Roger N. 1988. *Thanks to God and the Revolution: Popular Religion and Class Consciousness in the New Nicaragua.* New York: Columbia University Press.

Langewiesche, William. 1992. "The Border." *The Atlantic* 269 (May): 53-92.

Lanternari, Vittorio. 1960 [1963]. *The Religions of the Oppressed: A Study of Modern Messianic Cults.* New York: Signet Classics.

Leach, E. R. 1954. *Political Systems of Highland Burma.* London: G. Bell & Sons.

Lenski, G. H. 1963. *The Religious Factor: A Sociological Study of Religion's Impact on Politics, Economics and Family Life.* New York: Doubleday.

LeoGrande, William M., Morris Blachman, and Kenneth E. Sharpe. 1986. "Grappling with Central America: From Carter to Reagan." In *Confronting Revolution: Security through Diplomacy in Central America*, ed. Morris Blachman, William M. LeoGrande, and Kenneth E. Sharpe. New York: Pantheon Books.

Lernoux, Penny. 1989. *People of God: The Struggle for World Catholicism.* New York: Viking.

———. 1988. "The Fundamentalist Surge in Latin America." *Christian Century*, January 20: 51-54.

———. 1980. *Cry of the People: The Struggle for Human Rights in Latin America. The Catholic Church in Conflict with U.S. Policy.* London and New York: Penguin Books.

Lessa, William, and Evon Z. Vogt, eds. 1979. *Reader in Comparative Religion.* 4th ed. New York: Harper & Row.

Lincoln, Bruce. 1985a. "Introduction." In *Religion, Rebellion, Revolution*, ed. Bruce Lincoln. London: Macmillan.

———. 1985b. "Notes Toward a Theory of Religion and Revolution." In *Religion, Rebellion, Revolution*, ed. Bruce Lincoln. London: Macmillan.

Loescher, Gil, and John A. Scanlan, eds. 1986. *Calculated Kindness: Refugees and America's Half-Open Door, 1945-Present.* New York: Free Press.

Lynch, John. 1988. "Power in the Church: An Historico-Critical Survey." *Concilium* 197: 13-22.

MacGaffey, Wyatt. 1981. "African Ideology and Belief: A Survey." *African Studies Review* 24: 227-74.

Manz, Beatrice. 1988. *Refugees of a Hidden War: The Aftermath of Counterinsurgency in Guatemala.* Albany: State University of New York Press.

Marrus, Michael R., and Anna C. Bramwell. 1988. *Refugees in the Age of Total War.* London: Unwin Hyman.

Martinez, Demetria. 1989. "Group Documents Border Patrol Abuses." *National Catholic Reporter*, February 24.

Martínez, Oscar J. 1988. *Troublesome Border.* Tucson: University of Arizona Press.

McGovern, Arthur F. 1989. *Liberation Theology and Its Critics.* Maryknoll, N.Y.: Orbis Books.

McHugh, George. 1983. *An Analysis of U.S. INS Statistics on Refugees from El Salvador.* Dublin, Calif.: Social Justice Committee of St. Raymond's Catholic Church, July 22.

Mead, Sidney. 1975. *The Nation with the Soul of a Church.* New York: Harper Forum Books.

Melville, Thomas R. 1983. "The Catholic Church in Guatemala, 1944-1982." *Cultural Survival Quarterly* 7: 23-27.

Middleton, John. 1960. *Lugbara Religion: Ritual and Authority among an East African People.* Washington, D.C.: Smithsonian Institute.

Miller, Perry. 1961. "From the Covenant to the Revival." In *The Shaping of American Religion*, ed. James W. Smith and A. Leland Jamison. Princeton, N.J.: Princeton University Press.

Miller, Tom. 1981. *On the Border: Portraits of America's Southwestern Frontier.* Tucson: University of Arizona Press.

Miller, R. T., and R. B. Flowers. 1987. *Toward Benevolent Neutrality: Church, State and the Supreme Court.* Waco, Tex.: Baylor University Press.

Miranda, José. 1980. *Marx against the Marxists.* Maryknoll, N.Y.: Orbis Books.

Morris, Brian. 1987. *Anthropological Studies of Religion: An Introductory Text.* New York: Cambridge University Press.

Moyser, George. 1991. "Politics and Religion in the Modern World: An Overview." In *Politics and Religion in the Modern World*, ed. George Moyser. London and New York: Routledge.

Murrin, John M. 1990. "Religion and Politics in America from the First Settlements to the Civil War." In *Religion and American Politics: From the Colonial Period to the 1980s*, ed. Mark A. Noll. New York: Oxford University Press.

Mydans, Seth. 1991. "One Last Deadly Crossing for Illegal Aliens." *New York Times*, January 7.

Nash, J. 1979. *We Eat the Mines and the Mines Eat Us.* New York: Columbia University Press.

Nichols, J. Bruce. 1988. *The Uneasy Alliance: Religion, Refugee Work, and U.S. Foreign Policy.* New York: Oxford University Press.

Ortner, Sherry. 1989. *High Religion: A Cultural and Political History of Sherpa Buddhism.* Princeton, N.J.: Princeton University Press.

———. 1984. "Theory in Anthropology since the Sixties." *Comparative Studies in Society and History* 26: 126-66.

Osterweis, Rollin G. 1953. *Three Centuries of New Haven, 1638-1938.* New Haven: Yale University Press.

Panikkar, Raimundo. 1983. "Religion or Politics: The Western Dilemma." In *Religion and Politics in the Modern World*, ed. Peter H. Merkl and Ninian Smart. New York: New York University Press.

Pearce, Jenny. 1986. *Promised Land: Peasant Rebellion in Chalatenango, El Salvador.* London: Latin America Bureau.

Peck, Jane Cary. 1984. "Reflections from Costa Rica on Protestants' Dependence and Non-liberative Social Function." *Journal of Ecumenical Studies* 21: 181-98.

Pessar, Patricia R. 1988. *When Borders Don't Divide: Labor Migration and Refugee Movements in the Americas.* New York: Center for Migration Studies.

Pfeffer, Leo. 1974. "The Legitimation of Marginal Religions in the United States." In *Religious Movements in Contemporary America*, ed. Irving Zaretsyk and Mark Leone. Princeton, N.J.: Princeton University Press.

Quarles van Ufford, Philip, and Matthew Schoffeleers. 1988. "Toward a Rapprochement of Anthropology and Development Studies." In *Religion and Development: Toward an Integrated Approach*, ed. Philip Quarles van Ufford and Matthew Schoffeleers. Amsterdam: Free University Press.

Rahman, Fazlur. 1986. "Islam and Political Action: Politics in the Service of Religion." In *Cities of God: Faith, Politics and Pluralism in Judaism, Christianity and Islam*, ed. Nigel Biggar, Jamie S. Scott, and William Schweiker. New York: Greenwood Press.

Ranger, Terrence. 1987. "An Africanist Comment." *American Ethnologist* 14: 182-85.

———. 1982. "The Death of Chaminuka: Spirit Mediums, Nationalism, and the Guerilla War in Zimbabwe." *African Affairs* 81: 349-69.

Robertson, Roland. 1987. "General Considerations in the Study of Contemporary Church-State Relationships." In *Church-State Relations: Tensions and Transitions*, ed. Thomas Robbins and Roland Robertson. New Brunswick, N.J.: Transaction Books.

Robertson, Roland, and JoAnn Chirico. 1985. "Humanity, Globalization, and Worldwide Religious Resurgence: A Theoretical Exploration." *Sociological Analysis* 46: 219-42.

Robertson, Roland, and William R. Garrett, eds. 1991. *Religion and Global Order*. New York: Paragon House.

Rohter, Larry. 1990. "Mexico's South Fights Tide of U.S.-Bound Aliens." *New York Times*, April 10.

Ross, John. 1987. "Refugees Meet Brutality, Extortion on Mexican Border." *Latin America Press*, September 10.

Sahlins, M. 1981. *Historical Metaphors and Mythical Realities*. Ann Arbor: University of Michigan Press.

Sahliyeh, Emile. 1990. "Religious Resurgence and Political Modernization." In *Religious Resurgence and Politics in the Contemporary World*, ed. Emile Sahliyeh. Albany: State University of New York Press.

Saltzman, Philip Carl. 1988. "Fads and Fashions in Anthropology." *Anthropology Newsletter* 29.

Santiago, Daniel. 1990. "The Aesthetics of Terror, the Hermeneutics of Death." *America*, March 24.

Saunders, George R. 1988. "Introduction." In *Culture and Christianity: The Dialectics of Transformation*, ed. George R. Saunders. New York: Greenwood Press.

Scott, James C. 1985. *Weapons of the Weak: Everyday Forms of Peasant Resistance*. New Haven: Yale University Press.

Seidman, Steven. 1990. "Substantive Debates: Moral Order and Social Crisis—Perspectives on Modern Culture." In *Culture and Society: Contemporary Debates*, ed. Jeffrey C. Alexander and Steven Seidman. New York: Cambridge University Press.

Semonche, John E. 1986. *Religion and Constitutional Government in the United States: A Historical Overview with Sources*. Carrboro, N.C.: Signal Books.

Sharpe, Kenneth E. 1988. "U.S. Policy toward Central America: The Post-Vietnam Formula under Siege." In *Crisis in Central America: Regional Dynamics and U.S. Policy in the 1980s*, ed. Nora Hamilton, Jeffrey A. Frieden, Linda Fuller, and Manuel Pastor Jr. Boulder, Colo.: Westview Press.

Sheldon, Garrett W. 1990. *Religion and Politics: Major Thinkers on the Relation of Church and State*. New York: Peter Lang.

Shupe, Anson. 1990. "The Stubborn Persistence of Religion in the Global Arena." In *Religious Resurgence and Politics in the Contemporary World*, ed. Emile Sahliyeh. Albany: State University of New York Press.

Simpson, John H. 1991. "Globalization and Religion: Themes and Prospects." In *Religion and Global Order*, ed. Roland Robertson and William R. Garrett. New York: Paragon House.

Skocpol, Theda. 1985. "Bringing the State Back In: Strategies of Analysis in Current Research." In *Bringing the State Back In*, ed. Peter Evans, Dietrich Rueschemeyer, and Theda Skocpol. New York: Cambridge University Press.

Smith, Carol A. 1984. "Local History in Global Context: Social and Economic Transitions in Western Guatemala." *Comparative Studies in History and Society* 26: 193-228.

Smith, Carol A., and Jeff Boyer. 1987. "Central America since 1979: Part 1." *Annual Review of Anthropology* 16: 197-221.

_____. 1988. "Central America since 1979: Part 2." *Annual Review of Anthropology* 17: 331-64.

Smith, Christian. 1991. *The Emergence of Liberation Theology: Radical Religion and Social Movement Theory*. Chicago: University of Chicago Press.

Smith, Peter. 1986. "The Origins of Crisis." In *Confronting Revolution: Security through Diplomacy in Central America*, ed. Morris Blachman, William M. LeoGrande, and Kenneth E. Sharpe. New York: Pantheon Books.

Sonnichsen, C. L. 1982. *Tucson: The Life and Times of an American City*. Norman: University of Oklahoma Press.

Stanley, William Deane. 1987. "Economic Migrants or Refugees from Violence? A Time-Series Analysis of Salvadoran Migration to the United States." *Latin American Research Review* 22: 132-54.

Stephen, Lynn, and James Dow. 1990. "The Dynamics of Religion in Middle American Communities." (Also "Introduction.") In *Class, Politics, and Popular Religion in Mexico and Central America*. Washington, D.C.: Society for Latin American Anthropology Publication Series, vol. 10.

Stoll, David. 1990. *Is Latin America Turning Protestant? The Politics of Evangelical Growth*. Berkeley: University of California Press.

Stout, Harry S. 1990. "Rhetoric and Reality in the Early Republic: The Case of the Federalist Clergy." In *Religion and American Politics: From the Colonial Period to the 1980s*, ed. Mark A. Noll. New York: Oxford University Press.

_____. 1986. *The New England Soul: Preaching and Religious Culture in Colonial New England*. New York: Oxford University Press.

Swatos, William H., ed. 1989. *Religious Politics in Global and Comparative Perspective*. Westport, Conn.: Greenwood Press.

Tabb, William K. 1986. "Introduction: Transformative Theologies and the Commandment to Do Justice." In *Churches in Struggle: Liberation Theologies and Social Change in North America*, ed. William K. Tabb. New York: Monthly Review Press.

Taussig, Michael T. 1980. *The Devil and Commodity Fetishism in South America*. Chapel Hill: University of North Carolina Press.

Thompson, Kenneth. 1986. *Beliefs and Ideology*. London and New York: Tavistock Publications.

Thrupp, Silvia. 1962. *Millennial Dreams in Action*. The Hague: Mouton & Co.

Trudeau, Robert, and Lars Schoultz. 1986. "Guatemala." In *Confronting Revolution: Security through Diplomacy in Central America*, ed. Morris Blachman, William M. LeoGrande, and Kenneth E. Sharpe. New York: Pantheon Books.

Turner, Victor. 1974. *Dramas, Fields and Metaphors: Symbolic Action in Human Society*. Ithaca, N.Y.: Cornell University Press.

_____. 1969. *The Ritual Process: Structure and Anti-Structure*. Chicago: Aldine Publishing Co.

_____. 1964. "Betwixt and Between: The Liminal Period in Rites of Passage." Reprinted in *Reader in Comparative Religion*, ed. William A. Lessa and Evon Z. Vogt. 4th ed. (1979). New York: Harper & Row.

Ulin, Robert C. 1984. *Understanding Cultures: Perspectives in Anthropology and Social Theory*. Austin: University of Texas Press.

U.S. Committee for Refugees. 1991. *Running the Gauntlet: The Central American Journey in Mexico*. Washington, D.C.: American Council for Nationalities Service.

Wald, Kenneth D. 1991. "Social Change and Political Response: The Silent Religious Cleavage in North America." In *Politics and Religion in the Modern World*, ed. George Moyser. London and New York: Routledge.

_____. 1990. "The New Christian Right in American Politics: Mobilization amid Modernization." In *Religious Resurgence and Politics in the Contemporary World*, ed. Emile Sahliyeh. Albany: State University of New York Press.

_____. 1987. *Religion and Politics in the United States*. New York: St. Martin's Press.

Wallace, Anthony. 1966. *Religion: An Anthropological Approach*. New York: Random House.

Warner, William Lloyd. 1961. *Family of God: A Symbolic Study of Christian Life in America*. New Haven: Yale University Press.

Warren, Kay B. 1978. *Symbolism of Subordination: Indian Identity in a Guatemalan Town*. Austin: University of Texas Press.

Washington Post. 1988. "FBI Reportedly Probed Groups that Opposed Reagan Policies." Reprinted in *Hartford Courant*, January 1, 1988.

Weber, David R., ed. 1978. *Civil Disobedience in America: A Documentary History*. Ithaca, N.Y.: Cornell University Press.

Weber, Paul J. 1989. "Strict Neutrality: The Next Step in Religion in First Amendment Development?" In *American Politics*, ed. Charles W. Dunn. Washington, D.C.: Congressional Quarterly Press.

Weller, Robert P. 1985. "Bandits, Beggars and Ghosts: The Failure of State Control over Religious Interpretation in Taiwan." *American Ethnologist* 12: 46-61.

Whittier, Charles H. 1984. *Religion and Public Policy: Background and Issues in the 1980s*. Congressional Research Service Report No. 84-104 GOV 17 (October).

Williams, Raymond. 1981. *The Sociology of Culture*. New York: Schocken Books.

Wilson, J. F., and D. Drakeman. 1987. "Introduction." In *Church and State in American History: The Burden of Religious Pluralism*, ed. John F. Wilson and Donald L. Drakeman. Boston: Beacon Press.

Wilson, John F. 1990. "Religion, Government and Power in the New American Nation." In *Religion and American Politics: From the Colonial Period to the 1980s*, ed. Mark A. Noll. New York: Oxford University Press.

Wittner, Lawrence S. 1984. *Rebels against the War: The American Peace Movement, 1933-1983*. Philadelphia: Temple University Press.

Wolf, Eric, ed. 1991. *Religious Regimes and State Formation: Perspectives from European Ethnology*. Albany: State University Press of New York.

_____. 1984. *Religion, Power and Protest in Local Communities: The Northern Shore of the Mediterranean*. New York, Berlin: Monton.

Woods, James E. Jr. 1983. "Christian Faith and Society." In *Religion and Politics*, ed. James E. Woods Jr. Waco, Tex.: Baylor University Press.

_____. 1969. "Conscientious Objection and the State." *Journal of Church and State* 2 (3): 373-82.

Worsley, Peter. 1990. "Models of the Modern World System." In *Global Culture: Nationalism, Globalization and Modernity*, ed. Mike Featherstone. London: SAGE Publications.

_____. 1957 [1968]. *The Trumpet Shall Sound: A Study of Cargo Cults in Melanesia*. New York: Schocken Books.

Wuthnow, Robert. 1988. *The Structuring of American Religion: Society and Faith since World War II*. Princeton, N.J.; Princeton University Press.

Yanagisako, Sylvia. 1977. "Women-Centered Kin Networks in Urban, Bilateral Kinship." *American Ethnologist* 3: 207-26.

Zanger, Maggy. 1990. "Planes, Training and Automatic Weapons." *Tucson Weekly*, April 4.

Sanctuary Bibliography

Books/Journal Articles/Government Documents

Alles, Gregory D. 1987. "Sanctuary." In *The Encyclopedia of Religion*, ed. Mircea Eliade. vol. 13. New York: Macmillan.

Atkins, Henry. 1986. "Options Narrow for Sanctuary." *The Witness* 69 (June).

Bassett, Carol Ann. 1983. "Traveling with the Salvadoran Refugees." *Denver Post Magazine*, August 7.

Bau, Ignatius. 1985. *This Ground Is Holy: Church Sanctuary and Central American Refugees*. New York, Mahwah, N.J.: Paulist Press.

Bellamy, John. 1973. *Crime and Public Order in the Latter Middle Ages*. London, Toronto: Routledge & Kegan Paul, University of Toronto Press.

Bosniak, Lindie, and Jane Rasmussen. 1984. "Crackdown on Sanctuary: The Underground Railroad Surfaces." *Report on the Americas*, May/June: 4-7.

Brom, Thomas. 1983. "Church Sanctuary for Salvadorans." *California Lawyer*, July.

Burks, Paul. 1985. "This Is Sanctuary: A Reformation in Our Time." In *Sequoia: The Church At Work*. n.p.: Northern California Ecumenical Council.

Chicago Religious Task Force. 1985. "Organization, Purpose, Faith Commitment and Purpose of CRTF." *Basta!* January.

Cohn, Haim Herman. 1972a. "Blood Avenger." In *Encyclopaedia Judaica*. Jerusalem: Keter Publishing House.

_____. 1972b. "City of Refuge." In *Encyclopaedia Judaica*. Jerusalem: Keter Publishing House.

Corbett, Jim. 1991. *Goatwalking: A Guide to Wildland Living, a Quest for the Peaceable Kingdom*. New York: Viking.

_____. 1986. "Borders and Crossings." Vols. 1 and 2. Tucson, Ariz.: Xeroxed pamphlet.

_____. 1985. "The Covenant as Sanctuary." In *Sanctuary: A Resource Guide for Understanding and Participating in the Central American Refugee Struggle*, ed. Gary MacEoin. San Francisco: Harper & Row.

Coutin, Susan B. 1993. *The Culture of Protest: Religious Activism and the U.S. Sanctuary Movement*. San Francisco: Westview Press.

Cox, Charles. 1911. *The Sanctuaries and Sanctuary Seekers of Medieval England*. London: George Allen & Sons.

Crittenden, Ann. 1988. *Sanctuary: A Story of American Conscience and Laws in Collision*. New York: Weidenfeld & Nicolson.

Davidson, Miriam. 1988. *Convictions of the Heart: Jim Corbett and the Sanctuary Movement*. Tucson: University of Arizona Press.

Fitzsimmons, Kevin J. 1984. "American Sanctuary." *Los Angeles Reader*, May 11.

Gillet, Richard W. 1984. "Jailing Grand-Jury Resisters: Implications for Church Activists." *Christian Century*, September 26.

Golden, Renny, and Michael McConnell. 1986. *Sanctuary: The New Underground Railroad*. Maryknoll, N.Y.: Orbis Books.

Greenberg, Moshe. 1972. "Levitical Cities." In *Encyclopaedia Judaica*. Jerusalem: Keter Publishing House.

Hersh, Kathy Barber. 1984. "A Refuge for Refugees." *Mother Jones*, January.

Hull, Elizabeth. 1986. "Sanctuary Self-Defined." *Christianity and Crisis* 46 (February).

Ingwerson, Marshall. 1984. "More U.S. Churches Join Effort to Harbor Central Americans." *Christian Science Monitor*, July 25.

Jessel, David. 1983. "The Pimpernel of the Desert." *The Listener*, October 20.

Jorstad, Eric. 1986. "Reverberations from the 'Sanctuary' Trial: No Routine Smugglers." *Commonweal*, October 10.

_____. 1983. "A Theological Reflection on Sanctuary." *Commonweal*, October 31.

Jorstad, Eric, and Leon Howell. 1986. "Conversations on Sanctuary." *Christianity and Crisis*, September 22.

Kemper, Vicki. 1988. "Acquittals in Sanctuary Trial." *Sojourners*, November.

————. 1987a. "Court Rulings Provide Boost to Sanctuary Movement." *Sojourners*, June.

————. 1987b. "Stacey Merkt Released from Prison." *Sojourners*, June.

————. 1986a. "Convicted of the Gospel." *Sojourners*, July.

————. 1986b. "The Road to Conversion: Sanctuary Workers Focus on Refugees." *Sojourners*, December.

Kirby, L. 1989. "Sanctuary." In *New Catholic Encyclopedia*. Vol. 18, supplement 1978-88. Washington, D.C.: Catholic University of America.

————. 1986. *Sanctuary: A Canonical History of the Right of Asylum*. Canon Law Society of America.

Lorentzn, Robin. 1991. *Women in the Sanctuary Movement*. Philadelphia: Temple University Press.

MacEoin, Gary. 1985. "A Brief History of the Sanctuary Movement." In *Sanctuary: A Resource Guide for Understanding and Participating in the Central American Refugee Struggle*. San Francisco: Harper & Row.

Malcolm, Marion. 1987. "Overcoming Paternalism in the Sanctuary Movement." *Basta!* March: 21-25.

Matas, David. 1989. *The Sanctuary Trial*. Winnipeg: Legal Research Institute of the University of Manitoba.

Mazzinghi, Thomas John. 1887. *Sanctuaries*. Stafford, England: Halden and Son.

McClory, Robert. 1987. "Sanctuary: Should Parishes Break the Law for a Stranger?" *U.S. Catholic*, May.

McGrath, Peter, and Ron LaBrecque. 1982. "A Haven for Salvadorans." *Newsweek*, April 5.

McNamee, Stephen, and Donald Reno Jr. 1985. *Government's Trial Memorandum Statement of Facts*. CR 85-008-PHX-EHC. August 23.

Milgrom, Jacob. 1972. "Bloodguilt." In *Encyclopaedia Judaica*. Jerusalem: Keter Publishing House.

Molesky, Jean. 1986a. "Rio Grande: War Zone and Sanctuary." *The Witness* 69 (June).

————. 1986b. "Sanctuary in the Rio Grande Valley." *St. Anthony Messenger*, May.

Namuth, Tessa. 1983. "The Refugees of El Corralón." *Newsweek*, December 5.

Nikitas, Margo. 1986. "Sanctuary: Testimony the Court Didn't Hear." *People's World*, March 8.

Ovyrn Rivera, Rachael Jo. 1987. "A Question of Conscience: The Emergence and Development of the Sanctuary Movement in the United States." Ph.D. dissertation, City University of New York.

Pacheo, Patrick. 1984. "They Live Their Religion." *Ladies Home Journal*, December.

Quammen, David. 1986. "Seeking Refuge in a Desert: The Sanctuary Movement." *Harper's Magazine* 273 (December).

————. 1984. "Knowing the Heart of a Stranger." *New Age Journal*, August.

Rauber, Paul. 1984. "Conscientious Protectors." *San Francisco Focus*, September.

Riggs, Charles H. Jr. 1963. *Criminal Asylum in Anglo-Saxon Law*. University of Florida Monographs no. 18. Gainesville: University of Florida Press.

Rodriguez, Richard. 1988. "I Will Send for You or I Will Come Home Rich." *Mother Jones*, November.

Scharper, Stephen B. 1991. "Knocking on Heaven's Door: Sanctuary." *Maryknoll Magazine*, December.

Siebold, Martin. 1934. "Sanctuary." In *Encyclopaedia of the Social Sciences*. New York: Macmillan.

Slater, Nelle G. S., ed. 1989. *Tensions between Citizenship and Discipleship: A Case Study*. New York: Pilgrim Press.

Smith, Jeff. 1986. "They're Just Good, God-fearing Americans . . . Whose Kids Keep an Eye out for the Feds. Meet the Sanctuary Smugglers." *New Times*, February 26.

Sobrino, Jon. 1988. "A Theological Analysis of the Sanctuary Movement." *Today's Parish*, January.

Theiler, Patricia. 1990. "Double Standard? Is the Government Using a Double Standard in Its Handling of Illegal Aliens from El Salvador?" *Common Cause Magazine*, July/August.

Thornley, Isobel D. 1924. "The Destruction of Sanctuary." In *Tudor Studies Presented to the Board of Studies in History in the University of London,* ed. Robert W. Seton-Watson. London: Longmans, Green & Co.

Tomsho, Robert. 1988. *The American Sanctuary Movement.* Austin: Texas Monthly Press.

Trenholme, Norman M. 1903. "The Right of Sanctuary in England." *University of Missouri Studies*, 1:5.

Unsworth, Tim. 1989. "What the Church Has Taught Us about Sanctuary." *SALT*, July.

Urrutia-Aparicio, Carlos. 1978. *Diplomatic Asylum in Latin America.* Washington, D.C.: American University Press.

Walsh, James H., and Mary Ellen O'Neill. 1987. "Sanctuary: A Legal Privilege or Act of Civil Disobedience?" *Florida Bar Journal* 61 (2): 11-16.

Weller, Paul. 1987. *Sanctuary—the Beginning of a Movement?* London: Runnymede Commentary no. 1.

Westermarck, Edward. 1958. "Asylum." In *Encyclopaedia of Religion and Ethics*. Vol. 2. Ed. James Hastings. 4th ed. Edinburgh and New York: T & T Clark, Charles Scribner's Sons.

Witt, Linda. 1982. "Defying the Law: Jim Corbett Smuggles a Desperate Salvadoran Family to Safety in the U.S." *People Magazine*, August 9.

Yarnold, Barbara M. 1991. "The Role of Religious Organizations in the U.S. Sanctuary Movement." In *The Role of Religious Organizations in Social Movements*, ed. Barbara M. Yarnold. New York: Praeger.

Newspaper Articles

Allen, Teresa, and John Bach. "Border crossings: a conspiracy to commit justice." *Hartford Courant*, June 14, 1989.

Applebome, Peter. "In the Sanctuary Movement, unabated strength but shifting aims." *New York Times*, October 27, 1989.

Beckland, Laurie. "Tucson group provides bail for Salvadorans detained by U.S." *Los Angeles Times*, July 16, 1981.

Bishop, Katherine. "U.S. adopts new policy for hearings on political asylum for some aliens." *New York Times*, December 20, 1990.

Brooks, Geraldine. "Offered Sanctuary: Scores of U.S. churches take in illegal aliens fleeing Latin America." *Wall Street Journal*, June 21, 1984.

Browning, Daniel R. "Informant Cruz alters testimony after review of secret recording." *Arizona Daily Star*, January 10, 1986.

――――. "Informant questioned about testimony discrepancies." *Arizona Daily Star*, February 28, 1986.

――――. "Jury gets to hear one side of testimony about conditions in El Salvador." *Arizona Daily Star*, February 6, 1986.

――――. "Key federal witness contradicts U.S. prosecutor in Sanctuary trial." *Arizona Daily Star*, January 8, 1986.

Davidson, Miriam. " 'Admissible' evidence remains biggest question in Sanctuary trial." *Christian Science Monitor*, November 22, 1985.

_____. "Defense in Sanctuary trial hangs on a twig and jury compassion." *Christian Science Monitor*, November 15, 1985.

_____. "Government's case in Sanctuary trial hurt as key witness's credibility dims." *Christian Science Monitor*, December 26, 1985.

_____. "Sanctuary Movement under fire." *Christian Science Monitor*, October 22, 1985.

_____. "Sanctuary workers active, but cautious." *Christian Science Monitor*, March 12, 1986.

_____. "Sanctuary workers, buoyed by light sentences, vow to continue." *Christian Science Monitor*, May 9, 1986.

Elder, Jack. "The Sanctuary challenge." *Texas Observer*, June 27, 1986.

Farrell, Michael. "Sanctuary: Part of the bigger picture." *National Catholic Reporter*, September 14, 1984.

Fleck, John. "Path to Freedom: Claremonters join the movement to help refugees from Central America." *Claremont Courier*, October 10, 1984.

Galvan, Manuel. "Sanctuary Movement persists: First guilty verdict tests commitment of groups." *Chicago Tribune*, May 20, 1984.

Hall, Carla. "The Border Breaker: Jim Corbett's risky runs for refugees." *Washington Post*, July 23, 1983.

Healy, Eric. "Sanctuary Suit Settled; exits halted." *Arizona Daily Star*, December 20, 1990.

Hernandez, Ruben. "Court upholds convictions of eight Sanctuary workers." *Tucson Citizen*, January 15, 1991.

Hotz, William. "Salvadoran refugee's journey full of danger, intrigue." *Baltimore Evening Sun*, May 31, 1985.

Hyre, Meg. "Sanctuary trial ends in victory." *Catholic Worker*, September 1988.

Ingwerson, Marshall. "More U.S. churches join effort to harbor Central Americans." *Christian Science Monitor*, July 25, 1984.

Kahn, Robert. "No time to call end to Sanctuary Movement." *Oakland Tribune*, December 26, 1990.

Kenkelen, Bill. "Rights and church groups' 1985 lawsuit led to U.S. shift." *National Catholic Reporter*, December 28, 1990.

King, Wayne. "Leaders of alien sanctuary drive say indictments pose church-state issue." *Miami Herald*, February 3, 1985.

LeMoyne, James. "For relatives of Salvador's dead, anguish evolves into political activism." *New York Times*, February 2, 1985.

Leslie, Lourdes Medrano. "Sanctuary Movement wins landmark ruling limiting U.S. infiltration." *Arizona Daily Star*, December 12, 1990.

Maharidge, Dale. "Refugees' flight: A saga of pain." *Sacramento Bee*, August 26-30, 1984.

Martinez, Demetria. "Ruling on government spying seen as victory for Sanctuary Movement." *National Catholic Reporter*, December 21, 1990.

_____. "Sanctuary activists see legal move as vindicating efforts." *National Catholic Reporter*, December 28, 1990.

Mathews, Jay. "Church sanctuary movement for refugees grows in U.S." *Washington Post*, January 27, 1983.

McCarthy, Tim. "Sanctuary Movement: Crucible of crisis." *National Catholic Reporter*, February 1, 1985.

_____. "Sanctuary raids, spying tactics anger activists." *National Catholic Reporter*, January 25, 1985.

McManus, Jim. "Church and state speakers worlds apart on Sanctuary." *National Catholic Reporter*, May 15, 1987.

———. "Church officials give INS mixed reviews." *National Catholic Reporter*, October 23, 1987.

Medlyn, Beverly. " 'Underground railroad' still runs in the open." *Arizona Daily Star*, December 25, 1982.

Miami Herald. "Churches give sanctuary to illegal refugees who face deportation." April 18, 1983.

———. "Church gives sanctuary to refugees." March 29, 1983.

Miller, Kay. "Church shelters Salvadoran refugee." *Minneapolis Tribune*, December 12, 1982.

Millman, Joel. "In search of Sanctuary." *New Jersey Monthly*, May 1987.

Morrell, Lisa. "Churches sue U.S., claim win." *Arizona Republic*, December 11, 1990.

New York Times. "Clerics denounce curbs on aiding illegal aliens." March 1, 1985.

———. "Guatemalan family reaches refuge." March 25, 1984.

Oppenheim, Carol. "Salvadoran underground railway: Churches defy alien law." *Chicago Tribune*, May 4, 1982.

Roth, Michael. "The new underground railroad." *The Rebel*, February 27, 1984.

Rummler, Gary. "Defiant churches welcome three refugees." *Milwaukee Journal*, December 3, 1982.

Stammer, Larry. "Churches become part of illegal alien chain." *Los Angeles Times*, February 7, 1983.

Suro, Robert. "Pope lauds those who aid refugees of Latin America." *New York Times*, September 14, 1987.

Taylor, Stuart. "U.S. indicts 16 in smuggling of aliens." *Miami Herald*, January 15, 1985.

Turner, Mark. "Judge rules communion question out of Sanctuary trial." *Arizona Daily Star*, December 13, 1985.

———. "Sanctuary informant admits perjury in '82." *Arizona Daily Star*, December 13, 1985.

Wilkinson, Tracy. "U.S. agrees to reopen 150,000 asylum cases." *Los Angeles Times*, December 29, 1990.

Williamson, Michael. "Escape from El Salvador." *Sacramento Bee*, August 26-30, 1984.

Index

Compiled by Douglas J. Easton

Hilary Cunningham is assistant professor of anthropology at the University of Notre Dame in Indiana. In addition to teaching in the area of religion and politics, she is pursuing anthropological research on the role of religious groups and the social construction of power. Her research has taken her through central Canada, the U.S. Southwest, Mexico, and Guatemala.